# ASIO AND ITALIAN 'PERSONS OF INTEREST'

A History of Sydney's

Federation of Italian Migrants and their Families

(FILEF)

## Gianfranco Cresciani

Connor Court Publishing

Published in 2017 by Connor Court Publishing

Connor Court Publishing Pty Ltd.
PO Box 7257
Redland Bay QLD 4165
sales@connorcourt.com
www.connorcourt.com

Phone 0497 900 685


ISBN: 978-1-925501-45-2


Cover design, Maria Giordano

Printed in Australia

*To Jane*

# Publications of Gianfranco Cresciani

(Ed. with R.J.B. Bosworth) *Altro Polo. A Volume of Italian Studies* (1979).

*Fascism, Anti-Fascism and Italians in Australia. 1922-1945* (1980), Italian edition published in 1979.

(Ed.) *Australia, The Australians and the Italian Migration* (1983), Italian edition published in 1984.

*The Italians* (1985).

*Migrants or Mates. Italian Life in Australia* (1988).

(Ed.) *Giuliano-Dalmati in Australia* (1999).

*The Italians in Australia* (2003).

*Transfield. The First Fifty Years* (2006), second edition (revised) published in 2008.

*Per le vie del mondo. A short history of Apulians in New South Wales* (2009).

*Trieste goes to Australia* (2011).

*Amina Belgiorno-Nettis. A Life* (2012).

(Ed) *Ida Cerino-Zegna. Poesie* (2012).

(Ed. with Bruno Mascitelli) *Italy and Australia. An Asymmetrical Relationship* (2014).

(Ed with Jane Silversmith) *Carmela Lavezzari. Memoirs of a "person of interest"* (2014).

# Acknowledgements

To write the history of some communist party or communist 'front' organisation in Australia has always been a dangerous and difficult task, even after the troublesome years of the Cold War. Secrecy, reticence and the ever-present bogey of being a 'fellow traveller' hampered researchers and historians alike. When an organisation was an "ethnic' one, drawing support, ideas and inspiration from its foreign mentor, claims of sedition, treason, subversion and of being un-Australian were levelled without hard evidence, justified only by the abysmal ignorance of the motivations, aspirations and actual policies pursued by this organisation.

This was the case for the Federation of Italian Migrants and their Families (FILEF) in Sydney. Its members were spied upon by the Australian Security Intelligence Organisation (ASIO), ostracised by a large part of the Italian migrant community and its media, embarrassingly acknowledged by Italian diplomatic and consular representatives, fearful of losing their jobs because of their political beliefs, demonised by the Australian Establishment as the Trojan Horse of Italian communism, even when FILEF's members claimed to have a "human face".

After forty years of militancy, time has come to record FILEF's journey through Australian and migrant politics, welfare, arts, education and union activities. The idea to commission the author to undertake this task was originally vented by FILEF's current leaders, among them Frank Panucci, Francesco Raco, Bruno Di Biase and Claudio Marcello. To them goes the credit and my sincere thanks for having made this project possible by allocating the necessary financial resources. Leichhardt Municipal Council also generously contributed to this initiative with three grants for the archiving and digitising of FILEF's documents deposited at its Library and for the research and writing of FILEF's history. A particular thanks is due to former Mayor Cr Darcy Byrne who strongly supported this initiative.

Research was carried out in Australian and Italian archives. My particular gratitude goes to James Andrighetti and staff at the Mitchell Library in Sydney, that is holding FILEF's records between 1972 and 1986, and to Amie Zar, Alison Grellis and Marilyn Taylor of Leichhardt's Municipal Library, where the Federation's records to the present day are deposited. Their kind assistance is gratefully acknowledged. The National Archives of Australia, in both Sydney and Canberra, made available to me important documents for my project. In particular, I wish to thank Brendan Fenton of the Canberra branch and Kerrie Jarvis of the Sydney one.

In Italy, Cristiana Pipitone and Giovanna Bosman of the Archive of the Fondazione Gramsci in Rome have been most helpful in identifying documents in the Fondo Partito Comunista Italiano pertinent to FILEF-Sydney. Their contribution was invaluable, and for this I am indebted to them. I also wish to acknowledge the Director of the Archivio Centrale dello Stato in Rome, Dott. Agostino Attanasio, for having provided microfilm documents on FILEF's members of the Sydney Branch. I am also indebted to Canberra's staff of ASIO who, upon my request, released six files detailing FILEF's activities from 1972 to 1986. Without information diligently and painstakingly recorded in them, much of FILEF's history could not have been written.

Interviews with former and current members of FILEF have been most informative. In particular, I wish to thank for their contribution Francesco Raco, Bruno Di Biase, Claudio Marcello, Carmela Lavezzari, Rosalba Paris and Vera Zaccari.

My lifelong friend, Professor Richard Bosworth of Jesus College, Oxford University, a world authority on contemporary Italian history, in reading the manuscript of this book has been, as always, a precious source of advice, criticism and relentless testing of my assumptions. His at times vigorous challenges prompted me to look deeper into the facts and fiction of FILEF's history. For his dispassionate effort to assist me in my task I am heartily thankful to him.

As always, my family had to endure long periods of mental absence on my part, as well as my trips to Rome and Canberra to scour archives. For Jane's, Emilio's and Raffaella's patience and understanding I am truly grateful.

To paraphrase ASIO's historian David Horner, it needs to be emphasised that this history of FILEF is not FILEF's view of its history and its assessment of its own achievements. Rather, it is the history of FILEF written by an independent historian, based primarily on the Federation's own records. All eventual misinterpretations, omissions and errors are my own responsibility.

Gianfranco Cresciani

# Abbreviations

| | |
|---|---|
| ABA | Australian Bicentennial Authority |
| ABS | Australian Bureau of Statistics |
| ACLI | Associazione Cattolica Lavoratori Italiani |
| ACTU | Australian Council of Trade Unions |
| ALP | Australian Labor Party |
| ANESBWA | Association of non-English Speaking Background Women of Australia |
| APR | Associazione Progressista Repubblicana Italo-Australiana |
| ASIO | Australian Security Intelligence Organisation |
| BLF | Builders Labourers Federation |
| CFC | Circolo Fratelli Cervi |
| CGIL | Confederazione Generale Italiana dei Lavoratori |
| CIB | Criminal Investigation Branch |
| COMITES | Comitato degli Italiani Residenti all'Estero |
| COASIT | Comitato di Assistenza Italiano |
| CPA | Communist Party of Australia |
| CPC | Casellario Politico Centrale |
| DC | Democrazia Cristiana |
| DIEA | Department of Immigration and Ethnic Affairs |
| DILGEA | Department of Immigration, Local Government and Ethnic Affairs |
| EPT | Electric Power Transmission |
| ESL | English as a Second Language |
| FCC | FILEF Cultural Committee |
| FIG/PCI | Fondazione Istituto Gramsci, Rome, Fondo Partito Comunista Italiano |
| FPCIA | Federation of the Italian Communist Party in Australia |
| FTG | FILEF Theatre Group |

| | |
|---|---|
| GIA | Grant-in-Aid |
| IACC | Italo-Australian Community Centre |
| INCA | Istituto Nazionale Confederale di Assistenza |
| LLFC | Leichhardt Municipal Library, FILEF-NSW Collection |
| MCAR | Migrant Committee for Aboriginal Rights |
| ML MSS 5288 | Mitchell Library, Sydney, FILEF-NSW Collection |
| MSI | Movimento Sociale Italiano |
| NAA | National Archives of Australia |
| NESB | Non-English Speaking Background |
| OVRA | Opera Volontaria Repressione Antifascismo |
| PEAPS | Pilot Equity and Access Project |
| PCI | Partito Comunista Italiano |
| PCUS | Communist Party of the Soviet Union |
| PSI | Partito Socialista Italiano |
| SBS | Special Broadcasting Service |
| SPA | Socialist Party of Australia |
| UPI | Unione Pensionati Italiani |
| USSR | Union of Soviet Socialist Republics |
| WEA | Workers Educational Association |

# Contents

# 1

# Sydney's Italians and the PCI

*Non si pretenda che i lavoratori italiani portino qui*
*solo le braccia e lascino la testa a casa.*
(One cannot expect that Italian workers bring here with them
only their muscles and leave at home their brains).
FIG/PCI, 1978/482/60

"It's time". This slogan, emblematic of the coming to power of the Australian Labor Party in December 1972 under the leadership of Edward Gough Whitlam, had a profound effect on migrants of non-English speaking background. The venue chosen to launch the Party's electoral campaign on 13 November, the Blacktown Civic Centre, was significant. Blacktown hosted one of the largest concentrations of migrants in the country, especially Italians. The two largest Italo-Australian companies employing several thousands Italian migrants, Electric Power Transmission (EPT) and Transfield, had their construction factories in the Blacktown area, the former at Marayong and the latter at Seven Hills. EPT had also a workshop on Parramatta Road, Leichhardt, a suburb where many Italians resided. Leichhardt was something of an US-style "Little Italy" by reason of its strong Italian presence, with shops, businesses, restaurants, clubs and entertainment places being managed almost exclusively by Italians. It also hosted a bookshop, the *Libreria Italiana*.

Labor's appeal to the "New Australians", as the assimilationist lore of the time dubbed newcomers, found its reason in the refreshing policies introduced by the new government after more than twenty years of stifling, unimaginative, monocultural conservative rule. The White Australia policy was finally repealed. Its legal end is usually placed in the year 1973, when the Whitlam Labor government implemented a series of amendments preventing the enforcement of racial aspects of the immigration law. Multiculturalism was proclaimed, Australia opened to the world with the government recognising the People's Republics of Vietnam and China, as well as a spate of People's Republics of Soviet-controlled Eastern Europe

Australia was coming out of the Cold War and bringing home its troops from Vietnam, where some not yet naturalised Italian migrants had unwittingly been called to serve, thanks to the abhorred lottery system that forced people whose birthday date was drawn from the barrel to be compulsorily drafted. Some recently arrived young Italians had been influenced by the 1968 Italian student revolt, in the wake of the French one, that controversially preached *l'imagination au pouvoir*. They liked the imagination and drive manifested by the Whitlam government and were willing to take part in the process of making Australia a more progressive and egalitarian society. Multiculturalism became the dominant ideology of the time, paradoxically advocating the "levelling" of socio-economic differences by proclaiming slogans like "unity in diversity" and the rights of "ethnics". The invention of the "ethnic" and its "identity politics" furthered the obfuscation and then the destruction of class in the following decades and so paved the way to neoliberal hegemony.

For the first time in many years, migrants felt – one doubts how realistic their expectations were – that they were called to contribute to this nation-building process by bringing their experience, their culture and their aspirations to the fore of the political debate. For the first time, they felt being "consulted" and not ignored on the assumption that they were mainly interested in their families and their material well-being. They objected being treated just as factory fodder, prodded to assimilate to the way of life of the dominant Anglo-Celtic culture after having discarded, if that would ever be possible, their language, heritage and traditions. However, they soon realised that the road ahead was not easy, that they had to fight for the recognition of their rights to education, social assistance and political participation. To do this, they needed an organisation to put forward their claims.

Existing, long-standing Italian institutions were eminently unsuited to perform this task. Traditionally, they were linked to the Catholic Church, to the Italo-Australian business establishment that included importers of foodstuffs from Italy, wool buyers, bankers, shipping agents, traders and owners of the Italo-Australian Press. During the Cold War years, these institutions looked with disdain and concern at the presence of "left-wing"" or "communist" initiatives and of *focolai di sovversivismo* (subversive dens) such as the newspaper *Il Risveglio*, the Italo-Australian Club in George Street, Sydney and the Garibaldi Bar in Darlinghurst, owned or managed by Jewish refugees, anti-Fascist militants and former partisans.[1]

The Cold War years were also coincidental with the mass migration of Italians to Australia. In 1947-51 some 42,600 Italians settled in this country, in 1952-60 arrivals totalled 177.600, in 1961-65 67,300, in 1966-70 62,200, to drastically diminish during 1971-75, when only 18,500 arrived.[2] Those were also the years of the witch-hunt against alleged communist fellow travellers, of the Red Peril, of the policy of assimilation. Before emigrating, Italians were screened by the Australian Security Intelligence Organisation's (ASIO) Liaison Officer staffed at the Migration Office of Rome's Embassy and by the *Carabinieri* and if found to be a member of the Italian Communist Party, left-wing organisations or of the *mafia*, were excluded from being accepted. Those who made it were discouraged from supporting each other by forming in Australia their own political pressure groups, their enclaves, their commercial or cultural and formally apolitical Little Italies, and were prodded to instantly transmogrify from being a "weird mob" into "New Australians".

In 1976, Michael McKellar, Minister for Immigration, in stating his reason for deporting journalist Ignazio Salemi, stated: "He is, of course, an active organiser amongst Italian migrants on behalf of the Communist Party of Italy. The Government respects the right of people to hold varying political beliefs. However, it has been the view of successive governments that it is not in the interests of Australia or of the migrants in Australia that political differences in their countries of origin should be pursued in Australia".[3] Discrimination at school, in the workplace, in business, shops and places of public entertainment was of common occurrence, although it compared favourably with the inequity and corruption that compelled migrants, among other reasons, to leave Italy. A monocultural, dominant majority could hardly tolerate the assertion of their difference and of their rights by members of what in 1971 was the largest non-Anglo-Celtic community group in Australia, totalling, according the Census held in that year, 289,476 Italy-born people. The public perception was that "Italians" were "ignorant peasants", only too often willing in Australia, when forced by economic necessity, ignorance of industrial practices and union solidarity, to be *crumiri* (strikebreakers).

Often, prejudice, intolerance and discrimination prompted migrants to react, at times violently. The two most glaring instances of rioting against the unacceptable treatment to which they were victims were the Bonegilla riot in 1952 and the 1972 riot at the Ford car factory in Broadmeadows, Melbourne. Paradigmatically, they roughly marked the beginning and the end of Italian mass migration to this country. At the Bonegilla migrant reception centre, in July 1952, Italians, frustrated by the harsh camp conditions, a cold winter and delays in their employment, that had been assured by the Australian government, rioted. On 19 July Rome's newspaper *Il Tempo* carried the headline "Tanks out in Australia against 2,000 Italian emigrants" and stated that 200 soldiers and five tanks had been kept at the ready to intervene against the newcomers. The involvement of the military was confirmed in the memoirs of one eyewitness and leader of the disturbance, Giovanni Sgrò, who would become the Federation of Italian Workers and Families' (FILEF) Secretary in Melbourne: "when we arrived near... the administrative offices which were our destination, four tanks appeared, followed by over 200 soldiers.

When we saw them we stopped dead in our tracks". Of course, this incident was pretty minor if compared with some of the violent demonstrations at that time taking place in Italy and the murderous attacks on striking workers by *Carabinieri* and the Police. According to estimates by historian Emilio Sereni, working class repression between 1 January 1948-31 December 1954 resulted in 75 dead, 5,104 injured, 148,269 arrested, 61,243 sentenced to 20,426 years in prison and 18 life sentences. The data are incomplete because they refer to only 38 provinces. It is not surprising that many Italians opted to emigrate, even if Australia did not prove to be the Eldorado they dreamt of. One of the disaffected migrants, undoubtedly voicing what most of them believed, declared to the Italian Consul in Melbourne that *questa emigrazione è una truffa* (this emigration is a swindle). Australian authorities, historian Richard Bosworth reported, "were in no way prepared for a sudden influx of Italians whom they had long been taught were the racial inferiors of their Aryan selves".[4]

Likewise, the Broadmeadows riot was caused by harsh working conditions at the car plant. Its 4,000 strong workforce included 75% migrants of non-English speaking background. Conditions at the plant were notoriously unsafe, with workshops smothered in noxious fumes. One of the employees complained that "when the workers come to Australia they cannot speak English, they have no friends to help them and take an interest in their problems…they are obliged to work as cheap overworked labour…the company played the workers as they wanted. Because they can't speak English they work under inhuman conditions". As a matter of fact, Ford management used language difficulties to fob off worker complaints. On 18 May 1972 the workers went on strike, against their union's advice, and on 13 June occupied the plant, destroying company property and clashing with over 100 police. Ten weeks after the riot, Ford finally gave in. "The company agreed to slow the assembly line, hire more workers, hire women, increase the number of toilet breaks, repair leaking roofs and increase wages over and above their original offer". One of the strikers described the feeling of confidence and militancy as follows:

"We showed the company that we were not slaves…they started being very afraid of the workers and the union. They speak to us workers with respect. They don't address us like you would a dog, as they used to."[5]

The Broadmeadows disturbances were an isolated instance of direct action by migrants, despite the fact that they constituted the overwhelming majority of workers in some sectors of the economy. Italians were the feeblest in union membership and participation. The 1971 Census revealed that of the males and females employed as tradesmen, production workers, process workers and labourers, only 36% and 9% respectively were Australian born, while the greatest majority were non-English speaking migrants. Of the males, 62% were Italy born, 61% Greece born and 74% Yugoslavia born. Of migrant women, 49% were Italy born, 56% Greece born and 55% Yugoslavia born. Their working conditions and work-related health conditions were abysmal.[6]

To assist them in overcoming their health conditions, in 1977 a Workers Health Centre was established in Lidcombe. From 1977 to 1982, doctors at the Centre saw over 3,000 workers; migrant workers accounted for just over 50% of these patients, although in the months August-September 1982, 62% of clinical visits were from migrants. Of the 3,000 odd patients, doctors visited 60% on at least 4 – 6 occasions per year. In addition, approximately 30% came again to the Centre to either ask questions about their work environment and conditions or to see the interpreters about work related problems. 55% of migrants attending the Centre were women and nearly one third of them were diagnosed as having tenosynovitis and epicondylitis, respectively overuse of the hands and shoulder syndrome. Figures from the Centre indicate that about 6 times as many women as men contracted tenosynovitis or related conditions.

The high incidence of work-related ill health and accidents amongst migrant workers was due to their concentration in particular 'high risk' industries, in which conditions were very poor, in contrast with at the time widely held belief that migrants were stupid and clumsy, hence prone to having accidents, and were often termed 'malingerers' when physical injury was not obvious. There was no truth at all in these claims. Many migrant workers, especially women seen at the Centre, frequently took substantial doses of tranquillisers, analgesics and anti-depressants, prescribed after complaints to doctors of depression and of not being able to cope. A number of employers had installed dispensers of Bex and Vincents analgesics in factories where there was a high degree of noise and physical discomfort. Given the proven link between analgesic abuse and kidney problems, this measure was highly negligent on the part of employers and a poor alternative to changing work conditions that made drug abuse necessary.[7]

Recently arrived migrants, not being able to speak English (or even Italian, conversing only in their regional dialect), often threatened with dismissal if they complained or joined a trade union, unaware of their rights, ignored by monocultural and monolingual union representatives who spoke to their migrant members only in English, were at best ignored, and at worst discriminated, exploited and victimised by government agencies, employers and trade union officers alike. Following the Migrant Workers Conference, held in 1981 by the Australian Council of Trade Unions (ACTU), a survey carried out by FILEF, based on the returns of 200 questionnaires, revealed that 40% Italian members did not know anything about their union, 69% did not attend union meetings, 77% did not take part in discussions, 74% did not know the policies of their union, 46% needed an interpreter and 88% preferred a major amalgamation of unions in Australia. They were influenced by the Italian situation, where there were only three unions, the communist-oriented Italian General Confederation of Labour (CGIL), the socialist Italian Labour Union (UIL) and the Christian-Democrat Italian Confederation of Workers' Trade Unions (CISL).[8]

In the 1950s and 1960s, despite compulsory unionism, non-English speaking migrants, of whom Italians were the largest group, lacked a body that would speak in defence of their rights and would rally and organise them into a combative and assertive pressure group.

During the late 1960s the winds of change blew not only in the Italy of the "economic miracle" but also in the "Lucky Country", an ironic nickname for Australia, taken from the 1964 book of the same name by social critic Donald Horne. The Italian Socialist Party (PSI) became a member of the ruling coalition with the Christian Democrats (DC), and the Communist Party (PCI) went on in its apparently inexorable march to become *un partito di lotta e di governo,* (a Party of struggle and of government) as one of its slogans was claiming at the time. At the 1972 political elections it obtained 27.15% of the electoral vote (in 1976 its electoral support would peak at 34.4%). It is at this time that the PCI became involved in the affairs of Italian migrants abroad. In association with a number of trade unionists, artists and intellectuals and together with people militating in left-wing parties, environmentalists, libertarians and people without a definite political connotation, in November 1967 the Party set up in Rome the Italian Federation of Migrant Workers and Families (FILEF). This initiative was taken in spite of the fact that there was a continuing substratum of leftist Italian thought which viewed emigrants as traitors to the working class at home. This was a curious parallel to the Australian unionist position, loyal to class over ethnicity, that Italians were Catholic *crumiri.*

FILEF's founder was the writer and a victim of Fascist persecution Carlo Levi, author of the renowned autobiographical account *Christ stopped at Eboli.* The Federation was formed to promote and achieve equal rights for Italian migrants and their families in the cultural, social, educational, economic and political life of the countries to which they had emigrated. Migrants, as Levi wrote on 15 November 1968 in an article in the journal *Emigrazione*, and later in his preface to Paolo Cinanni's book *Emigrazione e unità operaia*, had to fight for their rights, and become *non più cose o passivi strumenti di lavoro, ma protagonisti* (no longer 'things' or passive labour providers, but protagonists). Following its formation in Italy, FILEF set up branches in other countries. In Australia, in 1972-73 it opened offices in Melbourne and

Sydney and, later, in Adelaide, Brisbane and Perth.[9]

FILEF (Sydney) was formed by migrant workers to deal with issues such as the lack of adequate interpreters, translators and other welfare services. Its chief goal was to assist Italian migrants in organising themselves around issues and problems concerning them. Through special projects, continuing activity, support for and provision of resources to the Italian community, FILEF encouraged the integration of Italian migrant workers and their families within the host society and provided the organisational conditions to enable them to defend and extend their rights along with the rest of the labour movement.

The maintenance and development of Italian language and culture was the central aim that underlaid each of the activities, as well as providing information and encouraging Italians to learn about, on the one hand, Australian society, its institutions, laws, culture and history, and on the other about their country of origin, including the developments that had taken place since their departure. Obviously, this information had a left-wing or PCI slant. Offering courses in Italian on a variety of topics was the most direct way in which these goals were achieved. Other FILEF activities included bilingual theatre productions, audio-visual exhibitions, the production of resource materials for the teaching of Italian in primary school and publications.

In Sydney, and perhaps elsewhere as well, FILEF was formed almost exclusively by the 'uneducated', that is, by people who had very little schooling in Italy – pensioners, labourers and some skilled workers – and who perhaps went through several migrations. Many, if not all, did not revisit Italy once they arrived in this country. Sociologically, they fitted perfectly the preconceived idea that the uneducated are also uncultured, and therefore unable to transmit anything of value from their homeland. It was, however, the Italian working class culture of FILEF which made it into an organisation with systematic links with modern Italy, and which absorbed from Italy not Ferrari or Armani, but the exceptional social development that marked that country's history in the 1970s.[10]

From the outset, several cultural and educational projects were created, encouraging workers to break out of their usual daily routine of home, work and television, and to take part in the daily life and decisions of the society of which they were an integral part. FILEF aimed at unifying Italian workers around issues that they considered important such as pensions, school and work-related problems, so that they could make their voice heard and influence the standards of living and the institutions of the society in which they were living.

In Sydney, FILEF rented premises at locations in Leichhardt. Its catchment area was primarily the inner City and Leichhardt, Drummoyne and Ashfield, but much of its work reached the Italian community throughout the Sydney metropolitan area. There were no other services similar to those offered by FILEF. Leichhardt was chosen because it was the focal point of Italian settlement. According to the 1971 Census, of the 67,000 Italian-born population in Sydney, 5,003 were living in the Leichhardt Municipality. By 1976, there were 175 Italian businesses in Leichhardt and 52% of the area's commercial establishments and social organisations were run by Italians, including bookshops, food outlets, butchers and delicatessen, optometrists, funeral directors, estate agents, bridal shops and regional clubs. It was in Leichhardt that the printers and publishers of the Italian newspapers *La Fiamma* and *Il Corriere di Settegiorni* were located.[11]

In 1981, according to a study of the population carried out by the Petersham Regional Office of the Department of Social Security, 54.3% of the population in this region were Italian born, and of these 37% were living in the Abbotsford-Five Dock area.

It was in the catchment area of inner-Western Sydney that the bulk of FILEF's supporters lived, however not exclusively. Italians living at Bankstown, Bondi, Blacktown, Fairfield and as far as Wollongong and Port Kembla became members of the Federation. From 1973 to 2002, FILEF-Sydney attracted the membership of over one thousand people, not an insignificant number considering the fact that in the eyes of the Italo-Australian Establishment it was considered to be an organisation militating on the 'wrong side' of the Cold War, stigmatised to be a Communist front agit-prop, receiving instructions from 'above' in Botteghe Oscure, supportive of radical and left-wing causes all over the world. Existing membership records attest that over the same period 961 people joined FILEF, however, many membership cards have gone missing. For instance, in 1990 the then President of FILEF, Claudio Marcello, declared that FILEF had 560 members, while surviving membership records attest to only 446 members.[12] The great majority of Italian migrants did not join FILEF for a number of reasons, including the stigma attached to militating during the Cold War years in a "subversive" organisation, fear of being dismissed from one's employment, geographical distance, preoccupation with family matters and the persistent media, consular, Catholic Church and Italian Establishment's campaign against FILEF. Ignazio Salemi, in a letter dated 21 February 1975 to Giuliano Pajetta, Head of PCI's Emigration Office, described this propaganda warfare as follows: "the sheer volume of fire against political activities that the Italian Coordination Committee is discharging at every opportunity, with the open support of the consul, is merely a continuation of the anti-communist terrorism of past times".[13]

An analysis of FILEF's social composition also gives the lie to the widespread prejudice that most members were dangerous agitators. A sample of 245 members reveals that 24% were pensioners, 9.3% industrial workers, 8% teachers, 7.3% housekeepers, 5% waiters, 2% invalids and 1.6% unemployed. The bulk practised working-class or lower middle class occupations and trades. Only 3 declared of being a contractor, 3 a lawyer, 1 a businessman. Only three out of 245 stated of being a 'political activist'. Of the 961 known FILEF members, 153 declared to also be card-carrying members of the Australian Branch of the Italian Communist Party (PCIA). Many of them militated in this organisation before emigrating to Australia, an interesting fact as it is raising doubts about the competence of the filtering process by ASIO and the *Carabinieri*, aimed at excluding communists and *Mafiosi*.[14]

Most communist sympathisers, emigrated to Australia, joined the PCI before and during the Cold War years; one, Giovanni Fede, in 1944, another four in 1945, three in 1946, two in 1947, two in 1948, one in 1949, one in 1950, one in 1952, one in 1953, two in 1955 and one in 1956. Between 1975 and 1980, marking the first years of FILEF's activities, another 16 took the PCI card.[15]

Obviously, since the beginning of mass migration from Italy in 1951, the policy pursued by Australia to screen prospective migrants and their next-of-kin proved a herculean task. Canberra wanted to find out the candidates' and their "close relatives' " eventual affiliation to, or "being sympathetic" to the PCI, the Italian Socialist Party (PSI), the Communist Youth Organisation, the "communist inspired" Peace Movement, the fascist Movimento Sociale Italiano (MSI), or having "any penal record, or any information on record for or against the applicant".[16] It soon became evident that Australia did not have the means to expeditiously process the swelling tide of applicants.

In 1951, ASIO acknowledged that "we are, perhaps, a little vulnerable in regard to our security check in that 1,069 out of 1,131 recommended for migration are awaiting security clearance". It was taking two months to clear an application, and by the end of 1951 some 37,500 applicants had been assessed by the Italian authorities, who rejected 10,000, and 27,500 were awaiting for Australian clearance.[17] The problem was that at the last general elections, held on 18 April 1948, 8,136,637 million Italians, or 30.98% of the electorate, voted for the PCI and the PSI, while the MSI attracted 526,882 voters (2.01%). It was impossible to screen this number of people. At a meeting with Italian Prime Minister Alcide de Gasperi, the Italian leader, rather tongue in cheek, tried to play down the ideological concerns of his Australian interlocutors, who reported to Robert Casey, Minister for External Affairs, that De Gasperi believed that "although the numerical strength of the Communist Party is approximately 1,500,000…less than 300,000 of them are active members of the Communist Party. The others have joined not out of sympathy for the cause but because they were ill-fed and unemployed, and Signor De Gasperi said that once in a new land such as Australia they would forget their temporary affiliation". In reality, De Gasperi was underestimating the number of Italians affiliated to the PCI, that in 1951 totalled 2,097.830 card-carrying members. Casey was also appraised of the fact that "the Italian authorities would like us to be guided by the Italian Department of Interior which keeps records of the active members of the Party rather than that we should continue, as at present, to go to the source for reports on the political affiliations of applicants and members of their families".[18] It is not surprising that many Italians, who militated in the PCI, slipped through ASIO's and the Italian Department of the Interior's screening nets.

Sydney's membership figures to the PCI for the period 1972-1980 are more or less confirmed from an examination of the records held in Rome at the Fondazione Istituto Gramsci in the Fondo Partito Comunista Italiano. The Fondo comprises 23 folders containing correspondence between FILEF in Australia and PCI's Ufficio Emigrazione and Sezione Esteri during this period. Documents beyond 1985 have not yet been catalogued. In his report to the Party Secretariat, following his trip to Australia on 14 April - 1 May 1973, Giuliano Pajetta made mention of "60-70 members in Sydney, 40-50 in Melbourne, 10-15 in Adelaide".[19] A year later, in September 1974, another Party official, Ignazio Salemi, a journalist from L'Unità who during the 1968 "Prague Spring" had been expelled from Czechoslovakia after he threw a flower pot on the head of a policeman while he was arresting a Dubcek's supporter, in his report on his stay in Australia, stated that in Sydney there were 84 members, while the overall Australian membership was 252.[20] In December 1975, Tino Colli, responsible in Melbourne for the Party's recruitment, reported that Sydney's members numbered 82, and 339 nationwide, while the target, aimed to be reached by 25 April 1976, was 500.[21] Claudio Cianca, FILEF's President from 1970 to 1985 and Member of the Italian Chamber of Deputies for the PCI from 1953 to 1972, following his visit to Australia on 3 - 31 October 1977, while overestimating the number of FILEF's supporters, reported that the overall Party membership in 1977 was 429, "while FILEF's supporters (*aderenti*) number some thousands".[22] However, by the late 1970s, anti-communism was still pervasive, and efforts to enrol new members were hampered by widespread fear and hostility. This situation was confirmed by Pierina Pirisi, who was in charge in Sydney of both FILEF's and PCI's activities. In her letter to Pajetta in February 1978, she said that "while enrolments to FILEF reached almost 100%, and we are confident to go by far beyond this percentage, there is more resistance to take the Party's membership…because of widespread fear, even fear of losing the pension or work if one joins the Party".[23] Fear also conditioned people's attitude towards FILEF. Salemi confirmed to Pajetta that, to some extent, the guiding role played by its communist members adversely affected FILEF's relations with other bodies: "the main Melbourne organisations are inviting us to attend their meetings, ministers are courting us, even if later they fear having compromised themselves, because they realise who is behind the organisation".[24] To combat widespread ostracism, Pirisi advocated a greater effort in order "to create conditions that would enable us to get out of this kind of 'working underground' that is so oppressive".[25] In 1974, an ASIO agent reported that, at a meeting of Party members, she announced that "in future the PCI would act under the name of FILEF; that we will be first and foremost communists, but we will act under the name of FILEF".[26] However, not all Australian institutions were reluctant to deal with communists. Leichhardt Council invited members of FILEF, who were also PCI's associates, to discuss issues affecting primary and secondary schools and strategies aimed to improve welfare assistance to needy Italians.[27]

Pajetta did not miss any opportunity to emphasise the importance of increasing the numerical strength of the Party in Australia. In a letter to Salemi, he prodded him to "remember the importance, for **many reasons**, of an increase in the membership".[28] In a previous letter, also to Salemi, he had emphasised that "the numbers are important and can be a measure, also for 'others', on how to judge progress". [29] The reason why Pajetta was so persistent in advocating a significant increase in PCI membership in Australia had its reason in his concern that FILEF would be seen essentially as a communist front organisation, and the Party as an inward-looking small group of affiliates. "For a thousand local reasons, the risk is", he wrote to Salemi, "for FILEF to merely become a 'socialist-communist mass party', and the Party a closed group of cadres…yet there is the need to have a mass Party…it is important and goes beyond the satisfaction – not exclusively statistical – to soon rely on hundreds of card-carrying members".[30]

Instead, for Pajetta, "FILEF, is, let us strongly remind everybody, an autonomous organisation. It must be clear in the first place that it is not a disguised organisation of ours, nor a political party 'a bit larger', but a democratic association (that we support with all our strength) committed to protect the material and moral interests of migrants and their families".[31] In a letter to the Sydney Branch, Pajetta reiterated that "FILEF is simply not a label, but a mass association including communist and non-communist members".[32] Given the fact that in 1975 ASIO had recorded Pirisi's assertion that "the PCIA must be kept separate from FILEF and INCA. However, the PCIA must be the force and brain behind them"[33], it is not surprising that Pajetta and his Sydney comrades were not sounding credible to sceptical outsiders when they were proclaiming FILEF's 'ecumenical' character.

Despite a sizeable minority of militants in PCIs ranks, most FILEF members, although supportive of left-wing policies and ideals, were not communist. The Federation's long-time President, Claudio Marcello, never became a PCI or a Communist Party of Australia (CPA) member. However, FILEF Sydney, being a Branch of FILEF Rome, from 1973 until the fall of the Berlin Wall drew most of its political, organisational, logistic and financial support, the latter in modest proportions, from the PCI, that at that time was partly funded by the USSR. Some of FILEF's members associated with the PCI founded parallel organisations in Western Sydney. The Circolo Culturale Italiano "Fratelli Cervi" (CFC) was set up in Fairfield, aiming to promote the social aggregation and the cultural development of

Italians residing in the Western suburbs, and to stimulate a relationship of cultural exchange and mutual understanding among Italians and the Australian community in general. Further, the CFC offered an information and welfare service to resident Italians. Article 2 of its Constitution stated that the CFC "is affiliated with FILEF...and shares the general aims of that organisation.[34]

From the outset, FILEF's leadership in Sydney endeavoured to clarify the role of PCIA's cadres who were also members of FILEF, as well as of other political bodies. An un-dated memorandum drafted by Bruno Di Biase, one of FILEF's long-standing Secretaries, put for the members' discussion "some considerations on the work by Communists in FILEF. As a mass organisation of Italian immigrants, FILEF naturally tends to openly support the party of the masses of workers in Australia, that is the Australian Labor Party (ALP). It is adopting this line because FILEF is not a party and is not tied to specific ideologies but is interested in resolving specific problems facing immigrants. Obviously, there is a greater opportunity to do this if you build a positive relationship with the party in government. This does not mean that FILEF supports the Labor Party at all costs and on all occasions, indeed our support should be 'dialectic', starting from positions and claims independently made. FILEF's work to convince Italians to vote in a certain way must have counterparts, commitments on the part of the ALP towards immigrant workers, made as most explicitly as possible. Communists working in FILEF will do everything to make these commitments a reality, and to have them respected by the candidates who are elected locally and, generally, by the Australian Labor Party".[35] It is not surprising that, given the pre-eminent role played by PCIA's members in determining FILEF's political stance, Australian authorities, in particular ASIO, and the right-wing Italian Press and Establishment in Australia exclusively saw FILEF as a communist front organisation.

There was a long history of concern by Australian authorities over communist activities. Already in 1927-1934 the NSW Security Service maintained a file on Italian communists.[36] In 1936-1939 the Commonwealth Investigation Branch, acting upon information given by a Maltese spy, who claimed that 10% of Italians in North Queensland were communist and 80% socialist, and that Sicilians were "a troublesome element", opened a file on "Italian Communists", although the reliability of the informer was questioned by the Branch: "the mere report that certain men are undesirable should surely require some corroboration, before they can be regarded as such, and the only way to obtain this would be through the person making the report being questioned". Again in Queensland, in March 1950 Josiah Francis, Minister for the Army, wrote to Harold Holt, Minister for Immigration, "concerning camouflage by Communists [at Wellington Point] who claim to be teaching the Australian way of life to Italians through the Italian-Australian Association". Holt replied that "the information…will be brought to the notice of the Security Authorities and you may rest assured that the danger of local Communists exerting influence on new arrivals in this country will be closely watched by my Department". A postscript on Holt's letter by the Assistant Secretary of the Department's Assimilation Division read: "please return file to me so that I may discuss this matter with ASIO".[37] Holt's assurance gave the political imprimatur for ASIO monitoring in future left-wing activities by Italian migrants.

From 1945 onward the Australian Labor Party accepted the assistance of an anti-Communist Roman Catholic movement, led by B.A. Santamaria to oppose communist "subversion" of Australian Trade Unions (Catholics being an important traditional support base). To oppose communist infiltration of unions Industrial Groups were formed to regain control of them. The groups were active from 1945 to 1954, with the knowledge and support of ALP leadership until after Labor's loss of the 1954 election, when federal leader Dr Herbert V. Evatt, in the context of his response to the Petrov affair, blamed the "subversive" activities of the "Groupers", for Labor's defeat. Many Australians were convinced of the danger of communism and believed that Australia's economic prosperity was threatened by communists who had infiltrated trade unions and the

Labor Party. In the Cinesound newsreels of the 1950s, anti-communist films explained that communism had subjugated 800 million people and that members of the Communist Party of Australia and their sympathisers were un-Australian and potential subversives.

At the peak of the Cold War, ASIO monitored nationwide CPA's proselytising among Italian migrants, in order to identify possible CPA agents.[38] In accordance with its charter, ASIO's formal function was "the collection, collation, evaluation and distribution of information on individuals, organisations and movements, whose objects or activities were considered subversive of the security of the Commonwealth". ASIO believed that if a person was a member of the CPA, PCI or of a front organisation, he or she was a potential subversive agent and needed to be watched. Some people, identified as "associated with communist activities", were threatened with deportation. This was the case for Mario Abbiezzi, then Secretary of Sydney's Italo-Australian Club, who was curtly told that unless he leave Australia by 17 February 1953, the Government would take action to enforce his departure.

*Archivio Centrale dello Stato, Rome. Casellario Politico Centrale. 1935. Photo of Mario Abbiezzi from his Police file (Courtesy ACS).*

Abbiezzi was not deported. Legal advice given to the Minister for Immigration pointed out that "because the activities of a migrant may cause some unrest this does not itself warrant action for his deportation. I feel that to take such action might create a dangerous precedent which could be used in future to the detriment of a person who could in no way be regarded as subversive, but whose political views were not in accord with those held by the government of the day".[39] During the 1950s, it was ASIO's common practice to film every year the participants in May Day marches, including "CPA... Italian, Albanian and Greek groups".[40] ASIO's concern for the CPA infiltrating Italian migrant organisations stemmed from the fact that some Australian communists were influenced by the line adopted by the PCI during the 1950s, returning to national traditions of socialism while ambiguously professing allegiance to the ideology of the USSR, the *stato guida*. Most migrants sympathising with the PCI espoused this line. Historian Alastair Davidson, in his book on the history of the CPA, mentions that "the writings of the Italians [PCIs publications] began to appear comparatively frequently in the CPA press after the war...the PCI *Foreign Bulletin* continued to arrive regularly, and the ideas contained in it caused a ferment in 1959-1960 among the Victorian younger cadres".[41]

By the early 1960s, as well documented by Mark Aarons in his book *The Family File,* detailing covert surveillance of members of his family who were prominent leaders of the Australian communist movement, ASIO had deeply penetrated the CPA and maintained files on his members, sympathisers and affiliated organisations. Aarons reveals that "according to a former ASIO deputy director-general, by the 1960s there was at least one agent in every CPA branch". According to Aarons, "much of the information in the files is inconsequential dross", albeit "by the 1970s there was little that communists successfully hid from ASIO's surveillance".[42] This surveillance was extended also to Italian migrants who were a member of the PCI in Italy or became a member in Australia, or joined the CPA or the Socialist Party of Australia (SPA). Screening of their movements and activities continued after they joined FILEF.

ASIO kept an interest in FILEF even before its establishment in Sydney in December 1973. Its first record dates 19 April 1972 and deals, among other issues, with FILEF's formation in Melbourne by Sgrò and Schiavoni. In July 2014 ASIO released to the author files number 1, 2 and 3, totalling 649 documents, dealing with FILEF's activities from 1972 to 1977. Further files covering the period 1978 to 1986, the last year before the 30-year closed period sets in, were released in September 2014. Material contained in these files documents that, like for the CPA and the PCI Branches in Australia, also FILEF was heavily infiltrated by ASIO agents. Most agents must have been Italian PCI members or sympathisers hired by ASIO, as the language spoken at FILEF's meetings was Italian. Their accounts of public as well as closed gatherings were relayed to an ASIO "case officer", who debriefed the agent and typed the information in English in a 'contact report'. Each of these detailed reports contains an evaluation of the reliability of the source and the credibility of information. Most of the information gathered dealt with petty issues, wrangles among members, organising events and ideological diatribes. It also reported on the time and location of planned meetings, on the physical details of people attending gatherings, on the owners of the vehicles used and on financial matters. For instance, In March 1975 ASIO's agent reported that at that time FILEF and the PCI in Australia were $320 in arrears with the rent for their premises at 26 Norton Street, Leichhardt.[43] Such was the secrecy of agent running that the name of the agent never appeared on the contact report. Instead, an alpha-numeric code was used (X for a member of FILEF or PCIA; Y for any other contact or informant), meaning that only the case officer knew the identity of the agent. All alpha-numeric codes were erased from documents made available to the author. Obviously, agent running was not the only source of information tapped by ASIO.

In January 1975 ASIO's Director-General regretted that "at the present time, we have no comprehensive paper on the activities of the PCI in Australia", and sent to ASIO's Liaison Officer in Rome several documents, with the request that "special care should be taken to protect these documents, which have been obtained from delicate sources and that no action should be taken on their content without reference back to this Organisation".[44] Again, in a letter to the Secretary of the Department of Immigration and Ethnic Affairs, dated 18 March 1977, ASIO's Director-General advised that "because they are based on intelligence from overseas liaison and from delicate secret sources within Australia neither our original summary nor the additional information above [on "communist influence in Italian ethnic groups"] should be disseminated further without prior reference to us".[45]

Indicative of ASIO's capillary and diligent screening is the case of Umberto and Carmela Lavezzari. Reaching Sydney on 23 January 1959 on board the MV *Flaminia*, they came to ASIO's attention in April 1961, when only their first name, "Umberto" and "Carmen", appeared in the CPA's newspaper *Tribune* as participants to the newspaper's annual picnic. In 2009 and 2010 the Lavezzaris were granted access, under the Freedom of Information Act, to volume 1 (up to 1973) of their files. Details of their surveillance reveal that on 28 June 1961 their identity was confirmed by an informant, obviously well conversant with Sydney's Italian community. On 31 October 1961 the Service was advised "by two sources [for the Lavezzaris] to be Communists who have stated that they were formerly active Communists before migrating to Australia". The accuracy of this information was verified by ASIO's station head at the Rome Embassy, who on 6 March 1962 advised that the Italian authorities had "no adverse trace recorded against [them] in any way" from a security or penal point of view. Despite this all clear verdict, consideration was given and, for the moment, deferred, to include their names in the Defence Warfare, War Book and Preparation for War, Emergency Measures – Special Index of Aliens – Aliens Included in the CPA Index.

Throughout the Cold War, Australia, like the United States,

believed that the chances of war with the USSR were quite high, despite their adhering to the M.A.D. strategic doctrine (Mutually Assured Destruction). Proponents of MAD believed that nuclear war could best be prevented if neither side could expect to survive a full-scale nuclear exchange as a functioning state. Despite the absurdity of their plan, ASIO made provision that at the outbreak of war, some ten thousand 'subversive aliens' would be arrested and interned. To this purpose, its Counter-Subversion Branch managed the War Book's Special Index of Aliens, that by 1958 included 2,220 names, mainly Russians, Yugoslavs and Czechs. However, left wing Italians figured prominently in the lists. Inclusion of the Lavezzaris' names would have sparked their immediate internment.

On 8 June 1961 they were on the list of employees, "to be definitely Communists", allegedly given to ASIO by the Management of Marayong's works of Electric Power Transmission. The company was headed by Enzo Oriolo, a staunch, unrepentant Fascist who maintained lifelong contacts with his former comrades of Mussolini's Social Republic. The day before, ASIO's Field Officer on the case tabled a confidential report claiming that there was a CPA Branch staffed by EPT's employees. At that time Umberto, a boilermaker by trade, managed his company, Lilac Structural Engineering, that carried out subcontracted work on behalf of EPT. On 17 November 1963 ASIO photographed Umberto Lavezzari attending a meeting at the CPA premises at 174 Day Street, Sydney.

For the following ten years (and longer, when their post-1973 files will be accessible), the Lavezzaris were reported being "very active on behalf of CPA in the Italian émigré community". On 30 May 1969 they were included in the Special Index of Aliens. Attendance at several CPA Seven Hills Branch meetings was duly recorded by the ASIO plant. Their names and addresses figured in the CPA's Sydney District Membership List "maintained by staff at the Sydney District Office, CPA Headquarters, 4 Dixon Street, Sydney", obviously procured to ASIO on 14 June 1974 by a mole operating inside the Party's premises. Lavezzari's 1976 subscription butt to the CPA's newspaper *Tribune*, bearing the note that "I would like not to see my name appear in the paper" was surreptitiously 'extracted' from the newspaper's premises in Dixon Street and ended in Lavezzari's ASIO file. In 1976-1977 the Lavezzaris became members of FILEF, where in the following years Carmela occupied leadership positions.[46]

What most concerned ASIO were the visits by Italian communist Giuliano Pajetta. In January 1932, at 17 years of age, Pajetta had left fascist Italy, where he had already been involved in PCI's underground activities, to go to Moscow. There, he attended Palmiro Togliatti's lessons on fascism. It was then that he received his political education at the "Leninist school" where, as a biographical note published in *L'Unità* mentioned, "he became a fully fledged soviet man" (*è diventato un sovietico in piena regola*). While in Moscow, he learned to speak Russian fluently, however his was Soviet Russian, not that spoken by the émigrés, as he was proud to tell the author during his stay in Sydney in 1976. In 1935 Togliatti sent him to Paris, to become the leader of communist youth. A political commissar of the 13th Brigade of the International Brigades during the Spanish Civil War, Pajetta also fought with the French *Maquis* and, during the Resistance, with the Garibaldi Brigades in Lombardy, where he came to know Mario Abbiezzi, at that time a partisan in Como. In October 1944 Pajetta was arrested by the SS and sent to the extermination camp of Mauthausen. A Member of the Italian House of Representatives and Senator-elect in 1963, Pajetta was a member of the PCI's Central Committee from 1945 to 1986, responsible for the Party's *Sezione Esteri* (Foreign Section), and from 1972 to 1981 in charge of its Emigration Office. ASIO was well aware of his importance. He was described as "the younger of two brothers both of whom hold leading positions in that Party. His older brother, Giancarlo, is presently a Member of Parliament and is considered to be one of the most authoritative and prominent members of the PCI".[47] Pajetta would come to Australia another three times, from 15 June to 8 July 1978, from 7 to 20 August 1979 and in May-June 1981. The visits were reported by FILEF's newspaper *Nuovo Paese* in its issues of 24 June and 8 July 1978, 19 August 1979 and 5 June 1981.

Giuliano Pajetta would die in Leghorn on 15 August 1988.

In April 1963 Pajetta visited Sydney in transit to and from New Zealand, to attend that country's Communist Party Congress where, according to ASIO, "the influence of the Chinese Communist Party on both the New Zealand and Australian Communist Parties would be one of the subjects for discussion". In April 1966 he returned to Australia, officially as Vice-President of the Italian Delegation to the Inter-Parliamentary Union Conference in Canberra. Amusingly, he was issued a visa by the Embassy in Rome unbeknown to the local ASIO officer, who on 4 April 1966 complained to Headquarters that he had to learn about Pajetta's visit by reading the PCI's newspaper *L'Unità* and that "Liaison Section (aka ASIO Rome) [was] not repeat not consulted before visa issued".

*Photo of Giuliano Pajetta on his way to Canberra, taken by ASIO on 14 April 1966 at Sydney airport. NAA, Series A9626, control symbol 169, barcode 7949855, Pajetta, Guiliano (sic).*

ASIO's agents reported that during his stay in Sydney, Pajetta held meetings with Laurence Aarons, CPA's General Secretary, his brother Eric and with Mavis Robertson, both Members of the CPA's Central Committee. On 10 April 1966 he also attended a meeting of Italians organised by Joseph Palmada, the CPA person responsible for Party security. On that occasion, he complained that out of 800 migrants to Australia from the township of Mantua, 200 of whom were PCI members, none had become a CPA member. One of the Italians present, Di Bella, said that many Italians were probably frightened of being deported if they associated with the CPA, while another, Dimitri Oliva, made the assertion that "only 20 Italians in the CPA were known to each other". Pajetta also decried the demise of *Nuovo Paese,* the Italian language bulletin sponsored by the CPA. Needless to say, also this meeting was attended by an ASIO plant, who obviously spoke or was Italian. He reported that Pajetta was surprised meeting Abbiezzi, whom he believed dead. According to the source, Pajetta revealed that Abbiezzi had been sentenced to death in Italy for stealing PCI funds, had escaped from Italy in 1948 following his exposure as a thief and this was the reason why he was anxious to remain in Australia and probably had been able to bargain with the security service over his naturalisation. Palmada also conspiratorially believed that Abbiezzi was an informer working for Security. To complete the innuendo of his report, the agent claimed that it was "rumoured that Abbiezzi [had] become a homosexual in the last few years".[48]

Three months later, an ASIO agent referred that Abbiezzi had written to Pajetta, asking for an explanation, and that the latter denied having made those allegations.[49] The culture of secrecy, suspicion and mistrust prevalent among PCI's members during the underground struggle against fascism and during the Resistance was understandable, given the network of spies and informers of the Regime that infiltrated and constantly wrecked communist cells. The efficient work carried out by these plants has been documented by Mauro Canali in his book *Le spie del Regime.*[50] It is not surprising that PCI cadres, even in countries of emigration, would have a manic fear of possible moles within their ranks, either from the fascist *Opera Volontaria Repressione Antifascismo* (OVRA) or later from ASIO, and give credit to unsubstantiated allegations.

Since the early 1960s the Communist Party of Australia had asked to have an experienced cadre from the PCI to work in Australia among Italian migrants. Only by mid-1973 the Party would formalise their request and offer material and logistic support. In a memorandum to the Direzione of the PCI, Pajetta endorsed this request, stating that "for many years our Australian comrades have been urging for one of our comrades to go there and perform a leadership role among our emigrants", but that "only recently the Australian comrades have formally detailed their commitment".[51] By "leadership role" Pajetta referred to the principles that would be spelled out in 1975 by Secretary Enrico Berlinguer at the PCI's 14th National Congress:

> One of our tasks, which we must not renounce, is to contribute to our utmost to the formation of a more solid consciousness among the workers and the people. But on what must this be founded today? Obviously, in the first place, it must be founded on rebellion against injustice and abuse and on conviction that collective struggle is necessary to create new social relations... The Party is the expression and the consciousness of the working class and the people, the highest result of the workers' drive for emancipation.[52]

The issue of having a Party organiser in Australia had become pressing in 1971, when Salvatore Palazzolo, Sydney's Secretary of the yet to-be-constituted Federation of the PCI in Australia wrote to Senator Ugo Pecchioli, a member of PCI's Direzione, asking for blank party membership cards.[53] Soon after, the PCI agreed to the establishment of a Federation in Australia. From the outset, Palazzolo, rather than seeking the collaboration of the Communist Party of Australia, antagonised them, and Pajetta as well. Palazzolo claimed that the CPA was "meddling in the affairs of the PCI in Australia... Aarons is a very arrogant person...wanted the names and addresses of all PCI members in Australia so as to try and win them over to the CPA".[54] In September 1972 the Head of the Emigration Office was compelled to send Palazzolo a blunt letter, "expressing our deepest disappointment for your behaviour on the occasion of your meeting with L. Aarons [Secretary of the CPA,] on 13 August 1972…what right do you have to think that our Australian comrades cannot know your problems…your behaviour is antagonistic, not towards the Australian Party but the Italian one". About Palazzolo's claim that he wanted his Sydney PCI Federation to be "autonomous" from Rome, Pajetta curtly ordered him to "renounce to the title autonomous".[55] In November 1972, Aarons wrote to Pajetta, complaining that "we have made several approaches for talks… there is no co-operation between our Party and the Federation leadership". Even worse, "a member of the Central Committee of the Federation sent a greeting to the Congress of the SPA, the splitting group from our Party".[56]

In February 1973, Aarons advised Botteghe Oscure that "the difficult situation has worsened recently…by a persistent rejection of all efforts to arrange discussions between our leadership and the Federation, going so far as not even replying to our letters".[57] This letter prompted Pajetta to send to all PCI members in Australia a long letter, complaining that "things are not going as we were hoping when we favoured the establishment of a PCI Federation in Australia" and making the point that "when we spoke of an autonomous federation we meant a Federation capable of taking autonomous political and propaganda initiatives, not in contrast with the general political line of our Party or of the comrades of the CPA".[58] An exasperated Aarons, facing a "very difficult position", on 27 March 1973 made a stinging attack against Palazzolo and his supporters. "First", the CPA National Secretary stated, "the present Federation leadership – and not just Palazzolo – are unable to develop any activity…Second, they are incompetent, lack drive, act bureaucratically, and are unable to develop any enthusiasm…the leading people live very much in the past, and are unable to see the new, and are also authoritarian…Third, at least some of the members of the Federation Committee are hostile to our Party, support the breakaway SPA".[59] Concerning Aarons' third accusation, the PCI swiftly took action. Armando Cossutta, a Member of the PCI Direzione, on 5 April 1973 wrote to Peter Symon, SPA's General Secretary, advising him that "your letter of 14 March cannot facilitate or initiate a contact or a collaboration between ourselves... we cannot accept the content and the tone of your comments on the CPA...we do not intend to establish a contact or collaboration that could be used against the CPA".[60] Concerning the other two points of criticism, Pajetta resolved to deal with them upon his arrival in Sydney in mid-April 1973.

Pajetta's visit took place from 14 April to 1 May 1973, to attend the first Congress of the Federation of the PCI (FPCIA) in Australia, held on 20-21 April in Sydney in the premises of the Building Workers' Industrial Union. ASIO surmised that "the National Congress of the FPCIA would not ordinarily warrant the presence of an official of Pajetta's rank, prestige and experience. His visit may therefore be an indication of PCI concern with the present serious rift within the Sydney leadership of the FPCIA".[61] Indeed, disunity marred relations between Sydney's PCI members.

On 27 February 1973, prior to his departure, Pajetta had sent them a letter, duly intercepted by ASIO, in which he hoped that they would adopt a "common orientation", carry out "ample political and mass work among the numerous Italian workers who live in Australia" and establish "a close collaboration and understanding firstly with our comrades of the CPA (our fraternal party and with which the PCI has excellent relations) as also...with other forces of the Australian Left".[62] The appeal of collaboration with the CPA was made rather tongue-in-cheek, as that Party was by then undergoing an irreversible ideological crisis in its struggle with the SPA and dissent with the line adopted by the Communist Party of the Soviet Union (CPSU). Nothing of the planned "political and mass work" had materialised. The only sign of activity was, Pajetta lamented, "a leaflet on Viet Nam distributed in Sydney and nothing else". Of greater concern to the PCI leader was the fact that he did not see it feasible to fund in Sydney the establishment of a newspaper. "The promise of particular help to start the publication of a newspaper was subordinate to the guarantee of an editorial group truly capable of carrying it out, a guarantee which up to the present time has not appeared and does not seem to exist".[63]

*Sydney, April 1976. Giuliano Pajetta addressing Italian migrants at Leichhardt Town Hall. (Left to right) Ignazio Salemi, Francesco Raco, Pajetta, Pierina Pirisi, Nicola Vescio (Courtesy Leichhardt Library FILEF Collection).*

Laurie Aarons, who spoke about the PCI and its similarity with the CPA, opened the National Congress of the Federation of the Italian Communist Party in Australia in the presence of 35 delegates, some of them obviously being ASIO agents, if one can judge from the lengthy verbatim reports filed with the Organisation. The initial report[64] listed the names of the attendees and their respective ASIO file number. ASIO also filmed each delegate to the Congress.[65] During the two days of proceedings, Pajetta commented that "it was terrible that the PCI membership in Australia was so small", and was also – incorrectly – reported by the ASIO agent as saying that it was "his instruction that all members of the PCI in Australia were to remain only as members of the PCI and not as members of the CPA".[66] Pajetta also admitted, using classical Stalinist phrasing, that "there were still some differences" with Moscow, but "attacked China on its incorrect policies". In view of this, he rather ambiguously reiterated, "you could not be a member of the PCI and the Socialist Party of Australia, but you could be a member of the PCI and the Communist Party of Australia". He interrupted the pro-Moscow speakers, among them Palazzolo and Abbiezzi, "saying he did not want to hear any criticism of the CPA". Dissent among the Sydney delegates was rife, some supporting the Marxist-Leninist stand of the SPA, others, among them Dimitri Oliva, "saying that the CPA had too much control in the affairs of the PCI", others still accusing each other and even Pajetta for his stand. One of the speakers, Lamarchesina, lambasted "the sectarian attitude of Italians towards one another". Pajetta concluded that "there had been general incompetence shown by the NSW Section leaders", and that "the Federal Secretariat would be better in Melbourne as there was no trouble there".[67] ASIOs analysis concurred with Pajetta's and went even further by confidently asserting that "the PCI in Australia will never be a stable organisation or one likely to have a strong political voice in the political arena".[68] In its final motion (*mozione conclusiva*), the Congress drew "a negative assessment of the political and organisational management of the outgoing Secretary and Federal Executive", namely Palazzolo and his supporters.[69] For his "political sympathy and practical collaboration" with the PSA and outright refusal to collaborate with the CPA, on 6 August 1974, Palazzolo and his wife, who were running INCA (Istituto Nazionale Confederale di Assistenza) in Sydney, were forced to resign, also in view of the fact that "comrade Palazzolo demanded money from clients for services given on behalf of INCA".[70] Nicola Vescio replaced them at the head of INCA.

During his brief stay, Pajetta had the opportunity to assess the local political situation, the opportunities offered to the PCI for the creation of a "mass" movement among Italian migrants and capacity of PCI cadres to establish the Federation as a viable force, able to influence Australian politics in a direction more favourable to the immigrants and with the aim to advantage the PCI, especially if there were ever to be a migrant vote. In a report to the PCI Direzione upon his return to Italy, Pajetta portrayed a dismal situation. Concerning the Australian trade union movement, he stated that "it is not aware of the **national** needs of the several groups of immigrants and, with some exceptions, the unions are not carrying out any specific initiative or program assisting the migrants". Coming to the CPA, he concluded that "its policies are not known, or almost ignored, by public opinion…and it is difficult that the CPA will at least become a "pressure group" of a certain strength". As far as Italian PCI militants were concerned, he observed that "all of them have a modest level of political and cultural preparedness… in Sydney personal issues are getting out of hand, mixing with political issues and causing a deep rift and break-up". Given this situation, Pajetta wondered whether "it is possible, and to what extent, to overcome the current, immense separation between our currently existing organisations and the great mass of Italians resident in Australia".[71] A year later his impressions would be shared by Ignazio Salemi, who wrote to him that "I have to admit that Italy and the Party in Italy are realities too far away, and not only geographically, in order to become a realistic element of cohesion between our cadres here".[72]

Despite the poor opinion of his Sydney comrades, Pajetta still trusted for his contacts with the CPA a young Sardinian woman, Pierina Pirisi. In July 1973 an ASIO operative reported that "officially, [the Federal Secretariat in Melbourne] is the only recipient of correspondence from Pajetta representing the PCI in Italy, however, it is known that Pierina Pirisi receives correspondence direct from Rome and passes it to Laurence Aarons' Headquarters where she is a full time employee".[73] In June, Pajetta had confirmed to FILEF Melbourne Pirisi's employment at CPA headquarters: "the new development is that comrade P. Pirisi is now working 'full-time' with our Australian friends".[74] In July, Pajetta had written to Aarons that "we are pleased that she has this new job…I think that Pierina is keeping you informed on our correspondence so there is no need to repeat myself".[75] One suspects that not all correspondence from Pajetta to Pirisi was forwarded to Aarons, in particular the instruction "to give priority to the PCI in Australia and not to the CPA, and that the PCI should work with all the left forces in Australia".[76]

Pajetta's papers contain several references to Pirisi's excellent work and his trust in her political acumen and commitment to the cause. In a letter to Salemi, he told him to encourage her: "we strongly recommend that you assist her and develop her journalistic work and any other thing she is able to do. We must help her morally and materially".[77] In another letter, he told her that "we are very concerned about your health and your personal situation. Remember that it is not 'revolutionary' to neglect your health and that you are for us a precious cadre".[78] Pajetta also assisted Pirisi in her political development by funding her attending a course at the Party school at Faggeto Lario, near Como, Italy.[79] The communist leader's regard for the Sardinian cadre – in one of his letters he would tell her that he considered her as the *de-facto* Vice-President of FILEF in Australia – was shared only in part by Salemi. In a letter to Pajetta, Salemi concurred that "your opinion is essentially correct, as she exudes good will and great honesty whilst dealing with many small and great practical things, but she lacks experience, that in a place like this should rather be cunning or trickiness, and a strong character that ultimately means ability to persuade others".[80] Obviously, Pirisi's managerial role was very taxing, given the dysfunctional character of the Sydney Branch and the internecine infighting among its members. In 1975 she, exhausted, decided to resign from FILEF and end her involvement in political activities. "My long-standing presence in the association had the result of wearing me physically and psychically, and of neglecting my studies. It helped FILEF to survive, not as a political organisation, rather as a motley crew who are at each other's throat". Her resignation was also reported to his 'agent master' (also bureaucratically classed by the Organisation as 'case officer') by the ASIO agent planted within the Party: "Pirisi's resignation from the PCIA Sydney Branch Executive was accepted. (Agent comment:

Pirisi intends to devote more time to her University studies)".[81] She was convinced to withdraw her resignation and to go on working for FILEF and the Party.

Pierina Pirisi had emigrated to Australia in 1970. An assessment made by the Selection Officer in Rome prior to her departure stated that Pierina Pirisi "has a very pleasant personality and appears a self confident and determined type of young lady". No mention was made of her political allegiance.[82] By 1973 Pierina was a member of the CPA and was accompanying Laurence Aarons on his speaking tours. She was with him in Granville on 19 June 1973, where she collected money for the Party.[83] Pierina Pirisi would become one of FILEF Sydney foundation members and would lead the Branch until her return to Italy in March 1984. During these years, ASIO kept her under surveillance and updated her file (NSW No. P/23/79). The same scrutiny was applied to members of the PCIA who would eventually join FILEF. For instance, Nicola Vescio, also one of FILEF's foundation members and responsible for the Benevolent Fund INCA, was "the subject of reporting since September 1971".[84]

On 26 April 1973, a few days after the FPCIA Congress, Pajetta visited the CPA Headquarters in Dixon Street, to attend a meeting with Joe Palmada. An ASIO agent, obviously a member of staff, tried to listen in to the conversation. "I overheard Pajetta", he or she reported, "talking with Richard Dixon in Gloria Garton's room. Pajetta said something about going to New Zealand on holidays and that Laurie Aarons was making all the arrangements".[85] Upon his departure from Australia, on 30 April 1973, Giuliano Pajetta left approximately $600 for the FPCIA.[86] As well as meeting Italian migrants and leaders of the CPA and SPA, Pajetta, as vaguely pointed out by an ASIO agent, "had important discussions on political problems in general and Italian emigration in particular with numerous Australian personalities, including Ministers Uren and Grassby and the President of the ACTU, Hawke".[87]

*Photo of Pierina Pirisi from her Selection Officer Report, Rome, December 1969. NAA, Series A2559, control symbol 1970/51/2142-2144 barcode 5337728.*

It was soon after Pajetta's visit to Australia that that some difference between policies respectively adopted by the CPA and PCI emerged, to the point that Pajetta felt compelled to issue a clear directive to the Party's Sydney Branch. "We must not forget that we are addressing ourselves to naturalised and non-naturalised Italians, who have a **specific** mindset, needs and particular grievances, different from those of Australian workers and of other nationalities. For this and other reasons we cannot and must not **identify** the activities of the PCI Branch with those of the CPA".[88] A year later the 'problem' persisted, and Pajetta advised Salemi that "the relations with Joe [Palmada] and friends …is not a simple issue and cannot be resolved in a day. It is important that another political line or other organisational measures be not imposed upon us". Pajetta went as further as to suggest a possible resignation by Pirisi from her employment at the CPA. However, in 2014, in an email to the author, Pirisi maintained that "she had never been forced by Pajetta nor by Salemi to leave [PCA's job], but resigned on her own will because she felt that CPA's leadership did not clearly understand what was her role, while she thought that she could be more useful by working for the Italian community".[89] In a curious and highly un-Marxist, nationalist statement, Pajetta strongly believed that "we have an 'Italian' way of working. This is the reason why PCI organisations do exist also in Australia…it is possible that CPA members of Italian background or nationality may not be interested in or agree with this way of working. We are not shocked, let them work as they deem fit in their organisations in the CPA, but they cannot impose upon us, in their name or of another party, to change our general line of work in emigration".[90]

*Leaflet advertising Pajetta's address to Italian migrants in Melbourne on 29 April 1973, the day before his return to Italy. The rally was organised by FILEF Melbourne (NAA, Series A6119, control symbol 3820, barcode 7949852, Pajetta, Guiliano (sic) Volume 1).*

While FILEF was established in Melbourne in 1972, by April 1973 there still was no Branch in Sydney. An ASIO report dated 9 April 1973, detailing the distribution of PCI Party Cards to the nine cells of the PCI in Sydney, mentioned "the possibility of establishing FILEF". Someone "suggested that a room on the first floor of a building in Norton Street, Leichhardt...could be used after renovations...it would appear that branches of FILEF would be responsible to local cells and that FILEF would be a mass organisation with members from other parties being allowed to join".[91] A week later, another ASIO operative noted that "all the cell leaders of the PCI will discuss the possible formation of FILEF... and the possibility of starting a coffee shop to supplement the operations of FILEF".[92]

On 20 June 1973 Pierina Pirisi alerted Rome to the fact that "comrade Palazzolo in Sydney wants to open a FILEF Branch here in Sydney...in the opinion of most members of the Branch, at this moment we could not take up this responsibility, better, we do not have the means to deal with it responsibly".[93] Pajetta immediately quashed Palazzolo's proposal. "We are not prepared to follow him on this dangerous path...initiatives such as FILEF must be co-ordinated with you [the Branch]...this is a kind of activity that cannot be 'launched' by someone known to be a communist, but by a group also inclusive of people not of our political persuasion".[94] Undaunted by the rebuff, Palazzolo's supporter in this initiative, Mario Abbiezzi, on 3 July 1973 called a meeting to discuss the possible foundation of FILEF in Sydney. It was a fiasco. ASIO's agent reported that, beside Abbiezzi, only another person attended.[95] Again, in November 1973, Mario Abbiezzi "said that an attempt should be made to form FILEF...in Sydney".[96] However, by December 1973 FILEF was established in Sydney. The ASIO agent on this case reported on 18 December that "FILEF has commenced operations in Sydney, and it has been set up at Nicola Vescio's residence at 358 Moore Park Road, Paddington".[97]

By the end of 1973, the need to put to rest internal dissent in the

PCI Sydney Branch became even more pressing for PCI officials. On 27 September 1973, Pajetta wrote to Colli, Head of the PCI Co-ordinating Committee in Australia, that "comrade Ignazio Salemi, who is now coming to Australia as FILEF representative to the Melbourne Conference, is the comrade who, by decision of the PCI Secretariat, should shortly be moving to Australia to direct the activities of the PCI organisations...the Party has made [efforts] to satisfy your long-standing request to have a skilled cadre to help you in your work".[98] The Party directed Salemi to stay in Australia for six months and ascertain the possibility of bolstering Party activities among Italian migrants. He was allocated three thousand Australian dollars (five hundred dollars per month) for his personal expenses, trips, etc. During his six-months stay, FILEF and the Party in Australia would be successful in raising an additional eighteen thousand Australian dollars to fund their activities. An analysis of the correspondence between Pajetta and FILEF in Australia during the years 1972 to 1980, kept in the Fondo Partito Comunista Italiano at the Fondazione Istituto Gramsci in Rome failed to unearth any significant financial support from the PCI, any "money from Moscow". Most remittances were made to help Pierina Pirisi. In January 1974 Pajetta told her that "we are making a small contribution (100 Australian dollars) for you personally ...a bit of help will not harm you".

In December 1974 Pajetta again wrote "it is good that you have received that small amount. We will try to send you another small Christmas present". During the same year Salemi advised Pajetta that he had contributed 400 dollars to Pirisi's travelling expenses to attend the Party's school at Faggeto Lario. FILEF's Secretary Bruno Di Biase confirmed that FILEF's initiatives in Sydney were funded through the financial support of its members and through government grants, raffles, dinners, *feste* and other promotional activities. Evidence of this was the fact that the organisation remained active for many years after the collapse of the USSR and the PCI.[99]

Salemi arrived in Victoria on 30 September 1973 on a tourist visa and returned to Italy on 10 August 1974. In October he attended in Melbourne the Migrant Workers Conference. He also urged, at a meeting of Party members, ironically gathered at the CPA Headquarters in Dixon Street, that "the PCI in Australia should work as one and should not be aligned to the CPA or the SPA. He said that if possible he would return to Australia and become a full time organiser for the PCI in Australia; if he could not come then another person from the PCI in Italy would be sent to Australia".[100]

Encouraged by the results of Salemi's initial stay, in September 1974 Pajetta asked the PCI Secretariat to approve another six thousand Australian dollars to fund Salemi's second tour, this time of one year, as well an additional two thousand five hundred Australian dollars in support of the recently established newspaper *Nuovo Paese*. Also, he forecast that Australian cadres would raise at least an additional twenty four thousand Australian dollars during that period.[101] On 30 October 1974 Salemi came back on a temporary entry permit. His arrival did not escape the scrutiny by ASIO, who on 21 October advised the Department of Immigration that it had "no objection to his entry". The Organisation kept him under surveillance and in 1976 advised the new Liberal Minister for Immigration and Ethnic Affairs that Salemi "has been a member of the propaganda office of the Italian Communist Party…during 1975 he actively participated in the affairs of the Italian Communist Party in Australia and acted as an organiser for the Party…he was a member of the Central Committee of the Italian Communist Party and it was his job to help run the Italian Communist Parties in other countries". However, the report concluded, "Salemi is not regarded as posing any substantial present threat to national security if, for reasons of policy, a further visa extension should be approved".[102]

Concerning FILEF, ASIO pointed out that "while FILEF is essentially an organisation controlled by the PCI (Italian Communist Party) it has the support of non-Communists and practically all of its activities in Australia are restricted to the field of social welfare amongst Italian migrants". The Italian Embassy confirmed ASIO's assessment. In another memorandum, ASIO reported that on 15 April

1976 "Dr Gesini, Counsellor, Embassy of Italy, Canberra, called at the Department [of Immigration]…He referred to application by Salemi for extension of stay and stated FILEF and Salemi do good work in the interest of Italian migrants in areas of social welfare. He stated also that his experience of Salemi indicated he was a moderate sort of person". Two days earlier, ASIO reported, "the Italian Ministry of Foreign Affairs approached our embassy in Rome to request that any order for Salemi to depart Australia be delayed 2 or 3 months. The Ministry was concerned that any requirement for Salemi to leave Australia might be linked with a recent visit to Australia by Mr Giuliano Pajetta, a leading member of the CPI (Italian Communist Party). The Embassy also pointed out risks attached to returning Salemi to Italy during national (Italian) election campaign and supported the request".[103] At that time, the Italian Communist Party was affording the government led by Christian Democratic Party indirect support by adopting that typically Italian, idiosyncratic formula of the *non-sfiducia* (not casting a no-confidence vote). Therefore, Italian diplomats were particularly sensitive to the political wishes of the PCI and continued in their efforts to defuse the situation.

On 12 April 1976, Pannocchia, Director-General of the Emigration Division of the Italian Ministry of Foreign Affairs, commented to Thawley of Rome's Australian Embassy that "although a PCI member, Pajetta was generally helpful and conciliatory".[104] On 16 August 1976, Ambassador Paolo Canali wrote to Lloyd Forrester Bott, Secretary of the Department of Immigration seeking information on the legal aspects of the case and took the opportunity to point out that "the view has been upheld that Mr Salemi has been unfairly denied the opportunity to fulfil his desire to remain in this country". As the language was almost harsh in diplomatic terms, Canali added an apologetic handwritten note to the letter: "You will excuse my causing you any inconvenience at such short notice. I have to refer back to our Ministry".[105]

On 2 February 1977, the Embassy in Rome contacted Pajetta directly, it is not clear for what specific reason. Their cablegram to the Department of Foreign Affairs in Canberra read as follows: "We spoke today with Giuliano Pajetta, member of the Communist Party's Central Committee and Head of the Party's Emigration Office. He referred to the Salemi case saying that the High Court had decided that it was up to the Minister for Immigration to give a definite statement on the Salemi case". While the PCI was kept abreast with the developments by its officers in Melbourne, the Embassy had "received no information of developments" from their superiors.

Despite ASIO's relaxed stand on the issue and hundreds of representations in support of allowing Salemi to stay in Australia, Michael McKellar, Liberal Member for Warringah and Minister of Immigration and Ethnic Affairs, determined to punish FILEF for having obtained political and financial support from his Labor adversaries, maintained a hard line. In his ruling, he stated that "[Salemi] is a man whose salary, by his own statement, is paid by the Rome Headquarters of a Communist front organisation, FILEF, and who has engaged in proselytizing among Italian migrants in Australia on behalf of the Communist Party of Italy". On 19 October 1977 Ignazio Salemi was deported to Italy. His work in Australia was appreciated by Pajetta, who proposed to the PCI Secretariat to appoint Salemi to FILEF's management committee (*gruppo dirigente*).[106]

As mentioned before, the Australian intelligence organisation had FILEF in its sight from its foundation. An ASIO report dated 5 February 1976 stated, quite accurately, although in a crude Cold War verbiage, what were FILEF's aims: "An official overseas source reports that FILEF (whose Headquarters is in Rome) was founded in 1967 by the PCI and that FILEFs aims are:

- To co-ordinate the activities of the various associations of communist inspiration founded in Italy and abroad with aims of assisting Italian migrants and their families;

- To penetrate Italian circles abroad, and families, so as to carry out propaganda of communist doctrine;

- To promote initiatives for the full recognition of equal treatment with local workers, in every aspect of work relations and the economic and civil life of the country of emigration, and for the exercising of all their rights in their own country.[107]

Concern for the pivotal role played by Salemi in bolstering the activities of FILEF in Australia barely one year after its formation transpires from several governmental documents. Already in July 1974, soon after Clyde Cameron became its Minister, Immigration reported, obviously overestimating *Nuovo Paese*'s print run, that Salemi was involved in:

- helping "organise" *Nuovo Paese*, "the official organ in Australia of FILEF...ten thousand copies are printed fortnightly and are normally bought in bulk by Trade Unions with large Italian membership;

- working also in FILEFs office as a welfare officer with Italian workers here;

- Mr Salemi works without salary but his living expenses are provided by FILEF members".[108]

FILEF, in a letter by its Secretary, Giovanni Sgrò, to Minister McKellar, dated 15 July 1976, supporting Salemi's stay in Australia, provided information on FILEF's wide-ranging activities: " Mr Salemi has helped in the preparation and distribution of 45,000 leaflets on health services in Italian and we are supplying bi-lingual material to 12 Australian Unions. He had helped to carry out research among 400 Italian families and has contributed to our work in an invaluable way".[109]

It is surprising that FILEF's limited impact on certain sectors of the alleged "Italian community", namely its pensioners, industrial workers and students, raised the concern of Australian authorities as well as the ire of some Australian and Italo-Australian Press. On 26 April 1975 Melbourne's *The Age* published on its first page an article entitled "Italian communists move in", illustrated by a photo of a grim-faced Salemi, claiming that FILEF was "making an all-out bid for political and social control of Melbourne's 250,000-strong Italian community". Brushing aside the accusation of being a communist publication, the paper recorded that during the previous 18 months FILEF had promoted the Migrant Education Conference, attracted 300 ethnic representatives and supported the establishment of the Ethnic Communities Council. *The Age* also acknowledged that "FILEF has successfully tackled many migrant problems which had previously been largely ignored by other Italian organisations".

Sydney's gutter sheet *Corriere di Settegiorni,* in an article on 22 July 1976, claimed that "the main purpose of FILEF is not to improve the lot of migrants…the organisation is always in the forefront of political demonstrations by extreme left unions…[and] pours out massive amounts of Marxist propaganda; almost traditionally, members of the Australian Communist Party appear at its social functions; FILEF is closely associated with groups, associations and individuals who profess the Communist faith". The other conservative paper, Melbourne's *Il Globo,* on 26 July 1976 added to the hysteria and bickering within the small, self-constituted *élite* of the "Italian community" by asserting that FILEF was "the long arm of the Italian Communist Party in Australia, a non-representative organisation which is ignored by the majority of Italian migrants in this country". The paper also criticised the financial support afforded by Prime Minister Fraser's Liberal-Country Party Coalition "to this same para-communist organisation". Ominously, the article concluded with the quotation "Whom the gods wish to destroy, they first strike blind".

As well as the Italo-Australian Press and conservative bodies, FILEF's policies were troubling Italian diplomats. Early in 1975, Salemi held discussions with the Italian consul in Sydney, aimed at seeking financial assistance for FILEF. The consul replied that he was "willing to help only if FILEF 'tone down' their political activities".[110] In January 1976, representatives of the Catholic Association of Italian Workers (ACLI) expressed their concern for FILEF's influence in Australia at a luncheon with the Australian Ambassador. "At the present time", ACLI's representative was reported saying, "ACLI is planning to establish a branch in Australia...their presence in Australia has been requested by persons resident there, such as Monsignor Baggio, who are worried by the sheer monopoly presently enjoyed by FILEF. The presence of FILEF in Australia tends to give in Italy a one sided view of the situation of Italians in Australia. FILEF's excessive influence in Australia was shown by its ability to have most of its nominees accepted as delegates to the recent Conference on Migration".[111]

The publicity raised by the Salemi case, his deportation and, even more, by the arson attack by unknown people on FILEF's Coburg office in Melbourne on the night of 13 May 1975, paradoxically drew Italian migrants' attention to this body. They came to its office, where there were people who could speak their language and understand their problems. The incident also had repercussions in New South Wales. One week before it, on 5 May, the Liberal Party issued a media release, lambasting Salemi and FILEF in view of their communist connections, and claimed that "the Italian community in Australia is being disrupted and disturbed by the activities of this overseas based organisation". Following the fire, on 15 May Pierina Pirisi wrote to Michael MacKellar, Liberal Member for Warringah and Shadow Minister for Immigration, lodging her "protest in the strongest possible terms against the act of violence against FILEF-Melbourne and against the violent press campaign that preceded it. In the light of the hate campaign that has been developed against FILEF, we see this latest act as an attempt to silence the voice of Italian workers who want to organise and to participate fully in the social and political life of this country". MacKellar, in his reply, questioned the malicious nature of the arson attempt: "you see this as an act of violence and I would like to know what evidence you have to substantiate your serious claim that the fire was deliberately started". Following his incredulous statement, the Shadow Minister issued a press release denouncing FILEF as "a blatantly left wing political organisation... only two weeks ago I warned of the disruptive effects this organisation was having within Australia". In a letter to his Liberal colleague A.

A. Street dated 23 May, MacKellar indirectly confirmed the intense lobbying carried out by the Italian Establishment in Australia against FILEF. He informed him that "the question of FILEF in Australia has been exercising my mind for some time and I have been in close touch with the Italian community particularly in Sydney and Melbourne about their efforts".[112] On its part, FILEF 'exercised its mind' to find out the culprits for the arson attack. Salemi, now in a conspiratorial mindset, as reported by an ASIO informer, believed that "there had been strange coincidence which have happened in Melbourne over the last two months. The...premises had been set fire to...his private vehicle had been stolen and smashed and other FILEF members' vehicles had been stolen and burned...detectives in Melbourne had come to dead-ends in their enquiries and Salemi blamed either the Fascists or the Secret Service for these attacks".[113]

Despite trenchant opposition from many quarters, from its inception FILEF Sydney created a structure that in the following years would enable the prosecution of its key strategies. The key committees and groups were:

| | |
|---|---|
| *Nuovo Paese* committee | established in 1973 |
| Women's group | established in 1973 |
| Cultural committee | established in 1977 |
| Finance committee | established in 1977 |
| Theatre group | established in 1984 |
| Publications committee | established in 1985 |

However, the most significant initiative taken by FILEF in 1974 was the founding of a national newspaper, *Nuovo Paese*. The reason for publishing a newssheet was spelt out, in rather poor English, in the first issue, that appeared on May Day 1974:

> Why another newspaper? There are quite a few Italian newspapers, but *Nuovo Paese* hopes to fill the vacuum that the many Italian newspapers that are printed in Australia are unable or do not want to fulfil. It is the emptiness of the reality of the world of labour, the lack of security, of the exploitation, lack of education and of the

thousand ways that the 'system' uses against those whose existence builds the immense wealth – of which after all, only few enjoy. *Nuovo Paese* proposes to fill the vacuum of the lack of information regarding the struggle and the successes of local workers, and of other countries that constitute the reality of this world – of which even Australia is part.

*Nuovo Paese* was printed fortnightly in Melbourne and attracted significant support from the Australian Trade Union movement. From the outset, the Trade Unions funded by 70-85% the cost of publishing the paper.[114] *Nuovo Paese*'s print run was of 8,500 copies, 4,000 of them being purchased by the Trade Unions.[115] Also, FILEF organised several campaigns to increase subscriptions, but with the passing of time they and the print run considerably decreased. Figures for the period 1988-1996, when compared with the 1970s ones, attest to this decline:

| | | |
|---|---|---|
| Copies mailed to subscribers in | 1988 | 401 copies |
| | 1993 | 513 copies |
| | 1994 | 415 copies |
| | 1996 | 842 copies |
| | plus | 400 copies distributed free. |

All in all, *Nuovo Paese*'s distribution was tiny. The paper was too overtly political and too devoid of the popular culture that *La Fiamma*, *Il Globo* and the Church commanded. Its critics claimed, with some reason, that it was a waste of money. The 1996 increase was due to the fact that in that year *Nuovo Paese* attracted 152 new subscribers (including 82 schools). However, during the same year trade Union support plummeted:

1991 Unions subscribing were 18,  getting 1,869 copies.
1996 Unions subscribing were 8,  getting 710 copies.

Reasons given for the decline were the amalgamation of Trade Unions and the retirement of Italian workers, who received the paper through their Union.[116] Despite brief periods registering an increase in distribution, *Nuovo Paese* was chronically in financial dire straits, despite becoming nationally available in newsagents in 1986 and turning into a 52-page magazine. For a short period, it almost doubled its run per issue to 10 thousand copies.[117] By 1988, it had accumulated a deficit of $2,300.[118] Even the purchase of a new typesetter in 1985, at a cost of $17,000, did not ameliorate the situation,[119] nor did the yearly lotteries in support of the paper. For instance, in 1990 Cammareri Travel gave one return ticket to Rome in exchange for advertisement space.[120]

The amount of work to produce the paper was considerable, and it affected other activities. In 1981 Pierina Pirisi and Edoardo Burani moved to Melbourne to assist the editorial office in the production of the fortnightly edition. From 1974 to February 1984, when it became monthly, *Nuovo Paese* was distributed twice a month. The 1984 change in the frequency of publication was the result of serious problems encountered in Melbourne, and later in Sydney, in the publication of the paper. In 1984 the editorial and publicity offices for *Nuovo Paese* were transferred to FILEF Sydney, at 423 Parramatta Road, Leichhardt. It was at this time that the future of the paper was seriously discussed by the FILEF leadership in Melbourne, Sydney, Adelaide and Rome. Dino Pelliccia, General Secretary of FILEF, Rome, favoured a fortnightly issue, but Sydney pointed out that it could not take the responsibility of an increased frequency, having to deal with *troppo lavoro* (too much work) and that for FILEF Sydney the priority was to increase the organisation's membership and influence: the "organisational work" is "of central importance ... [to] ensure that the work we do will help to grow and strengthen the organisation and increase its influence among the Italian community and society in general". When Adelaide proposed to turn *Nuovo Paese* into a weekly publication, Sydney rejected this proposal, and the editorial office of the paper was transferred to Adelaide.

The search for the best way to inform Italians in Australia about FILEF's policies and activities had not been without robust internal discussion. In 1984 Adelaide complained that "what seems to be missing is being in touch with the workers, plain language, shorter articles and the contribution by people outside of our organisation".[121] On its part, Sydney lamented unwarranted criticism and the lack of constructive proposals. Two letters by Salemi, *infelici e provocatorie* (unfortunate and challenging) criticised FILEF for not insisting in its request for an Italian government contribution of 5-6,000 dollars, although he was a member of the committee deciding the grants. Another criticism was that "we were reproached at the end of last year, because we had not submitted new proposals on the content and the look of the NP monthly ... During the year we received no details nor ideas or contributions from the other branches nor from FILEF headquarters-Rome".[122]

From its beginning, FILEF, both in Melbourne and in Sydney, was involved in the process of defining what were the 'rights' it aimed to defend on behalf of the migrant community. It soon became apparent that three were the areas of immediate concern: the right to work, to education and to retain their cultural traditions, however "invented", foremost their language. Education and Cultural Committees were formed in Melbourne and Sydney in 1972 and 1977 respectively, and links with the Trade Union movement were actively sought. The Education Committee comprised teachers of Italian and parents. FILEF was particularly active in this area, campaigning for the introduction of Italian and other community languages in primary schools. Through the employment of a full-time teacher and a part-time liaison officer, it produced Italian resource materials for teachers of Italian. This material made a valuable contribution to the maintenance and development of the language of children of Italian background. The main objective of activities undertaken by the Cultural Committee was to allow the participants to gain a better knowledge of their culture of origin and to creatively contribute to the cultural and social development of Australia as a multicultural society. One of the ways to achieve this aim was to collect the life stories of immigrants. FILEF embarked on this task since 1975, when historian Morag Loh began to record the experiences of 35 Italian immigrants. In the climate of widespread racism and discrimination against non-

Anglo-Saxon newcomers, also present in the Trade Union movement, it was felt that, as Loh stated, "although twenty-seven per cent of Australia's workforce were born overseas, the immigration process had not been well understood and this had created divisions among working people who needed to understand and accept each other, to stand together so that they could know their rights and fight for them and have an effective voice in Australian society".[123] Morag Loh's research was published in 1980 in a book entitled *With Courage in their Cases*. During the 1980's, FILEF Sydney expanded this initiative, by setting up a publishing company, FILEF Italo-Australian Publications, that over the years produced a number of books in the areas of education, linguistics, social research and cultural endeavours.

The 1970s had been hard times for FILEF. It found itself ostracised by the self-appointed 'representatives' of Sydney's Italian community, kept under close and unremitting watch by ASIO, lambasted by the right-wing Italian Press in Australia, shunned by Australian political parties, of both Liberal-Agrarian and Labor persuasion, and by some sections of the Trade Union movement. Despite this, FILEF embarked in a courageous and determined campaign to motivate recently arrived migrants, in the main Southern, illiterate, Catholic *contadini* (peasants), to know their rights and to assert them. To compound its difficulties, FILEF's proselytising among Catholics, even if nominal, was hampered by the Decree against Communism, issued on 15 July 1948 by the Catholic Church. This document, by Pope Pius XII, excommunicated Catholics collaborating with communist organisations, or even for reading the PCI's daily *L'Unità*. The Decree, confirmed in 1962 by Pope John XXIII, resulted in one of the largest formal excommunications in the history of the Catholic Church. Also, FILEF's charity and welfare initiatives could hardly compete with those of the Church and its related organisations like the Italian Committee of Assistance (Co.As.It). It is not surprising that Italian migrants, having escaped from Christian-Democratic rule only to plunge in anti-communist, Cold War Australia, accustomed to unquestioningly obey the diktats of the priest and the *padrone*, were loath demanding what Salvador Allende's *campesinos* were at the same time clamouring for, *el derecho de vivir en paz,* the right to live in peace, and with dignity.

*FILEFs delegation meets Enrico Berlinguer, Secretary of the Italian Communist Party. (From left) Claudio Crollini, Bruno Di Biase, Margaret Gloster, Enrico Berlinguer, Frank Barbaro, Nicola Vescio, Rome, 1978. (Courtesy Leichhardt Library, FILEF Collection).*

Only during the 1980s the lessons of the Whitlam government, the consequences of the Vietnam War, the quizzical effect of multiculturalism on Anglo-Saxon Australia and the arrival of young people who had experienced the revolutionary fervour of the 1968 student revolt, woke up in many Italian migrants the conscience of their worth, their culture, their rights, their place in Australian society. FILEF was then ready to take up this challenge on their behalf, just as neoliberalism began to take control.

# Notes

[1] On Australian Security Intelligence Organisation's (hereafter ASIO) surveillance on *Il Risveglio*, and on the Italo-Australian Club see: National Archives of Australia (hereafter NAA), Series A9108, Control symbol ROLL 7/12, barcode 1743161, Investigation of communist influence in the Italo-Australian Club. On surveillance on Abbiezzi, Mario, owner of the Garibaldi Bar, see: NAA, Series A432, Control symbol 1953/2096, barcode 1110644, Deportation powers – security aspects – Mario Abbiezzi. On Abbiezzi and the Garibaldi Bar, see: Cavadini, Fabio, *The Other side of the Coin (Il rovescio della medaglia)*, Frontyard Films, Sydney 2012.

[2] Australian Bureau of Statistics (hereafter ABS), *Overseas Born Australians 1988. A Statistical Profile*, Canberra 1989, p. 46.

[3] NAA, Series A10756, control symbol LC1634, item barcode 8861347, Cabinet Note on submission 1601, 24 August 1977.

[4] On Bonegilla, see: Sgrò, Giovanni, *Mediterranean Son. Memoirs of a Calabrian migrant*, Scoprire il Sud, Coburg 2000, pp. 26-28. On working class repression in Italy, see: http://www.fondazionecipriani.it/carlo.htm, accessed 10 December 2014. Also: Bosworth, Richard, 'Conspiracy of the Consuls? Official Italy and the Bonegilla Riot of 1952', in: *Historical Studies*, No. 22, 1987, pp. 547-567.

[5] www.takver.com/history/fordriot.htm, accessed 2 September 2013.

[6] Leichhardt Library, FILEF Collection (hereafter LLFC), box 6, file 5, Migrant Workers and Occupational Health and Safety, p. 3a.

[7] LLFC, box 6, file 5, Lidcombe MHC report, un-dated.

[8] *Nuovo Paese*, 31 July 1981.

[9] Levi, Carlo, *Emigrazione*, no. 1, 15 November 1968. For a history of the establishment of FILEF in Melbourne and its activities between 1972 and 1980, see: Battiston, Simone, *Immigrants Turned Activists. Italians in 1970s Melbourne*, Troubadour Publishing, Kibworth Beauchamp, UK 2012. See also: Sgrò, Giovanni, op.cit., pp. 69-70. See also: Battiston, S. 'Salemi v MacKellar revisited: drawing together the threads of a controversial deportation case', in: *Journal of Australian Studies*, 84 (New Talents issue) 1-10, 2005. Also: Battiston, S., 'La federazione si sviluppa e si consolida: il partito comunista italiano tra gli emigrati italiani in Australia (1966-1973)', in: *Studi Storici*, 50(2): 555-571, 2009. Also: Battiston, S. and Sestigiani, S., 'Percorsi d'emigrazione e di militanza politica: donne italiane in Australia tra gli anni settanta e ottanta del Novecento', in: Luconi, S. and Varricchio, M. (eds), *Lontane da casa: Donne italiane e diaspora locale dall'inizio del Novecento a oggi*, Torino: Accademia University Press, pp. 175-205, 2015. Also: Battiston, S. and Sestigiani, S., 'A lucky country? Il viaggio inchiesta di Diego Novelli de *l'Unità* nell'Australia del 1971', in: *Altreitalie*, 48(1): 40-57, 2014. Also: Pojmann, Wendy (Ed.), *Migration and Activism in Europe since 1945*, Palgrave Macmillan 2008.

[10] LLFC4/1, Halevi, Joseph, *FILEF*, paper un-dated.

[11] Solling, Max and Reynolds, Peter, *Leichhardt: On the Margins of the City*, Allen & Unwin, Sydney 1997, p. 229.

[12] LLFC, box 1, file 7, Marcello, Claudio, to Kirby, Elisabeth MLC, 22 October 1990.

[13] *l'enorme volume di fuoco antipoliticizzante che il Comitato Italiano di Coordinamento esprime in ogni suo momento, con l'appoggio dichiarato del console, non è altro che la continuazione del terrorismo anticomunista di una volta* – FIG/PCI 1975/334/144, Salemi to Pajetta, 21 February 1975.

[14] A long-standing communist member was Agresta, Antonio, who joined the Party in 1921, the year of its foundation in Leghorn. Agresta arrived in Sydney on the *MV Toscana* on 7 May 1951. When, in 1957, he applied for a Certificate of Naturalisation, Sydney's Deputy-Director of the Commonwealth Investigation Service stamped on his form "not adversely recorded". The Service should have been alerted by the fact that Agresta's application had been endorsed by Antico, Giovanni Terribile, an anarchist well known to the CIB since the late 1920s, when Antico, father of the starkly more conservative Antico, Sir Tristan, was playing the piano in Melbourne's anarchist Matteotti Club. Agresta joined FILEF in 1974 (On Agresta, Antonio, see: NAA, Series C321, control symbol N1969/11924, item barcode 12049387, Agresta, Antonio [Italian migrant; immigration file] [Box 93]).

Incidentally, by the passing of time Antico had toned down his anarchist fervour. Like other Italian anarchists in fear of being deported to Italy for their anti-fascist sentiments, on 18 January 1930 he obtained his Certificate of Naturalisation from the Scullin Labor government. During the previous years, Sydney's Italian Consul, Carosi, Mario, obviously not conversant with the ideological differences tearing apart the Regime's enemies, reported to his superiors in Rome that the 'subversive' Antico, who had emigrated to Australia in 1924, was the leader of the local Anti-Fascist League, was contributing to the anarchist newspaper *Il Risveglio* (The Awakening), maintained anti-Italian feelings (*principi anti-italiani*) and was the Secretary of the Communist Party. By 1940 Antico had 'assimilated' to the Australian "way of life" by adopting the name "Terry", no longer signing himself as "Terribile" (*Terrible*). However, once a 'wog', always a wog. During that year he was harassed by his neighbour, a Mrs J. McCarthy, who shouted to him that, as Antico reported to the Police, "we [Italians] are all spies, we should be interned like all the Germans; we rob the Australians their work; we are dirty dagos and pretty soon we all be interned and, if Italy goes to war, our boys will fix the filthy people, and we will have many houses at our disposal". In 1942 some formerly interned Italians again harassed Antico because suspected to be a Police informer. Having investigated the matter, Military Police Intelligence decided to drop the case, on the ground of "Antico, like all Italians, [having] not much moral courage… and has convinced himself that he is a marked man, and is frightening himself accordingly" (NAA, Series C123, control symbol 14556, item barcode 8773837, Antico, Terribile (Italian born – naturalised British subject) [Box 445]. See also: Archivio Centrale dello Stato, Rome, Ministero dell'Interno, Divisione

Affari Generali e Riservati, J5/10, Antico, Giovanni Terribile).

Another communist who evaded the authorities' screening was Abbiezzi, Mario, who took the PCI card in 1926. Born at Casorate Primo in Lombardy in 1907, a draughtsman by profession, like many communists he had incurred the wrath of OVRA, Fascism's secret police. His file in the Casellario Politico Centrale at the Archivio Centrale dello Stato in Rome documents that between 1935 and 1945 he was kept under surveillance after he had been sentenced by the Special Tribunal for State Security. A Memorandum by the Prefect of Novara, dated 3 May 1935, to the Ministry for the Interior, details Abbiezzi's biographical note as follows: "He soon proved to have a good character, possessing ability and organisational skills, so much so that, having enrolled in the same year [1932] in the PNF, he was entrusted with prominent trade union tasks. However, in April 1934 he was arrested after it was ascertained that he had agreed with a certain Tambussi Luigi, his father's name being Celestino, to attempt at the life of H.E. the Head of Government by exploding bombs against the train, at the inaugural opening of the railway line Biella-Novara, which was carrying beside H.E. Il Duce, several of the Regime's VIP's. For this crime, on 27 March 1935 he was sentenced by the Special Tribunal to eight years in prison with two years of conditional amnesty, the perpetual disqualification from public offices and to be kept under security surveillance" (*si dimostrò subito buon elemento rivelando anche capacità ed attitudini organizzative, tanto che, iscrittosi nello stesso anno [1932] al PNF, gli furono quì affidate importanti cariche sindacali. Senonchè nell'aprile 1934 egli venne tratto in arresto essendo venuto a risultare che si era messo d'accordo con tal Tambussi Luigi di Celestino per attentare alla vita di S.E. il Capo del Governo mediante esplosione di bombe contro il treno inaugurale del tronco ferroviario Novara-Biella nel quale avrebbero dovuto trovarsi oltre S.E. il Duce, numerose personalità del Regime. Per tale delitto venne condannato con sentenza 27 marzo 1935 del Tribunale Speciale ad otto anni di reclusione col condono condizionale di anni due, alla interdizione perpetua dai pubblici uffici ed alla libertà vigilata* – ACS/CPC, busta 5, codice identificativo A00102, Abbiezzi Mario, Novara's Prefect to Ministry for the Interior, 3 May 1935).

Abbiezzi was the son-in-law of Ramella, Secondo, a former socialist Member of Parliament, having married his daughter Vanda. At that time Ramella was also kept under surveillance by OVRA (ACS, CPC busta 4216, codice identificativo R00874, Ramella Secondo Giovanni). Abbiezzi's comrade in 'crime', Tambussi, Luigi, also a communist, was given a shorter period of detention, four years (ACS, CPC, busta 5017, fascicolo 120807, codice identificativo T00622, Tambussi, Luigi Teodoro). Both were incriminated, as Ramella claimed in a letter to Bocchini, Arturo, Chief of Police, "concerning the planned bombing, following testimonies given by communist detainees" (*in merito al progettato attentato le deposizioni di accusa provenivano da detenuti comunisti*). While in detention, Abbiezzi wrote to Mussolini and to the King, seeking their pardon and an early release. While admitting that the Tribunal had justly condemned him, "because in effect there was wicked evidence against me", he professed to the man he had planned to murder, his "faithfulness to Your Sacred Person and to the Fascist Regime". In his letter to the King, like many turncoats (*voltagabbana*) who constellate the history of Italian anti-fascism, also Abbiezzi gave the impression of having abjured communism: "there are political detainees who do not have a bar of pardon, because they follow a chimerical and utopian belief, but I only think of my family". Abbiezzi was incarcerated in the penal establishment at Castelfranco Emilia until 17 April 1938, when he benefited from an amnesty. The Prefect of Novara advised the Ministry for the Interior that Abbiezzi, "in view of his being dangerous, should be kept in jail until after the Führer visit to Italy" (*data la pericolosità dell'Abbiezzi, sarebbe opportuno trattenerlo in carcere fin dopo la venuta in Italia del Führer*). Following his release, the fascist authorities, to the very end of the dictatorship, regularly monitored his whereabouts. In February 1945, Milan's *Questura Repubblicana* reported to the Ministry for the Interior that Abbiezzi "in October 1943 was residing at Lambrugo (Como), from where in September 1944 he left for an unknown destination", and Como's *Questura Repubblicana* confirmed during the same month that the "subversive, since last January wanted by this *Questura*, has not been seen in this location, nor were we able to find out his current whereabouts…It was not possible to ascertain his participation in attacks or sabotage and his degree of dangerousness" (*dal gennaio scorso, siccome ricercato da codesta Questura, non è più stato notato in questo Comune nè è stato possibile conoscere ove si trovi attualmente…circa la capacità di commettere attentati o atti di sabotaggio ed il grado di pericolosità, non è possibile precisare* – ACS, CPC, Abbiezzi Mario, busta 5, codice identificativo A00102. Abbiezzi's appeals to Mussolini and to the King, un-dated; Ministry for the Interior to CPC, 1 April 1935; Prefettura di Novara to Ministero dell'Interno, 3 May 1935, 27 November 1937 and 8 April 1938; Ramella to Bocchini, 3 April 1936; Questura Repubblicana di Milano to Ministero dell'Interno, 18 February 1945; Questura Repubblicana di Como to Ministero dell'Interno, 12 February 1945). Obviously, the fascist *repubblichini* authorities were unaware that Abbiezzi had already joined the partisan brigades operating on the mountains overlooking Como.

In 1953 legal advice to the Australian Cabinet stated that Abbiezzi "was admitted as a business visitor in 1949 and in regard to whose permanent stay a security objection was raised on the ground that he was a member of the executive of a communist-penetrated organisation and a financial contributor to a communist publication". Security's objection was prompted by Abbiezzi's anti-fascist record published on 14 January 1953 in the CPA's paper *Tribune*: "1934 His anti-fascist activities resulted in his arrest and sentence to eight years in Mussolini's jails. 1942. Was arrested in May and sentenced to death in August of that year. 1943. He was freed by the patriots and in October was in the first fight against the fascists as a member of the patriotic forces…He was commander of the partisan forces in Milan during the political strike against the German invaders…as commander of the partisan forces of the zone of Como and Sondrio…he gave the order to his partisan group at Dongo to arrest Mussolini and his 19 Ministers…he was elected Chief of Police of Sondrio". Abbiezzi is quoted in Pavone, Claudio, *Una guerra civile* as being in July 1944 the political commissar of the 40th Garibaldi Matteotti brigade by the battle name of "Ario". Abbiezzi joined FILEF in 1974, and in 1975, in a conversation with a person, unbeknown to him to be an ASIO informer, indicated that "he was tired of working in the coffee shop…and that he would sell the shop and work full time for

FILEF" (NAA, Series A6122, control symbol 2671, item barcode 13031175, FILEF vol. 1, - 2323 - confidential report, 21 May 1975). Abbiezzi died on 20 March 1986 in the Sacred Heart Hospice, Darlinghurst. (On Abbiezzi, Mario, see: NAA, Series A432, control symbol 1953/2096, item barcode 1110644, Deportation powers. Also, *Tribune*, 14 January 1953. Also: Pavone, Claudio, *Una guerra civile. Saggio storico sulla moralità nella Resistenza*, Bollati Boringhieri, Torino 1998, pp. 133, 675 and 797).

Another prominent communist militant who slipped through the net was Braida, Dante. He arrived in Sydney on 1 August 1952 on board the *MV Castel Bianco*, a political as well as economic emigrant. During the Second World War, from April 1944 to June 1945, Braida was a partisan in the communist-led Garibaldi Division Left Tagliamento "Sergio and Battisti", Brigade "Calligaris", Battalion "Cairoli". After the war, his friendship and siding with Yugoslav partisans brought him into a collision course with the PCI, that was following Stalin in his condemnation of Tito's brand of communism, and he was expelled because accused of "Titoist heresy". Braida joined FILEF in 1978. (On Braida, Dante, see: NAA, Series SP908/1, control symbol ITALIAN/BRAIDA DANTE, item barcode 8796497).

[15]   LLFC, box 9, items a, c, f, g, h.

[16]   NAA, Series A4556, barcode 280136, Australia: Immigration policy – Migration Agreement with Italy. Australian Legation, Rome, Information required of all applicants over the age of 14 years who apply for permanent residence in Australia, un-dated.

[17]   Ibid., ASIO to Casey, 13 November 1951.

[18]   Ibid. On PCI's membership figures, see: http://it.wikipedia.org/wiki/Partito_Comunista_Italiano accessed 3 July 2014. For general histories of the Italian Communist Party, see: Spriano, Paolo, *Storia del Partito Comunista Italiano*. Vol. 1 to 5, Einaudi, Torino 1967-1975. Also: Spriano, Paolo, *Intervista sulla Storia del PCI*, Laterza, Bari 1979. Also: Pons, Silvio, *Berlinguer e la fine del comunismo*, Einaudi, Torino 2006. Also: Gozzini, Mario, *Oltre gli steccati: cattolici, laici e comunisti in Italia, 1963-1993*, Sperling & Kupfer, Milano 1994)

[19]   Fondazione Istituto Gramsci, Rome, Fondo Partito Comunista Italiano (hereafter FIG/PCI), 1973, busta 217, fascic. 244.

[20]   FIG/PCI, 1974/262/14, Salemi, Relazione sulla permanenza in Australia, September 1974.

[21]   FIG/PCI, 1975/334/144, Colli to Sezione di Organizzazione, 9 December 1975.

[22]   FIG/PCI, 1977/415/33, Cianca, Informazione sulla sua permanenza in Australia, un-dated.

[23]   *mentre con la FILEF siamo quasi al 100% e contiamo di superarlo notevolmente, col partito incontriamo più resistenze, dovute…a una diffusissima paura, c'è persino paura di perdere la pensione o il lavoro se ci si iscrive al partito!* – FIG/PCI, 1978/482/60, Pirisi to Pajetta, 21 February 1978.

24    *i principali comitati della città ci convocano a tutte le riunioni, i ministri ci fanno la corte anche se poi hanno il timore di compromettersi perchè capiscono e sanno chi c'è dietro* – FIG/PCI, 1974/276/111, Salemi to Pajetta, 17 June 1974.

25    *dovremmo pensare di più a come creare le condizioni per uscire da questa specie di 'clandestinità' che ci pesa tanto* –FIG/PCI, 1978/482/60, Pirisi to Pajetta, 21 February 1978.

26    NAA, Series A6122, control symbol 2671, item barcode 13031175, FILEF vol. 1, 117 – confidential report, date censored.

27    FIG/PCI, 1974/262/14, Salemi, relazione sulla permanenza in Australia, September 1974.

28    *ricordati quanto è importante per molte ragioni un incremento degli iscritti* – FIG/PCI, 1975/334/144, Pajetta to Salemi, 9 October 1975.

29    *comunque ricordati che i numeri hanno la loro importanza e possono servire da elemento di giudizio anche per "altri"* – FIG/PCI, 1974/276/111, Pajetta to Salemi, 18 November 1974.

30    *il rischio di avere una FILEF 'partito di massa socialcomunista' e un partito chiuso e di 'quadri' esiste per mille ragioni ambientali…la necessità di avere un PCI di massa ci sembra esistere…ci sembra molto importante e va molto al di là della soddisfazione – non puramente statistica – di contare presto alcune centinaia di tesserati* – FIG/PCI, 1974/276/111, Pajetta to Salemi, 23 April 1984. In Sydney, the recruitment of members to the Party was hampered by public quarrels and disunity among Branch members. Salemi made this point in a letter to Pajetta: *"C'è un altro compagno…l'ho reclutato io un mese fa. Ma è veramente impegnatissimo: lavora in una azienda industriale, insegna italiano e storia all'Università, sta facendo accurate ricerche sul movimento antifascista in Australia dal primo dopoguerra ad oggi e abita a venticinque miglia da Sydney…l'ambiente di Sydney non è certo quello più adatto per utilizzare un tipo come quello…vorrei evitare che rimanesse sconvolto dalla situazione di Sydney dalla quale si è mantenuto sempre ai margini perchè impegnato in altro modo* – FIG/PCI, 1974/276/111, Salemi to Pajetta, 17 June 1974. Also, see: FIG/PCI, 1975/334/144, Salemi to Pajetta, 31 October 1975.

31    *la FILEF è, ricordiamolo bene a tutti, una organizzazione autonoma. In primo luogo deve essere chiaro che non si tratta nè di una mascheratura nostra, nè di un partito "un po' più largo" ma di una associazione democratica (che noi appoggiamo con tutte le nostre forze) che si occupa della tutela degli interessi materiali e morali degli emigrati e delle loro famiglie* – FIG/PCI, 1978/ 482/60, Pajetta to PCI Organisations in Australia, 18 October 1978.

32    *la FILEF non è una semplice etichetta ma una associazione di massa comprendente comunisti e non comunisti* – FIG/PCI, 1973/234/14, Pajetta to Sydney Branch, 30 June 1973.

33    NAA, Series A6122, control symbol 2672, item barcode 30485694, FILEF vol. 2, - 144 -, confidential report, date censored.

34    LLFC, box 6, file 15, CFC Constitution, Article 2.

35    LLFC, box 2, file 7, Di Biase, Bruno, Il ruolo del PCI nelle elezioni australiane. Appunti per una discussione, un-dated.

36  NAA, Series C320, control symbol CIB615, barcode 305090, NSW Security Service File – Italian Communists.

37  NAA, Series BP242/1, control symbol Q10422, barcode 335288, 'Undesirable Italians'. Also: NAA, Series A437, control symbol 1950/6/153, item barcode 75139, Italian-Australian Association – Assimilation of Italians, Francis to Holt, 9 March 1950; Holt to Francis, 31 March 1950.

38  NAA, Series A6122, control symbols 376, 380, 381, 382 and 629, barcodes 368164, 368180, 368204 368206 and 5470967 respectively, 'CPA – Activities and interest in Italian community. For a history of ASIO from its establishment, in March 1949, to 1990, see: Cain, Frank, 'ASIO and the Australian Labour Movement – An Historical Perspective', in: *Labour History,* No. 58, May 1990, pp.1-16. See also: McKnight, David, *Australia's Spies and their Secrets,* Allen & Unwin, Crows Nest 1994. Also: Burgmann, Meredith, *Dirty Secrets. Our ASIO Files,* Newsouth, Sydney 2014. Also: Moorhouse, Frank, *Australia under Surveillance,* Random House, 2014. Also: Horner, David, *The Spy Catchers. The Official History of ASIO. 1949-1963,* Allen & Unwin, Crows Nest 2014.

39  NAA, Series A432, control symbol 1953/2096, barcode 1110644, Deportation powers – security aspects.

40  NAA, Series C5431, control symbol 32/1/320.3, barcode 8402042, May Day March Melbourne 1957 (surveillance footage recorded by ASIO).

41  Davidson, Alastair, *The Communist Party of Australia. A Short History,* Hoover Institution Press, Stanford University, 1969, p. 166.

42  Aarons, Mark, *The Family File,* Black Inc., Melbourne 2010, p. X-XI and p. 276.

43  NAA, Series A6122, control symbol 2671, item barcode 13031175, FILEF vol. 1, - 172 – confidential report no. 1044/75, 9 April 1975.

44  NAA, Series A6122, control symbol 2671, item barcode 13031175, FILEF Vol. 1, - 145 - Director-General, ASIO to Liaison Officer, Rome, 7 January 1975.

45  NAA, Series A6122, control symbol 2673, item barcode 30485695, FILEF Vol. 3, - 104 - Director-General, ASIO to Secretary, Department of Immigration and Ethnic Affairs, 18 March 1977.

46  NAA, Series A6119, control symbol 4747, barcode 30820415, Lavezzari, Umberto, Volume 1. See also: NAA, Series A6119, control symbol 4640, barcode 30030851, Lavezzari, Carmela, Volume 1.

47  NAA, Series A6119, control symbol 3820, barcode 7949852, Pajetta, Guiliano (sic) Volume 1, ASIO report no. 38/73, dated 5 April 1973.

48  Ibid., ASIO report no. 1482/66, dated 23 May 1966.

49  Ibid., ASIO report no. 2873/66, dated 24 August 1966.

50  Canali, Mauro, *Le spie del Regime,* Il Mulino, Bologna 2004.

51 *da molti anni i compagni australiani sollecitano l'invio di un compagno nostro in grado di svolgere una attività di direzione politica tra i nostri emigrati... solo recentemente i compagni australiani hanno precisato in modo formale il loro impegno* – FIG/PCI, 1973/217/244, Pajetta to Direzione PCI, 19 July 1973.

52 Berlinguer, Enrico, Opening Report to the XIV National Congress of the PCI, in: *The Italian Communists, Foreign Bulletin of the PCI*, N. 2-3, March-May 1975, pp. 66 and 73.

53 FIG/PCI, 1975/334/144, Palazzolo to Pecchioli, 12 October 1971.

54 NAA, Series A6122, control symbol 2671, item barcode 13031175, FILEF Vol. 1, - 68 – confidential report, 29 November 1973.

55 *vogliamo innanzitutto esprimervi il nostro più vivo disappunto per il vostro contegno in occasione dell'incontro con L. Aarons del 13.8 scorso...con quale diritto voi pensate che i compagni australiani non possano conoscere i vostri problemi...ogni altro vostro atteggiamento si oppone non al partito australiano ma al partito italiano* - FIG/PCI, 1972/170/191, Pajetta to PCI Federation in Australia, 20 September 1972.

56 FIG/PCI, 1972/177/254, Aarons to Pajetta, 28 November 1972.

57 FIG/PCI, 1973/217/244, Aarons to PCI Central Committee, 14 February 1973.

58 *le cose non vanno come speravamo quando abbiamo favorito la costituzione di una Federazione del PCI in Australia...quando parlavamo di una federazione autonoma intendevamo una Federazione capace di prendere iniziative politiche e propagandistiche autonome non in contrasto con la linea politica generale del nostro Partito o dei compagni del PCA* – FIG/PCI, 1973/234/13, Pajetta to PCI members in Australia and to the PCA, 27 February 1973.

59 FIG/PCI, 1973/234/12, Aarons to Pajetta, 27 March 1973.

60 *la vostra lettera del 14 marzo non può facilitare o avvicinare un contatto o una collaborazione fra noi...sono per noi inaccettabili sia il contenuto che il tono dei vostri riferimenti al CPA...non intendiamo stabilire nessun contatto o collaborazione che possano essere utilizzati contro il PCA* – FIG/PCI, `973/234/12, Cossutta to Symon, 5 April 1973.

61 NAA, Series A6119, Control symbol 3820, barcode 7949852, Pajetta, Guiliano (sic), Volume 1, ASIO report no. 38/73, dated 5 April 1973.

62 FIG/PCI, 1973/234/13, Pajetta to PCI members in Australia and to the PCA, 27 February 1973.

63 NAA, Series A6119, Control symbol 3820, barcode 7949852, Pajetta, Guiliano (sic), Volume 1, ASIO report no. 2103/73, dated 22 March 1973.

64 Ibid., ASIO report no. 2537/73, dated 2 May 1973.

65 Ibid., ASIO HQ File no. 2/20/11, dated 29 May 1973.

66 Ibid., ASIO report no. 2728/73, dated 23 April 1973.

67    Ibid., ASIO report no. 2537/73, dated 2 May 1973.

68    Ibid., ASIO report no. 3890/73, dated 25 July 1973.

69    *esprime un giudizio critico sulla gestione politica e organizzativa del Segretario e dell'Esecutivo Federale uscenti* - FIG/PCI, 1973/234/12, Mozione conclusiva, un-dated.

70    *il compagno Palazzolo si è fatto pagare per le prestazioni date a nome dell'INCA* – FIG/PCI, 1974/275/110, Salemi to Francisconi, un-dated. See also: FIG/PCI, 1974/262/14, Salemi, Relazione sulla permanenza in Australia, September 1974. Also: FIG/PCI, 1974/276/111, Salemi to Pajetta, 15 April 1974.

71    *non sono avvertite le esigenze nazionali dei vari gruppi di emigrati e, tranne qualche eccezione, i sindacati non hanno nessuna iniziativa particolare o forma di lavoro particolare verso gli emigrati... le sue politiche sono sconosciute o quasi alla grande opinione pubblica...è difficile che il PCA sia almeno un "gruppo di pressione" di una certa forza...sono tutti di livello modesto...a Sydney le questioni personali degeneravano, confondendosi con questioni politiche e portavano a una profonda spaccatura e a una rottura...si pone a questo punto la questione se, e in che misura, è possibile superare l'attuale, immenso distacco tra le nostre attuali organizzazioni esistenti e la gran massa degli italiani residenti in Australia* – FIG/PCI, 1973/217/244, Pajetta, Informazione sul soggiorno in Australia, aprile-maggio 1973.

72    *mi pare di dover costatare che l'Italia e il partito in Italia, sono cose troppo lontane, e non solo geograficamente, per poter costituire un serio elemento di coesione dei nostri organizzati quì* – FIG/PCI, 1974/276/111, Salemi to Pajetta, 15 April 1974.

73    NAA, Series A6119, Control symbol 3820, barcode 7949852, Pajetta, Guiliano (sic), Volume 1, ASIO report no. 3889/73, dated 30 July 1973.

74    *il fatto nuovo è che la compagna P. Pirisi lavora adesso a 'tempo pieno' con i nostri amici australiani* – FIG/PCI, 1973/234/13, Pajetta to Colli, 18 June 1973.

75    FIG/PCI, 1973/234/12, Pajetta to Aarons, 19 July 1973.

76    NAA, Series A6119, Control symbol 3820, barcode 7949852, Pajetta, Guiliano (sic), Volume 1, ASIO report no. 1143/74, dated 8 March 1974.

77    *ti raccomandiamo vivamente di utilizzarla e valorizzarla per il lavoro giornalistico o altro che può fare. Occorre aiutarla moralmente e materialmente* – FIG/PCI, 1974/276/111, Pajetta to Salemi, 18 November 1974.

78    *noi siamo molto preoccupati della tua salute e della tua sistemazione. Ricordati che non è 'rivoluzionario' trascurare la propria salute e tu sei un nostro quadro prezioso* – FIG/PCI, 1974/276/111, Pajetta to Pirisi, 7 January 1974.

79    FIG/PCI, 1974/276/111, Salemi to Pajetta, letter un-dated.

80    *i giudizi che tu dai sono sostanzialmente giusti ed essa profonde buona volontà ed onestà a piene mani in una serie di cose piccole e grandi di carattere pratico, ma le mancano esperienza, che in un ambiente come questo dovrebbe chiamarsi piuttosto astuzia o malizia, e forza di carattere che in fondo significa capacità di essere convincente* – FIG/PCI, 1975/334/144, Salemi to

Pajetta, 21 February 1975. See also Salemi's more damning assessment of Pirisi in a letter of 1974, where he maintained that *Pierina, poverina, ha tanta volontà ma anche moltissimi limiti, di personalità, di comunicabilità, di iniziativa, di memoria, di organizzazione, di ordine, e bisognerebbe dire anche di presentazione e di qualche cos'altro. Alterna lunghi momenti di scoramento a brevi momenti di entusiasmo disorganizzato e disorganizzante. Il tutto frammisto a periodi di poca salute* – FIG/PCI, 1974/276/111, Salemi to Pajetta, 17 June 1974.

[81] *la mia continuata permanenza nell'organizzazione serve soltanto a logorarmi fisicamente e psichicamente e a farmi trascurare i miei studi. Serve tutt'al più a far sopravvivere la FILEF, ma non la FILEF come un'organizzazione politica, bensì la FILEF come un'accozzaglia di individui che si scannano l'uno con l'altro* – FIG/PCI, 1975/334/144, Pirisi to Pajetta and Salemi, 6 September 1975. See also: NAA, Series A6122, control symbol 2672, item barcode 30485694, FILEF vol. 2, confidential report, - 134 -, date censored.

[82] NAA, Series A2559, control symbol 1970/51/2142-2144, barcode 5337728, Pirisi Pietrina (sic), born 13 August 1950.

[83] NAA, Series A6119, control symbol 4640, barcode 30030851, Lavezzari Carmela, volume 1, ASIO report no. 3606/73, dated 26 June 1973.

[84] NAA, Series A6119, control symbol 3820, barcode 7949852, Pajetta, Guiliano (sic), Volume 1, ASIO Regional Director, Sydney, to Headquarters, 16 January 1974.

[85] Ibid., ASIO report no. 2558/73, dated 3 May 1973.

[86] Ibid., ASIO report no. 3040/73, dated 31 May 1973.

[87] Ibid., ASIO report no. 4465/73, dated 20 June 1973.

[88] *non bisogna dimenticare che noi ci rivolgiamo agli italiani, naturalizzati o no, ma che hanno una mentalità* specifica*, bisogni e rivendicazioni particolari, non uguali agli altri lavoratori australiani o di altre emigrazioni. Per questo e anche per altri motivi non possiamo e non dobbiamo* identificare *l'attività della sezione del PCI con quella del CPA* – FIG/PCI, 1973/234/14, Pajetta to PCI Branch Sydney, 18 June 1973.

[89] *le relazioni con Joe e amici…non è una questione semplice e non si risolve in un giorno – importante è che non vi sia una imposizione di altra linea o di altre misure organizzative…Vedrete voi, con calma, se è meglio che [Pirisi] si disimpegni dalla sua posizione ufficiale con la ditta di Joe* – FIG/PCI, 1974/276/111, Pajetta to Salemi, 5 December 1974. Edoardo Burani's account is that *"per quanto riguarda l'impiego di Pierina al CPA, non ha mai subito alcuna pressione nè da Pajetta nè da Salemi per lasciarlo, ma si è dimessa spontaneamente perchè non le risultava che la direzione del CPA avesse ben chiaro il suo ruolo, mentre riteneva di poter fare qualcosa di più concreto lavorando nella comunità italiana* –Burani, Edoardo and Pirisi, Pierina, email to author, 18 July 2014.

[90] *noi abbiamo una linea di lavoro 'italiano'. É questo lo scopo dell'esistenza di organizzazioni del PCI anche in Australia…É possibile che dei membri del CPA, di origine o nazionalità italiana, non siano interessati o non siano d'accordo con questo tipo di lavoro. Noi non ce ne scandalizziamo, lavorino come credono opportuno nelle loro organizzazioni del CPA ma non ci possono imporre in*

*nome proprio o di un altro partito di cambiare la nostra linea generale di lavoro nell'emigrazione* –
FIG/PCI, 1974/276/111, Pajetta to Pirisi, 4 December 1974.

91 NAA, Series A6119, control symbol 3820, barcode 7949852, Pajetta, Guiliano (sic),
Volume 1, ASIO report dated 9 April 1973.

92 Ibid., ASIO report dated 17 April 1973.

93 *il compagno Palazzolo di Sydney ha intenzione di aprire una sezione della FILEF qua a Sydney...a
parere della maggior parte dei membri del Comitato a questo momento non potremmo assumerci
l'incarico, o meglio, non abbiamo la possibilità di occuparcene in modo responsabile* – FIG/PCI,
1973/234/14, Pirisi to PCI Rome, 20 June 1973.

94 *non siamo disposti a seguirlo su una strada pericolosa...iniziative tipo FILEF devono essere coordinate
con voi...questo è un tipo di attività che non può essere 'lanciata' da qualcuno conosciuto come
comunista, ma da un gruppo comprendente anche gente non nostra* – FIG/PCI, 1973/234/14,
Pajetta to PCI Branch Sydney, 18 June 1973.

95 NAA, Series A6122, control symbol 2671, item barcode 13031175, FILEF Vol. 1, -
43– confidential report, 23 July 1973.

96 NAA, Series A6119, control symbol 3820, barcode 7949852, Pajetta, Guiliano (sic),
Volume 1, ASIO report dated 29 November 1973.

97 NAA, Series A6122, control symbol 2671, item barcode 13031175, FILEF Vol. 1, -
67– confidential report, 19 December 1973.

98 FIG/PCI, 1973/234/13, Pajetta to Colli, 27 September 1973.

99 FIG/PCI, 1974/275/110, Pajetta to PCI Secretariat, 9 September 1974. Also: FIG/
PCI, 1974/276/111, Pajetta to Pirisi, 7 January and 4 December 1974; ibid., Salemi
to Pajetta, letter un-dated; Bruno Di Biase, interview with author, 24 January 2014.

100 NAA, Series A6119, control symbol 3820, barcode 7949852, Pajetta, Guiliano (sic),
Volume 1, ASIO report no. 5320/73, dated 29 November 1973.

101 FIG/PCI, 1974/275/110, Pajetta to PCI Secretariat, 9 September 1974.

102 NAA, Series A6980, control symbol S203645, barcode 6936595, Salemi Ignazio –
Part 4, ASIO, Summary of Information, Mr Ignazio Salemi, un-dated.

103 NAA, Series A6980, control symbol S203645, barcode 6936595, Salemi Ignazio –
Part 4, ASIO, Memorandum, History of principal events, un-dated.

104 NAA, Series A6122, control symbol 2672, item barcode 30485694, FILEF vol. 2, -
208, 209 – cablegram, 13 April 1976.

105 NAA, Series A6980, control symbol S203609, barcode 6946508, Salemi Ignazio –
Part 2, Canali to Bott, 16 August 1976.

106 FIG/PCI, 1977/448/205, Pajetta to PCI Secretariat, 31 October 1977.

107 NAA, Series A6980, control symbol S203645, barcode 6936595, Salemi Ignazio –

Part 4, ASIO, Summary of Information, Mr Ignazio Salemi, un-dated.

[108] NAA, Series A6980, control symbol S203609, barcode 6946508, Salemi Ignazio – Part 2, ASIO, Memorandum, un-dated.

[109] Ibid., Sgrò to McKellar, 15 July 1976.

[110] NAA, Series A6122, control symbol 2671, item barcode 13031175, FILEF Vol. 1, - 203– confidential report, date censored.

[111] NAA, Series A6122, control symbol 2672, item barcode 30485694, FILEF vol. 2, - 139–, ASIO's Liaison Officer, Rome, note to Ambassador, 6 January 1976.

[112] NAA, Series M4174, Control symbol 73, item barcode 31110403, Documents concerning FILEF.

[113] NAA, Series A6122, control symbol 2672, item barcode 30485694, FILEF vol. 2, - 130 –, confidential report, date censored.

[114] LLFC, box 1, file 1, Di Biase to FILEF Adelaide, 23 May 1985.

[115] LLFC, box 1, file 1, FILEF Sydney memorandum, September 1984. See also: FIG/PCI, 1974/262/14, Salemi, Relazione sulla permanenza in Australia, September 1974.

[116] LLFC, box 1, file 1, Bianco, Adelaide, to Editorial Offices in Melbourne, Sydney and Perth, 12 July 1996.

[117] LLFC, box 1, file 1, Pettini, circular letter, 7 February 1986.

[118] LLFC, box 1, file 1, Panucci to members, 10 March 1988.

[119] LLFC, box 1, file 1, Panucci to FILEF Adelaide, 13 September 1985.

[120] LLFC, box 1, file 1, Zaccari to Cammareri, 4 June 1990.

[121] *ci sembra che manchi quel contatto con i lavoratori, il linguaggio semplice, l'articolo più breve e l'intervento stesso di persone fuori della nostra organizzazione.* - LLFC, box 1, file 1, Enzo (Adelaide) to Pierina, 17 February 1984.

[122] *ci si rimproverò, alla fine dell'anno scorso, di non aver presentato delle proposte nuove rispetto agli eventuali contenuti e forme del NP mensile…Nel corso dell'anno non ci sono pervenute idee o contributi particolari nè dalle altre sedi e nè dalla FILEF centrale-Roma* – Ibid.

[123] Loh, Morag, *With Courage in their Cases,* FILEF Publications, Melbourne 1980, p. 1.

# 2

# FILEF during the 1980s: "no longer 'things' or passive labour providers, but protagonists".

*Per questa gente, va bene parlare di multiculturalismo,*
*finchè si tratta di pizza e spaghetti,*
*ma non quando si tratta di politica.*
(It is acceptable for this people to talk about multiculturalism,
while it is about pizza and pasta,
but not when it is about politics).
FIG/PCI, 1978/482/60

The 1970's, at least until 1978, were halcyon years for left-wing parties in Italy. After that, it was downhill all the way as neoliberalism arrived, in Australia ironically mostly through politics introduced by governments led by the previous union leader Robert Hawke and by Paul Keating. American scholar Robert W. McChesney defined neoliberalism as "capitalism with the gloves off". Any short-term gains were illusions as unions were destroyed and inequality advanced, although there is a neoliberal case that can be made. It is about global growth and catch up through free trade, the end of quite a bit of self-indulgent government waste and a tracking down of prosperity to the majority in a process that is at least arguable to 2008. In an Australia that quickly went through the exhilarating experience of change under Whitlam, only to be confronted by the backlash of conservatism under Malcolm Fraser, the first years of FILEF were understandably difficult. An early, un-dated circular letter, written early in 1974, announced the publication *a brevissima scadenza* ("in a short while") of a newspaper, *Nuovo Paese,* that would be FILEF's *organo ed espressione fondamentale* (mouthpiece and main advocate). It also advertised the formation of a provisional committee, based in Melbourne and Sydney, operating from the private residences of Giovanni Sgrò in Coburg and Nicola Vescio in Paddington. The letter also proclaimed the organisation's goals, drawn from the statute of FILEF's headquarters in Rome. They included the defence of migrants' rights, their participation in the affairs of their country of election, welfare programs, the promotion of cultural activities, the maintenance of the Italian language and treatment equal to that enjoyed by local labour. But of course fundamental and ironical was the switch from class to 'identity politics'.[1]

One of FILEF's immediate concerns was to find an appropriate venue from where to operate. Soon, Paddington's private premises proved inadequate and in 1974 a venue was rented at 26 Norton Street, Leichhardt. The Spanish Communist Party in Australia and the Migrant Action Group shared the building with FILEF. Soon, the tenants were in arrears over their rent, and FILEF repeatedly threatened to evict them. FILEF's Dimitri Oliva, who also was a member of the pro-Moscow Socialist Party of Australia, reflecting the conspiratorial mindset of the time, attacked the CPA "for supposedly not paying the rent on behalf of the Migrant Action Group so as the PCI Sydney Branch would collapse". An ASIO informer reported that the Group's dues were 14 weeks late because "Pierina Pirisi, who controlled the Migrant Action Group, is currently in Italy and this Group has become moribund".[2]

In May 1975, compelled to relocate by reason of the unaffordable rental cost, FILEF moved to 85 Parramatta Road Annandale, and in January 1977 to 558 Parramatta Road, Petersham.[3] Eventually, as membership increased and adequate funds were raised, FILEF leased suites 1 and 2 on the first floor at 423 Parramatta Road, Leichhardt, from where it carried out its activities until 1993. However, in October 1992 FILEF advised the lessor: "I regret to inform you that our organisation is not at present in a position to commit itself to another three year term. We are confident only of the near future and therefore ask that you consider offering a shorter lease or continue on a monthly basis".[4] In December 1992 FILEF paid the last monthly rental and forfeited reimbursement of security money. The reason why it terminated the lease was that "FILEF has not received any major government funding in the last two years".[5]

FILEF's premises at 423 Parramatta Road, Leichhardt, 1980s (Courtesy Leichhardt Library, FILEF Collection).

Although FILEF was a federation, inclusive of members belonging to disparate political affiliations, the communist element, adopting a very old "Leninist" tactic, as mentioned in chapter 1, played a pivotal role. Edoardo Burani, one of FILEF's stalwarts from the early days, admitted it in 1978, although overestimating the numerical strength of PCI's members: "In those years the Italian Communists established INCA (Istituto Nazionale Confederale di Assistenza Benevolent Fund), laid the foundations of FILEF, a mass anti-fascist organisation, whose members included workers of different political beliefs, in which the Communists played a vanguard role because they were the most numerous and the most active".[6]

However, the political environment in which FILEF had to make inroads was difficult, when not overtly hostile. As Burani stated, "since the early years of the organised presence of PCI in NSW, late in 1971 or early in 1972, the comrades had to deal with obstacles of a different nature: economic, logistic, misunderstandings with workers' organisations in Australia, difference of views between comrades themselves, but above all the difficulty to reactivate the Italian comrades, emigrated during the 1950s, who remained for a long time and for different reasons on the edge of Italian and Australian political life".[7] At that stage, the main strategy aiming to reach sympathetic migrants was the provision of written information, alternative to that spread by the Italo-Australian conservative press, represented by Sydney's *La Fiamma* and *Il Corriere di Settegiorni*. At the 1978 congress of the NSW section of the PCI, Burani reported: "the need for a more honest and democratic information in the Italian community was seen as one of the priorities of the nascent organisation of the PCI in Australia". That is why in the 1960s Italian communists affiliated with the CPA began distributing a bulletin in Italian, *Il Nuovo Paese*. It was subsidised by the Communist Party of Australia, and it was sold for sixpence, while the cost of production was one shilling and sixpence per copy.[8] It had a troubled life, not only financially. Few migrants were interested in it. Local Italian communists naively believed in the effectiveness of print propaganda among Italian migrants, who were in many cases illiterate or semi-literate, preoccupied in rebuilding their life in a country largely hostile to their politicisation, especially if communist-inspired, and fearful of retribution if caught supporting what was considered by the dominant culture an alien, subversive ideology. In June 1965 three hundred invitations were sent out to first-generation Italians to attend a meeting, to discuss the newspaper's future. Other than its committee members, only two other Italians turned up, one being Carmela Lavezzari, who was drafted in the executive group.[9] Other committee members were Giuseppe Cortelessa, Francesco Di

Bella, Nicola De Franco, Vittorio Magistrale and Dimitri Oliva.

In 1973 ASIO reported that Mario Abbiezzi had for some time been on the committee of *Il Nuovo Paese*.[10] In September 1965 only 300 copies were sold in Leichhardt.[11] Another reason for its poor circulation was police harassment. An ASIO agent reported that "the bulletin was being distributed in Leichhardt on a Saturday morning when Police officers, who were thought by the Italians to be from Security, stopped them from handing out the bulletin because there was an incorrect address shown at the foot of it, vis. a post office box number instead of an actual address".[12] By 1966, the bulletin had ceased publishing. An ASIO plant reported that Giuliano Pajetta, during a meeting of Italians organised by the CPA at Surry Hills, "commented on the failure of *Il Nuovo Paese* and said he could not understand this when the Greek newspaper *Neos Kosmos* was managing to do so well".[13] Obviously, Greek left-wing migrants were more militant and better organised, following 30 years of national division between the forces of the left and the right. Their activism can be traced to the resistance against the Axis occupation of Greece during World War II, the bitter divisions of the subsequent civil war, climaxing in the dictatorship of the Greek military junta between 1967 and 1974.

Following the demise of *Il Nuovo Paese*, in 1973 *Voce Libera* (Free Voice) was born, a monthly newsletter of the first organisations of the PCI in Australia, which was distributed in all states, and sometime sold on the street. It was edited by Pierina Pirisi, who in July-August 1973 was able to issue its third number.[14] In September, Pirisi informed the PCI's Ufficio Emigrazione that "we have printed 1,000 copies of *Voce Libera*". About 500 were sent to Melbourne, 50 to Adelaide, 15 in Western Australia, 15 to Wollongong and 15 to Newcastle. "The remaining copies were distributed in Sydney, only few people paid for them...it is necessary that people in the first place begin being accustomed to us and to the bulletin".[15] Despite the hesitation, mistrust or fear on the part of Italian migrants to read a communist sheet, Pirisi's work was appreciated in Rome. ASIO reported that "Pirisi, who has been the most active member of the Sydney Branch, is also a member of the National Committee of the CPA".[16] In September 1973, Pajetta wrote to Laurie Aarons that "we are very pleased with the bulletin that Pierina and her friends are publishing".[17] Following the publication in May 1974 of FILEF's *Il Nuovo Paese*, not to be confused with the previous PCI bulletin, *Voce Libera* was replaced by an internal bulletin, *Unità Reprint* (Unity Reprint) ... but most communist activities concerning information, organisation and mobilisation would be carried out through FILEF, in order to try to gradually overcome the deeply rooted anti-communism of Australian society.[18] The ever-present ASIO informant reported that "due to the poor quality of the PCIA newspaper *Voce Nuovo* [sic, instead of *Voce Libera*], it has been decided not to produce this paper any longer. The main political line will be placed in the *Nuovo Paese*".[19] As reported by Burani at the above mentioned congress, until December 1975 the main activities carried out by the Sydney Branch of FILEF were the following:

- sent to FILEF Rome a survey on the situation of children of immigrants in local schools and Saturday schools;

- launched a petition against the abolition of maritime passenger services with Italy (1,200 signatures);

- launched a petition on the right to be granted an Italian pension and on the right to have recognised the contributions made to it during the period of work in Australia;

- submitted a report to the first conference of migrant workers held in Sydney in 1973;

- took part in the struggle to keep in employment more than 300 workers, almost all immigrants, at IXL Newtown;

- met Italian Under-Secretary Granelli on the occasion of his visit to Australia and advocated the needs of the community, handing him a second petition of 800 signatures supporting the transferability of pensions;

- on 1 May 1974 *Nuovo Paese* was launched in Melbourne. The first copies arrived in Sydney and were distributed a few days later;

- in August 1974 a Youth Club was established;

- FILEF took part in the campaign for the municipal elections in Leichhardt;

- three delegates from Sydney attended the National Conference on Emigration in Italy;

- organised a public meeting to discuss with Social Security Minister John Wheeldon the draft law on compensation, opposed by the liberal - agrarian opposition;

- cultural initiatives were undertaken with screenings of films and discussions;

- in May 1975 FILEF changed abode, moving to Annandale. Its comrades made a great effort in restoring the new premises;

- started English and Italian courses and collected books for a library;

- Governor-General Sir John Kerr dismissed the Labor government, new elections were held: at FILEFs premises several immigrant organisations met and formed a Migrant Workers' Electoral Committee that took part in the election campaign.

As mentioned in chapter 1, the first PCI Branch in Sydney was formed in September 1971, on the occasion of an Australian tour by Diego Novelli, *L'Unità* journalist and Mayor of Turin. Italian migrants Mario Abbiezzi, Salvatore Palazzolo, Francesco De Bella and Dimitri Oliva were members of its executive committee.[20] However, it was during Giuliano Pajetta's visit to Australia in 1976 that the dismal PCI membership was acknowledged and strategies adopted to improve it. Again, as Burani remarked, "it was at this time that some new comrades, encountered during the activities carried out by the party and by FILEF in previous years, entered the organisation and *si presero responsabilità di lavoro* (engaged themselves in party activities). In December 1974 a Circolo Giuseppe Di Vittorio was already operating in Haberfield, and a Federation of Italian Communist Youth (FGCI) was established at the same time, comprising the paltry number of seven members. ASIO noticed that "they attended an introductory course at Minto between 12 and 17 January 1975, which was conducted by comrade Ignazio Salemi".[21]

During the first two months of 1977, another Party cell was established in the western suburbs of Liverpool-Fairfield, the Circolo Fratelli Cervi. The two cells, numbering only a few dozen members, kept regularly in contact with each other. For instance, on 23 February 1986 PCI's Di Vittorio's Branch held its Seventh Congress in the premises of the Circolo Fratelli Cervi at Fairfield. Its main theme was "The development of the Left in Australia and the contribution given by Italian communists", without, understandably, admitting there had not been any.[22] The Circolo Di Vittorio also printed a "Bulletin of the PCI Organisations in Australia", entitled *Risveglio* (Awakening), that by May 1985 had reached ten issues. The cells were also formally affiliated to FILEF. A meeting of FILEF's committee in 1991 formalised this association: *Circolo PCI Di Vittorio si chiama Circolo della Sinistra G. Di Vittorio. Associare Circolo con FILEF – e FILEF con circolo. Invitare un rappresentante del Circolo alla segreteria della FILEF per fare da tramite tra le due associazioni.*[23] Under the Ethnic Affairs Commission of NSW Welfare Grants Program, the Circolo Culturale Fratelli Cervi received in 1982/83 a grant of $2,000 towards the salary of a casual organiser, renting of equipment and premises for activities with pensioners and a bus trip to the Blue Mountains and Terrigal. Not quite a revolutionary program, and reminiscent of similar initiatives taken by the Church, so much better at such things.[24]

As well as in the above listed activities, during 1975-1977 FILEF Sydney was engaged in two major campaigns: that of lobbying against the deportation of Ignazio Salemi, and that in support of the teaching of community languages in the state's primary schools. The Salemi campaign ended on 19 October 1977 with his deportation, but the second one eventually was a resounding success. It began during the second half of 1976 and, as Burani stated, it made FILEF aware of Italian parents' keen interest in pursuing what they deemed it to be "their right". For that campaign, FILEF produced a leaflet claiming that Italian was also an Australian language (*anche l'italiano è una lingua australiana*). By 1983, FILEF's campaign, orchestrated in 1976, persuaded the government to employ 50 community language teachers and to introduce community languages in primary schools.

*The Cervi Brothers were the seven sons of Alcide Cervi and Genoveffa Cocconi. They belonged to a family of Italian anti-fascists. Taken prisoners at Reggio Emilia, they were shot by the fascists on 28 December 1943. Giuseppe Di Vittorio was the Secretary of the Italian General Confederation of Labour (CGIL). His charisma made him the most popular leader of Italian workers. In 1957, his funeral was attended by more than three million people, coming to Rome from all over Italy (Courtesy Leichhardt Library, FILEF Collection).*

According to Bruno Di Biase, FILEF's Secretary from 1974 to 1989, with the wisdom of hindsight, the Salemi campaign had a negative effect on the Branch's activities: "in a sense, it detracted from, it paralysed FILEF in Sydney. All activities were too focused on a character, Salemi, while we were trying to understand the problems of the community, not the political ones, and we did a lot of activity in his support. This campaign was too long, there was a wrong perception of what FILEF was, because the community was saying: you see, these are communists. We spent a couple of years defending Salemi, there was not much else that could be done".[25] Di Biase's assessment was shared by FILEF's President, Claudio Cianca, who in 1977 advised the Party that "the resistance and the struggle against the Australian government's anti-democratic decision were correct, but we were totally engrossed by them and made of them the exclusive reason for mobilising our comrades".[26] Despite this drawback, the campaign had the positive effect of putting FILEF in touch with other left-wing migrant organisations, namely in the Serbian, Spanish, Portuguese and Palestinian communities, seeking their help against the deportation of the Italian journalist. Their support spilled over to FILEF's campaign in favour of community languages and, more widely, of the assertion of migrants' cultural rights. In 1975 FILEF formed a musical group, Bella Ciao, that performed in schools, teaching Italian children songs in the Italian language. It was also involved in theatre productions and in music courses. This was one of the first formal cultural forays by FILEF. Bella Ciao sang songs on the Italian resistance, the women's movement and the movement of workers and peasants. It was an important initiative for first-generation Italian migrants, who knew and heard those songs again, but also for the new generation, born in Australia, who learnt about the struggle of their parents. The group broke up in 1982-3 when several of its members left Australia.[27] Although it did not have a lasting impact, it was a novel initiative for that time.

Also, FILEF's staff went, accompanied by Italian parents, to local schools and churches, lobbying school principals and priests for the introduction of Italian in the classroom and during mass. Australian historian Richard Bosworth argued that a case could be mounted against Italian being taught since, on a global scale, it is a relatively minor language and it was not of course generally the mother tongue of the immigrants who spoke their variety of dialects. In terms of employment, languages like Chinese, Spanish and French were potentially more useful. Except in the short-term, the 'community language' may be little more than a chimera.

This sudden, bold assertion of one's cultural rights, despite the fact that "Italians" had so many, different and conflicted ways of possessing "Italian culture", took by surprise members of the dominant culture as well as pliant Italian *notabili* (members of the Establishment, literally "people who should be noted"). They not only were accustomed to the traditional subservience of the "Italians" of the many Italies, an attitude not unknown among Italian "intellectuals" of whatever definition, but were also unwittingly brainwashed by the policy of assimilation, that postulated the racial superiority of the dominant class and the duty of the migrant to unconditionally adapt to it. It is not surprising that *The Bulletin*'s interviewing journalist was aghast at Di Biase's statement, when he dryly quipped that "we Italian migrants did not come here just with our hands but also with our heads and we claim the right to think and to contribute with our ideas".[28] The novelty of this proactive policy confused and dumbfounded some Italian migrants and Australians alike, although it is doubtful whether anyone who mattered did care about what Di Biase said. He recollected the visceral campaign against FILEF orchestrated at that time by the conservative (if not altogether reactionary) Italo-Australian press in Sydney. In particular, journalist Pino Bosi, from the columns of *La Fiamma*, lamented the 'politicisation' of Italians. FILEF's reply did not take long to come. In a letter to the Editor, Pierina Pirisi retorted that "immigrants, from whichever country they are coming, bring with them in the country of immigration not only their recipes and their tongue, but also ideas and values that are part of the culture of their country ... so, Italian parties are not "coming" to Australia by who knows what mysterious way, but are part of the cultural identity of those migrants who have been a member of these parties in Italy or who share their policy and method of work".[29] Both Bosi and Pirisi were wrong in their assumptions. Politicising Italian migrants was very difficult for the very reason that they, even if PCI members, had not translated their political allegiance and militancy to the new Australian reality. Italian migrants were recalcitrant to respond to FILEF's overtures. Again, Di Biase remembered the difficulty in distributing *Nuovo Paese* among them: "Pierina Pirisi and I used to go to De Martin & Gasparini [a specialist concrete placing business] behind the Children's Hospital, and to distribute the newspaper was not easy, they were not taking it willingly, they were all Italian...De Martin & Gasparini were mainly hiring Italian labour".[30]

One of the the main, crucial stumbling blocs to Italians having their rights recognised was the attitude of the trade union movement, that subscribed to the thesis that class ought to be treasured over ethnicity. Generally, Di Biase acknowledged, its leadership was sensitive to the problems of the migrant workforce, "the rank and file rather less".[31] This attitude is confirmed by Edoardo Burani, who at the second congress of the PCI in Australia, held in Sydney in 1978 (the first congress was held in 1973), complained that "almost never the Australian left was able to organise the participation of immigrants in Australian politics, as demonstrated by the very low presence of immigrants in Australian left-wing parties, either as members or as leaders ... small or almost insignificant is their presence in leadership positions". Among the reasons put forward by Burani for the negligible participation by Italians in Australian left-wing politics was "the Cold War climate that the present liberal-agrarian government is stoking and the keeping of files by police on militants or sympathisers of the left".[32]

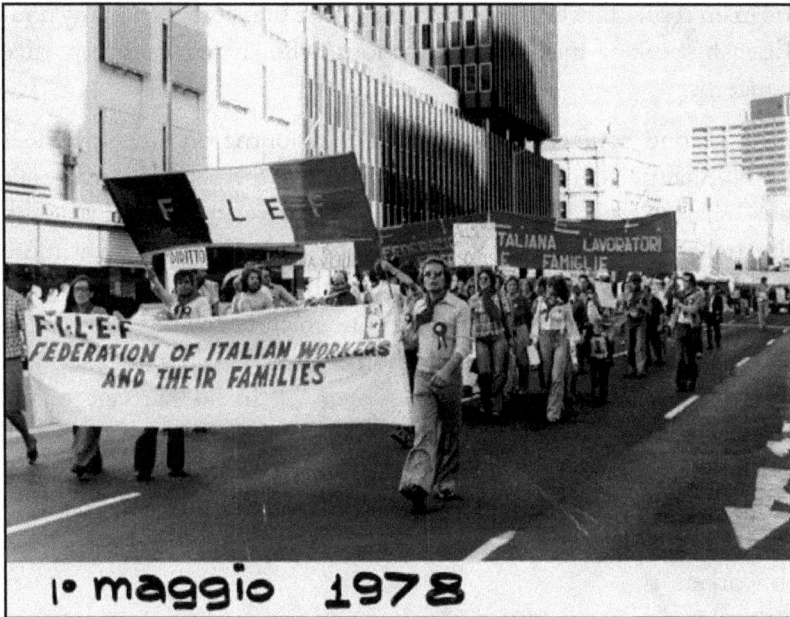

*May Day 1978 (Courtesy FILEF Collection).*

Historically, the move to alert the Australian Trade Union movement to the problems facing newcomers of non-English speaking background came from the migrants themselves, who organised a Conference of Immigrant Workers in Melbourne on 5-7 October 1973, attended by 200 delegates, and in Sydney on 3-4 November 1973. In an un-dated note, drafted in 1975, probably by Salemi, it was confirmed that "the move to convene the conference came from some fellow immigrants within the CPA who, with the support of the CPA, decided to launch the idea of a conference ... with the consent of the unions, which have generally given their support, at least formally, to the conference".[33] The conference had two main aims: to encourage migrant participation in union affairs and activities, that is "to break the language barrier", and to work for improved opportunities for migrant education and for the promotion of ethnic languages and cultures. Apart from raising these important issues, no "specific outcome" was expected from this first gathering. Its main result, however, was to bring under the same roof many non-English speaking migrant organisations, who shared their respective concerns.

A second conference was held in Melbourne on 7-8 November 1975. Again, according to Ignazio Salemi, "the second conference was characterised by a more massive presence by FILEF and the Italian workers, and by the attempt by FILEF to give a more 'strategic' and pugnacious character to the conference, focusing on the right to work as the main claim on which to focus, and to avoid a conference that would lead to another useless 'shopping list', with no direction, combativeness and strategy".[34] In his message to the second conference, Salemi emphasised that "FILEF considers this conference, as it did for the first one, to be, most of all, a show of industrial union, of union within the trade union movement, because the unions represent, as always, the only defence mechanism available to workers".[35]

Migrant participation and involvement in union affairs was dismal indeed. In his address to delegates to the second conference, its

Secretary, George Zangalis, unequivocally stated that "almost 50% of Australian male industrial workers and 60% of Australian female industrial workers are post-war migrants, overwhelmingly of non-English speaking origin. The great majority of these workers do not participate in the affairs of their unions because they cannot do so".[36] The main outcome of the conference was the establishment of a Migrant Union Centre, funded by the unions. Its realisation, more than to the Unions admitting past neglect, was due, as Salemi surmised, "to the growth of migrant workers' organisations, which increased their pressure on the unions, and to an increase in union awareness of the problem, even if their viewpoint was not always coincidental with the one expressed by immigrant workers".[37]

On 29-30 June 1981 the Australian Council of Trade Unions called in Melbourne another Migrant Workers Conference, to discuss issues pertaining to migrant workers in Australia. Among the issues to be canvassed were:

- Teaching of English language on the job
- Migrant workers participation in unions
- Problems of communication (unions-employers-governments)
- Migrant women workers
- Immigration and ethnic affairs policies
- Workers' rights on the job – intimidation, discrimination, industrial democracy, health and safety for migrant workers.
- Job security.

In preparing its submission to the conference, FILEF - Sydney controversially raised the question of "why has so little really changed since the passing of the ACTU migrant policy in 1979? Until the question why implementation of policy has been nearly non-existent is addressed and hopefully resolved, there does not appear much point in trying to expand or improve existing areas covered by policy. When the ACTU migrant policy was passed, no really effective new structure was set up nor existing ones modified to address the task of implementing the policy. A specific organisation with its sole purpose to be servicing migrant workers and implementing the ACTU migrant policy could be a step towards redressing the implementation imbalance...Provision of a full range of interpreting and translating services for general and specific needs is essential... The organisation must be able to take initiatives, including going into individual workplaces and determining what the needs and demands of the workers are in that particular place".[38]

An indication of the uphill struggle that, still in 1984, FILEF had to undertake in order to convince unions to accept Italian migrants in their fold is given by the following report, drafted by Frank Panucci, then engaged as a FILEF Grant-in-Aid (GIA) worker: "A working relationship has been developed with a number of GIA workers in trade unions; the AMFSU, FMWU and the CATU. Initially, these contacts were harder to establish than first thought. This was due to the fact that the role of these workers had not been completely developed by the unions. At the moment contacts with trade unions and shop committees who do not have GIA workers are being established. The unions we have contact with are attempting to implement programmes that will lead to an increase in the participation of their migrant members. Our role has been one of advice and counselling, hopefully this will lead to direct participation by FILEF in these developments and contact with rank and file workers...developing proposals for services that could be offered to trade unions and other organisations. These include an interpreter group and a group prepared to attend workplace meetings or training courses for migrant workers".

Panucci also pointed out that "we are preparing a publication that will include Italian texts of the ACTU and NSW Labour Council Migrant Worker Policy, as well as other information concerning the rights of migrant workers. It will also include information on workers rights in Italy. Another activity in this area is the translation of material for trade unions, shop floor groups and labour councils. This work is essential not only for the preparation of more material in community languages but also it creates a concrete contact with these organisations and shows that multilingual information is seen as essential by more worker-related organisations".[39]

It would be simplistic to assume that there was a uniform attitude to migrants' participation in union activities on the part of the union leadership, rank-and-file members and migrant workers. Interviews with union members and migrants carried out in 1988 by FILEF's Caterina De Re brought to light a variety of attitudes and problems. Builders Labourers Federation's (BLF) Viri Peres remembered that "we could not get an organiser who spoke Italian...the concrete yards were dominated 80-90% by Italian workers. Particularly Northerners, from Trieste, good unionists, well organised. Whereas with Southerners we had more problems...they don't have that industrial, that union tradition".[40] Another BLF organiser, Kevin Cooke, confirmed that "there were a lot of Italians who had a good trade union background and came from the Communist Party in Italy, so they were very progressive". However, they were given the worst jobs. Again, Cooke admitted that "they mostly did concreting and formwork – not so much rigging – probably because of their lack of English. There were a lot of Italians helping out with scaffolding jobs. Mostly involved in concreting, formwork, excavations, all the hard, dirty jobs...The bosses used to say: 'get the wogs to do this, get the wogs to do that', and every time that was said you knew it was a dirty, filthy job. And what they were saying is that only migrants would do this. White people wouldn't do this... ".[41] Peres reckoned that at times Anglo-Saxon unionists discriminated against their migrant mates: "sometimes they gang together and for the sake of a few dollars they say 'bugger him and let him do the hard work'. Sometimes the Anglo-Saxons are like that".[42] Yet another BLF unionist, Bud Cook, reiterated that "it was always the Italians who got the menial work. Unfortunately for them the language was always a big problem. It was always frustrating for the poor buggers...the Italians would come in [the union office], frustration would set in because they couldn't be understood and so they quietly went away, but utterly frustrated... Days later...the Italians in sheer desperation would bring in their children...they would have been no more than 8 or 12 years old... The kids did not know the jargon...stuff like the talk of jack hammers etc.".[43] The BLF, in particular, tried to overcome the language barrier. Jack Mundey witnessed that, while he was its Secretary, during the

Green Bans in the 1960's, the BLF "would have up to eight different translations at the mass meetings...the Italian Club down near the Haymarket [the left-leaning Italo-Australian Club in George Street] was very good...we used to get their translators out at the meetings and then the Italian workers merged. At one stage 30% of the Builders Labourers were Italian...Workers used to speak in their own language and be translated by an interpreter. This gave them a lot of confidence".[44] Bud Cook remembered the incredible admiration the Italians, always standing in awe of a charismatic leader, be him Benito or Berlusconi, had for Jack Mundey. "After many attempts at communication [with BLF officers], they would often ask for 'Mr Jack, Mr Jack'. 'No mate. It's not "Mr" Jack, just Jack', Cook used to tell them. But they would insist, 'Mr Jack' ". Cook said that Mundey was particularly patient with non-English speakers, would take time and persevere until they were understood, and for this reason he was respected and requested by migrants.[45]

By the early 1980s, the demographics of FILEF's membership and of the Italian migrant population, and the nature of FILEF's activities significantly changed. As well put by Joseph Halevi, an economist and FILEF member, "FILEF, an organisation that started out as completely working class, developed its own more or less solid intellectual framework thanks to an accurate perception of the relevant aspects of contemporary Italy, a perception which is virtually absent among young Italo-Australians. From the late 1970s on, FILEF began to attract a special type of newcomer: no longer the typical migrant, since mass migration had ceased, but the solitary person usually with a university degree, who for a variety of reasons (including environmental considerations) had decided to leave Italy. These newcomers were essential in maintaining and expanding existing ties with Italy's culture. Education in this sense mattered, but it was education acquired in Italy, not in Australia. Without such an influx it would have been difficult to develop other activities for which FILEF is also well known, such as the theatre".[46] In result of it, also FILEF's activities had to adapt to the new situation.

*Bruno di Biase (Centre), Secretary of FILEF (Sydney) and committee members at the 1st congress, held on 25 September 1977.*

From the outset, FILEF's policies, strategies and goals were discussed at its state congresses, although Bruno Di Biase played down their importance, since at times they tended to degenerate in a talkfest: "we were right in not dealing too much with issues of form ... we had a more practical than theoretical outlook".[47] One could argue that the congresses were more about rubber-stamping what the leaders, on democratic centralist advice from Rome, had determined. The first one was held on 25 September 1977 at the Five Dock Council Library. In his circular letter, inviting Italians to attend, FILEF's Secretary Di Biase stressed that the congress aimed to have a "practical effect in the transformation of this society with our ideas, our values and our united action" and to "awaken and stimulate [the migrants'] conscience and will to fight, for too long immobilised... thwarted by some of the local, reactionary *notabili* and by the Liberal government".[48] The congress agenda included the following:

- critically examine FILEF's developments and activities from its foundation until 1977.
- discuss the activities to be undertaken according to FILEF's

constitution.
* devise the means and ways to carry out united action with other immigrant groups and the Australian working class, provided that FILEF can effectively link with their organisations.
* achieve a more incisive role within the Italian community.
* bring about the establishment of the Consular Committees.
* Increase the distribution of the newspaper *Nuovo Paese*.

Ignazio Salemi, who a few days' earlier had been deported, sent a message, *forzatamente dall'esterno* (forcibly from the outside), to congress delegates. In it, he reiterated that FILEF's task was to go forward in search of better employment and living conditions in a more equitable society, because "the immigrants are the ones who pay the highest price with unemployment, marginalisation, with the high cost of living... workers can achieve their goals only by being united, never when divided".[49] In particular, Salemi charted the benchmarks that FILEF should set out to achieve. They were:

* Achieving a social security agreement between Italy and Australia.
* Recognition of Italian professional qualifications.
* Recognition of Italian degrees and diplomas.
* Exchange of teachers between the two countries.
* Teaching of Italian language and culture in Australian schools attended by Italian children.

The resolutions adopted at FILEF's first Congress were also endorsed at the Second Congress of the PCI in NSW, held on 9 April 1978. In addition, the communiqué released at the end of the PCI's congress decried "the still too small number of members and militants" (*il numero ancora troppo limitato di iscritti e di attivisti*) and advocated "the greatest effort to recruit new members in order to strengthen its cells...the strengthening of the links with other organisations of migrant workers, with the trade unions and with Italian workers in the factories...the dissemination of accurate and correct information on Italy...and the involvement in the organisation of an increasing number of women and young people".[50] One of the reasons for the failure in mass recruiting migrants to the Party was given a year earlier to an ASIO plant by an unsuspecting Di Biase, when he stated that "the PCI want mostly young Italians and not the older ones who still live under the shadow of the Pope".[51]

FILEF's third congress, held on 1-2 October 1983, following the second one on 27 September 1980, reflected the changed political and social situation affecting Italians in Australia. Its agenda put on notice the impact of the policy of multiculturalism, deplored the lack of progress by the trade union movement to act on the migrants' log of claims and the equally paternalistic attitude by Anglo-Australia, and raised the issues of welfare for elderly migrants and the isolation of second generation Italians. While the interpretation of multiculturalism by the most conservative or reactionary sector of the population implied "to give a new vest to old prejudices, dressed this time in paternalism and in so-called tolerance", to FILEF it meant "1) that the structures of Australian society must change in order to give practical recognition to the right of immigrants to maintain and develop their own language and culture and to fully take part in Australian society in all its aspects. Also, to foster a relationship of mutual understanding, and therefore of respect and dialogue, between the various components of society, in order to achieve integration on the basis of equality. 2) that immigrants have the right to make their contribution, according to their own ideas and concepts, to the social, cultural and political development of Australian society, without any discrimination".

The document complained that "the claims, advanced at several conferences on migrant workers, to which FILEF made a significant contribution, and then taken up by the ACTU conference on migrant workers, and thereafter by the ACTU Congress, for 90% remained on paper". Similarly, "assistance to immigrants is still heavily influenced by a paternalistic attitude that does not permit the participation of users to determine the nature and management of these services ... there is fear that immigrants freely express their ideas, which may be different from the dominant Anglo-Saxon ones".

*FILEFs 3rd Congress. (From left) Bruno Di Biase, speaking, Franca Arena, Consul-General Alvise Memmo, Claudio Marcello, Peter Baldwin, Labor MHR for Leichhardt, Dino Pelliccia, Member of the Central Committee of the Italian Communist Party and FILEF's National Secretary and Paolo Totaro (Courtesy FILEF Collection).*

The Congress asserted that FILEF's main weakness was its inability to grow fast enough to meet its obligations and raised the issue of increasing the distribution of *Nuovo Paese*, as if that would have been of any use. Concerning youth, it was admitted that "they are suspended between two conflicting cultural poles, being 'Australian' during the day and 'Italian' in the evening [or 'American' while watching TV. Few migrants watched SBS, they rather preferred the commercial channels. This was of course ironically class and not ethnic behaviour, N.d.A]. We often organise parties or other activities that to them are irrelevant. Often it is assumed that they are, at least culturally, Italian. But we're wrong. [They attend] an aggressively assimilationist school... [their] social and cultural life is not particularly rich in Italian stimuli...[their parents] are still anchored to values and habits that no longer exist [in Italy]".[52] What is striking in the above resolution is the national stereotyping of "Italian culture" and "Italian values", and how far it is from Marxism.

By the early 1980s, in order to fulfil its policy in support of Italian migrants and newcomers in general, FILEF had set up a complex organisational structure, as shown in this table:[53]

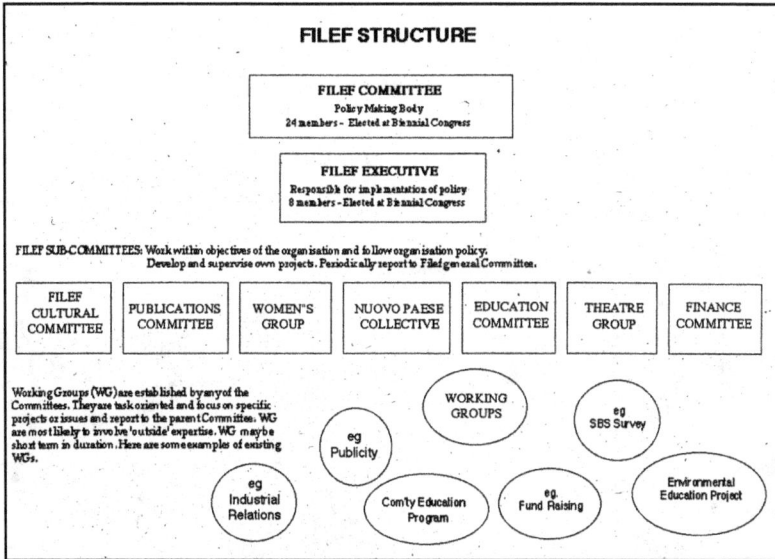

**FILEF STRUCTURE**

**FILEF COMMITTEE**
Policy Making Body
24 members - Elected at Biennial Congress

**FILEF EXECUTIVE**
Responsible for implementation of policy
8 members - Elected at Biennial Congress

FILEF SUB-COMMITTEES: Work within objectives of the organisation and follow organisation policy. Develop and supervise own projects. Periodically report to Filef general Committee.

| FILEF CULTURAL COMMITTEE | PUBLICATIONS COMMITTEE | WOMEN'S GROUP | NUOVO PAESE COLLECTIVE | EDUCATION COMMITTEE | THEATRE GROUP | FINANCE COMMITTEE |

Working Groups (WG) are established by any of the Committees. They are task oriented and focus on specific projects or issues and report to the parent Committee. WG are most likely to involve 'outside' expertise. WG maybe short term in duration. Here are some examples of existing WGs.

WORKING GROUPS

eg SBS Survey

eg Publicity

eg Industrial Relations

Com'ty Education Program

eg Fund Raising

Environmental Education Project

The 4th FILEF congress, held on 4-5 December 1987, in the premises of the Associazione Puglia in Renwick Street, Leichhardt, reiterated the key policies and resolutions adopted at the 3rd congress. However, particular emphasis was given for FILEF to be a more effective organisation in the pluralist society that Australia had become following the mass migration from the 1950s to the 1970s. One of the means to become more relevant and incisive in influencing Australian society was to promote cultural and educational development. This theme had become a *leit-motiv* during the 1980s: the conference program stated that "FILEF must be able to give an answer, with improving its organisation, to the standing issues of rights and multiculturalism, in government, in political parties, the trade unions, also because we are convinced that there cannot be economic development without a parallel development in culture and society".[54]

Yet again, FILEF claimed the migrants' right to take part in Australian affairs and, in so doing, change society. The long-discredited policies of assimilation and integration (by it meaning blind acceptance to the dominant cultural values) were rejected outright. Even the policy of participation, promoted by the Ethnic Affairs Commission of NSW since July 1978, was accepted with reservations. According to FILEF, the rules of the game had to be changed. The congress' concluding document stressed that "to us, multiculturalism means democracy, not as purely formal process, but as a participatory process, defending and promoting our democratic rights, particularly the ones of the migrants and, given the multicultural context in which we live, of the minorities".[55]

*FILEF rally in support of the introduction of community languages in State schools, 1980s (Courtesy FILEF Collection).*

One of the emerging issues during the 1980s had been that of second-generation Italo-Australians, in particular how to involve them in community affairs and convince them to take part in FILEF's activities. It was believed that culture and the arts would have been the ideal magnet to secure their participation. Eventually, it proved a delusion. During the previous four years, as it will be detailed in chapter three, FILEF had embarked in a spate of high profile initiatives aimed at achieving this end. The congress' document mentioned "among the activities that have been extensively developed since the last FILEF Congress, undoubtedly are the artistic initiatives carried out and supported by the organisation in order to involve young people and particularly the second generation. The three shows put on during the last three years have made a unique contribution to the development of a "theatre of emigration", in particular the multi-media exhibitions developed and staged under the direction of Dennis del Favero. All these activities have brought prestige to the organisation and made it grow".[56]

The end of Italian mass migration, the progressive ageing of first-generation migrants and the coming of age of second-generation migrants, coupled with the arrival of young activists who had witnessed and taken part in Italian left-wing and ultra-parliamentarian political activities caused problems and division within FILEF. This situation was reflected in the final congressional document where, in dealing with youth issues, it stated that "our countrymen in Australia are holding moral values. If we want [young people] to join our organisation, we cannot ignore these values. Not ignoring does not mean accepting. One of the reasons for [older people] leaving FILEF is undoubtedly the fact that the organisation has given too much space to groups of young 'trendies' who do not want to have anything (or very little) to do with the moral values of the older generation and in some cases not even show any respect in this regard".[57] Delegates at the 4th Congress pledged that in future FILEF would continue to carry out initiatives in the areas of political and social rights, Italian community, trade unions movement, schools, cultural and artistic promotion and information.[58]

FILEF's 5th Congress was held two years later, on 3-4 November 1989 at the Annandale Neighbourhood Centre. In attendance was also Claudio Balzamonti of FILEF's headquarters in Rome. The issue of adopting a more pronounced political profile for the organisation was discussed, in particular the relationship with left-wing organisations and the ALP, its wider social and political ramifications, if and when FILEF should take a stand, either at national and/or state level.[59] Again, as in previous congresses held during the 1980s, also this forum dealt with the issues of the community's longevity and of the problematic relationship with second-generation Italo-Australians. The congress' agenda for discussion emphasised that "today 80% of our community, that is our first-generation, is in Australia for more than 20 years and is relatively established in this country. The ageing of our community and the emergence of new generations (which now outnumber those who are born in Italy) today pose new problems that FILEF should also help to address. Among them pre-eminently are a greater demand for cultural recovery and support services for the elderly".[60]

The congress made also mention of the ongoing crisis in the Soviet empire, albeit doubting the veracity of reports on its progressive disgregation, that were dubbed "misinformation". Incidentally, what destroyed the Empire was ethnic politics and multiculturalism, Soviet style, and nationalism, notably in Poland as backed by Pope John Paul II. More telling was the reference made to the disillusionment, "confusion" and disorientation reigning among FILEF's members. Its program admitted that "it is possible that there have been instances of exhaustion, also due to a breakdown of communications, and perhaps fatigue, affecting both [FILEF's] headquarters and its peripheral branches. Added to these symptoms is the state of misinformation concerning the events happening in the socialist world, the forces of the left in Italy and so on. All this caused some confusion, and the Federation could not have had, because of the amount of activities nearing completion, the necessary moments of discussion, political orientation, verification and also, why not, encouragement and social interaction".[61] It is difficult to accept the validity of this self-interested exculpation, in view of the terminal crisis provoked by the invasion of Czechoslovakia in 1968 and Gorbachev's proclamation of *glasnost* in 1986, a policy that called for increased openness and transparency in government institutions and activities in the Soviet Union. Yet again, adherence to strict Leninist ideology precluded FILEF's cadres from seeing the real reason of their "exhaustion", "fatigue" and "confusion".

Symptoms of the ideological malaise and the lack of co-ordination affecting FILEF as well as PCI members had become evident since 1985, and arguably even before this date. At a meeting held in Melbourne on 26 August 1985 by PCI cadres in Australia, it was acknowledged that "the organisation of the PCI in Australia until 1982 had become a federation and from that year we played an increasingly smaller role and carried out less and less activity because the financial means and the relationship with the Emigration Section disappeared... The absence of formal relations with the Emigration Section caused a gradual political disorientation at various levels of the organisation, resulting in insecurity and uncertainty in our activities. We tried, on several occasions, to clarify with the Immigration Section what kind of relationship and commitment it wanted to maintain with Australia ... however, we did not get a reply that could drive at a resumption of a mutual dialogue".[62] The reasons for what would become the PCI's terminal crisis were manifold. In the first instance, what precipitated the break with the Soviets and other Communist parties was Party Secretary General Enrico Berlinguer's condemnation of the USSR intervention in Afghanistan in 1980 and his declaration in 1981 that "the progressive force of the October Revolution had been exhausted". His "heresy" outraged, in Italy as well as Australia, diehard Stalinists within the Party, who claimed that he had turned a workers' party into a sort of bourgeois revisionist club. Berlinguer's sudden death on 11 June 1984 and, even more significant, Giuliano Pajetta's leaving the direction of the Party's Ufficio Emigrazione in 1981, marked the end of the PCI's plans for its influence in Australia.

Isolation and lack of co-ordination were also felt by PCI members in Adelaide. Vincenzo Soderini, the local Branch Secretary, complained that "in recent years we had no contact, just when it would have been crucial, with branches in other States".[63] The seriousness of the problem was acknowledged by Gianni Giadresco, responsible for PCI's Emigration Section in Rome, who in 1986 wrote to Party branches in Australia that "the understandably difficult conditions, also due to the distance from Italy are making more and more difficult a frequent and direct relationship between us... it is necessary to enhance the relationship between party organisations in Australia and headquarters in Rome in ways that will gradually be possible, also in consideration of the great financial difficulties in which we are finding ourselves, that often undermine the best of our intentions".[64]

One of the episodes causing disaffection and division within the ranks of left-wing organisations in Sydney was the ongoing rift between FILEF and INCA. The Istituto Nazionale Confederale di Assistenza (INCA) was founded by CGIL (Confederazione Generale Italiana dei Lavoratori – General Confederation of Italian Workers) on 11 February 1945 and had been operating in Sydney since 1972. For 16 years, until 1988, INCA was based in Leichhardt at 26 Norton Street and later at 423 Parramatta Road, sharing premises with FILEF. Due to the fact that their room in Leichhardt was not situated on the ground floor, as easy access was essential to attract clients, INCA moved to 4/34 East Street, Five Dock and later to 106 Elswick St. Leichhardt. INCA was a not-for-profit organisation defending the welfare rights of workers and their families in Italy and abroad. Its main function was to assist the Italian community in obtaining from the Italian government pensions owed by law and ensuring regular payment of the correct sum with no undue delays. INCA was instrumental in negotiating the Bilateral Social Security Agreement between Italy and Australia that was signed on 23 April 1986. In 1989, FILEF still provided support to INCA-CGIL, the largest *Patronato* (Italian pension office) in NSW. Four FILEF members, in addition to FILEF's Grant-In-Aid worker, were members of the INCA's Management Committee.

By the late 1980's the relationship between the two organisations worsened for institutional and personal reasons. In June 1987 FILEF's National Secretary Giovanni Sgrò objected to INCA planning to part ways from FILEF: "I would like to remind the

INCA comrades in Rome that more than half their clients that go to INCA for information and assistance are sent to them by FILEF throughout Australia". INCA was resentful of FILEF's "hegemony" and fearful of being taken over by it, claiming that union bodies had to be autonomous from political organisations and from the Party. Their fear was clearly spelled out in a letter to Circolo Di Vittorio: "it is clearly evident that it is your intention not to take into due consideration the autonomy of INCA as an institution, but rather [from your letter] emerges the will to put INCA in a subordinate position". In August 1990 FILEF complained of a conflict of interest on the part of a member of INCA's committee and of a rift between the two bodies: "The presence on the Sydney INCA committee of people who run a private agency that provides pension services for payment is contrary to the policy of both organisations [INCA and FILEF] and represents a severe case of conflict of interest ... [INCA's management have taken] the decision to exclude the Circolo Di Vittorio from INCA's Committee... FILEF's representative on INCA's committee was denied access to correspondence which specifically related to the formation and functioning of the committee".[65]

By September 1990 FILEF felt compelled to refer the rift to PCI and FILEF headquarters in Rome. Cesare Popoli, then a committee member, thus described the situation: "The need to acquaint FILEF and the PCI about the rift arose from the progressive deterioration of the relationship between FILEF and the Party on the one hand and INCA's Sydney office on the other. A deterioration that dates back several months and that, from mutual collaboration has now broken out into open hostility and outright refusal on their part to co-operate and carry out political work with FILEF and with the Party...Equally questionable ...[was] the decision to reduce the pension advisory service in our office in Leichhardt from weekly to fortnightly. After our protest... INCA decided to terminate that service...Another very questionable decision was to reject the appointment of a fellow party member to the INCA committee. No justification was given for that refusal, adding moreover that INCA considered 'unnecessary' the presence of a representative of the Party in their committee...With the latest response, we were informed that INCA simply does not want to have anything to do with us".[66]

Delegates to the 5th FILEF congress in 1989 acknowledged the political damage resulted in the physical separation of the two organisations and in their internecine squabbling. Its communiqué read as follows: "The disruption brought about by the shift of INCA's office from Leichhardt added to the problems facing FILEF. It was a necessary step, according to INCA's Italian headquarters, that wanted a more spacious and modern office. The fact that INCA now does not have a presence in Leichhardt resulted, in our opinion, in weakening both organisations - INCA because they lost political drive and only responded to administrative and not social and political needs, and FILEF because people who are still coming here to seek pension assistance now must be redirected to Five Dock and because those who go to Five Dock are now missing the opportunity, existing beforehand, to also be in touch with FILEF".[67] In effect, rivalry between the two PCI controlled organisations reflected the crisis besetting the Party, that by the end of the 1980s proved in effect unable to provide leadership to its organisations in Australia, the more so in the absence of the "paternal" and authoritative managerial style that characterised Giuliano Pajetta's mandate from 1972 to 1981. A style that Edoardo Burani and Pierina Pirisi characterised, in an email message to the author in 2014, as "allowing great autonomy on the things to do in Australia because [Pajetta] had a great ability to understand our point of view and to encourage our initiative".[68]

Despite the worsening of the political and ideological crisis affecting the communist world, that no doubt had a demoralising effect on many FILEF members, the Federation carried out during the 1980s an amount of activities, spanning, as had been the case during the 1970s, across many fields. As already mentioned, particularly relevant were the initiatives in the artistic, cultural, educational and linguistic sectors, that will be examined in chapter 3. However, FILEF's mainstay remained industrial relations, in particular workers' health and safety.

Approximately one in three workers in NSW were born overseas. Their provenance was a constant reminder of the violence and strife affecting their country of origin: the Greeks were followed by the Yugoslavs, who preceded the Vietnamese, followed by pre-Tiananmen Square Chinese, mostly from Vietnam, as well as other nationalities. Like the rest of society, FILEF, with the exception of occasional manifestations of solidarity for their grievances, found it hard to adapt to the new immigrants, their cultures, histories and languages. "Ethnicity" was, as ever, a hypocritical playing card in a tiny and in the end pointless struggle for minority prestige and advantage. Migrant workers were often forced to do the most dirty and dangerous jobs. 80% of coke oven workers at the Port Kembla Steelworks were migrants; they were exposed to cancer-causing coke oven emissions. Migrant workers got no information or training about their jobs in their own languages. One in four, working with noise at the legal maximum of 90 decibels for four hours, lost some hearing. Fast, repetitive movements, poor job design and the bonus system caused tenosynovitis and other injuries. Many migrants working as unskilled labourers had to repeatedly lift, push or carry heavy loads. Women in NSW were not allowed by law to lift more than 16 kilograms; there was no maximum weight for men. Shift work caused digestive problems, sleeping difficulties, tiredness and upset family life. There were no laws forcing employers to label dangerous chemicals or give information to workers. Chemicals could cause dermatitis, headaches, breathing problems, kidney and liver damage, and cancer. Out-work done at home, mainly by migrant women, was not covered by any health and safety laws.

Working conditions in Italy, at that time, were also not ideal. Trade unionism was in decline and most paid-up union members were retired workers. The influence of the unions declined due to the reduction of the workforce in the industrial sector, the skepticism with which the trade union elite was perceived, and government policy aimed at weakening the unions. Much that was achieved by the unions was abolished or was on the verge of being dismantled. Privatisation, liberalisation, and budget cuts reduced the protection network, and businesses had a far freer hand in dealing with the workforce. Consequently, employers' contributions towards pensions were slashed, and overtime was not as well paid. The pressure of international competition and the necessity to maintain a healthy budget meant that labour costs had to be cut in both the private and public sectors. In order to preserve jobs, the trade unions and employers entered into a pact by which workers moderated their requests and accepted cuts in exchange for job security.

Already in 1974 FILEF, supporting the federal Compensation Bill, had issued a statement, advocating its enactment. "The Labour Government National Compensation Bill, 1974", FILEF's communiqué read, "is inspired by a basic principle of any human society: the responsibility of that society for the sick and the injured. For far too long Australian society has been based upon the law of the jungle. Sickness and injury have been used to exploit even further those who are unfortunate enough to suffer from them, in the sacred name of profit. Our organisation, FILEF, considers the adoption of the Bill as an urgent question that can no longer be delayed. Our organisation has promoted a petition and called a public meeting to discuss the Bill on 10 March 1975 at Leichhardt Town Hall. The Minister for Repatriation and Compensation, Senator John Wheeldon or his private Secretary, Dr Jim Anthony, will address the meeting and answer questions. Interpreters will be available for migrants". Dr Anthony replaced Senator Wheeldon as guest speaker. The ASIO agent monitoring the meeting reported that during question time Anthony was asked who would pay for the Repatriation and Compensation scheme. Barely disguising his or her antipathy towards the obviously Labor-supporting public servant, the agent wrote that "at this point Mr Anthony burst out and said: 'If we can pay for the Vietnam war and large Army expenditure we may pay for this'. He continued by saying: 'It is the fault of the capitalists for poverty and they should pay for their sins'. At the conclusion of the meeting Abbiezzi referred to

Mr Anthony as being 'a real socialist' ".[69]

In response to the recognition by workers and a number of trade unions of the lack of attention that was being paid to issues of occupational health and safety, in 1977 a Workers Health Centre was established Lidcombe. The Centre was responsible for the first public campaign on the issues of tenosynovitis, asbestos and noise, and the more general issues of the lack of enforcement of existing legislation, and the failure of governments at the level of administration and policy. The election of the national Labor government in March 1983 enabled the long-awaited recognition of the Centre's work. In August, Neal Blewett, Minister for Health, announced a grant to the Centre of $100,000 a year for three years. FILEF worked closely with Centre because it gave high priority to the specific problems confronting migrant workers and was the first organisation to translate information in major community languages. The most important factor for FILEF was that the Centre believed that any attempt to resolve specific problems had to firstly be negotiated through the relevant trade union. This policy had the twofold effect of arousing awareness and increasing participation by migrant workers in trade union activities and, secondly, of making the unions more aware of the specific needs of their migrant members. In the process, the unions found new members whom they could recruit.[70] At its 1981 Congress, the ACTU adopted many recommendations in support of migrant workers, urging unions to negotiate for the provision of English classes on the job, without loss of pay, for access to trained interpreters, for job induction programs and safety programs in appropriate languages, for clear and easily understood symbols and multilingual safety signs, and for paid study leave for trade union education. The Congress also passed a number of recommendations to strengthen the participation of migrant members in union affairs, as well as reaffirming their opposition to all forms of racial discrimination.[71]

In 1979, the NSW Government appointed Commissioner TG Williams to lead a commission of inquiry into occupational health and safety. Commissioner Williams' *Report of the Commission of Inquiry into Occupational Health and Safety*, dated 3 June 1981, recommended sweeping legislative changes. The Williams report, advocating self-regulation, did not discuss the problems migrant workers were facing on the job. The 150-page report specifically referred to migrants and women in two sentences, stating that Williams did not feel qualified to make any specific recommendations on this. Williams did not place any advertisements of the Inquiry in any of the ethnic media. Also, the union movement objected strongly to the recommendation that health and safety committees should only be established in workplaces with more than 50 employees, a move that excluded about two thirds of the NSW workforce. The Ethnic Affairs Commission of NSW was critical of the Williams recommendations and advocated that migrants, including women, should be included in direct proportion to their numbers in the workforce and that the government should provide interpreters and information material in ethnic languages. The Commission also rejected the self-regulation approach and the report's tendency to deny that occupational health and safety were an industrial issue. It also advocated the right of an employee to refuse to perform unsafe work. The Occupational Health and Safety Act 1983, a law enacted on 4 May 1983, put remedy to some of the migrants' concerns. The Labor Council of NSW issued a leaflet in Italian, detailing the legislative provisions.[72]

On 9 March 1984, FILEF made a submission to the Interim Commission preparing a report on occupational health and safety for the federal government. In it, the Federation advocated, among other measures;

- The recognition of the fundamental role of workers and trade unions in the prevention of occupational disease and injury, and thus the provision for worker health and safety representation in the workplace.
- The incorporation of ACTU policy regarding representation and training into state and federal legislation.
- The recognition of Workers Health Centres as a key element in the development of a worker-based national strategy to combat occupational disease and injury.

When the Report was released, nowhere in the document was it acknowledged that occupational health and safety was an industrial issue and nowhere was there a clear provision made for unions and workplace delegates to effectively participate in the decision-making processes at a national level. The Report refused to acknowledge that the toll of dead and injured was a result of the contradictions between the goals of management and workers. Management was concerned with maximising profit, therefore it was not in their interest to ensure a safe, healthy working environment because it could be costly and erode profits. Workers, on the other hand, were exposed to the hazards, so their primary concern was with a safe working environment.

FILEF did not limit itself to draft submissions, advocate legislative reforms and lobby trade unions. It also involved itself directly in assisting workers and their families to overcome their grievances. To this purpose, in January 1984 FILEF was awarded a three-year grant by the federal Department of Immigration and Ethnic Affairs. A second grant was awarded on 7 January 1987 and terminated on 6 January 1990. At first, Frank Panucci filled that position, and in July 1986 Vera Zaccari was appointed Grant-In-Aid worker. They handled workers compensation, Italian and Australian social security pensions and benefits and re-entry to Italy. In 1988, FILEF had given assistance to 184 clients and a further 2,080 enquiries requiring information or referral were taken. The statistics of 1988 "can be considered to be an average annual figure for our agency".[73] Seven groups operated, giving assistance to the GIA worker: Women's group, Bilingual Community Theatre Group, Music group, Cultural group, Social group, Migrant Committee for Aboriginal rights and a Children's bilingual play group. The program objectives were:[74]

- Action on welfare issues
- Advocate welfare rights
- Consultant to unions, community groups and government bodies
- Community development activities, providing information on settlement
- Needs of migrant women

In 1987, FILEF published a leaflet in Italian warning workers doing repetitive work about the dangers associated with the tenosynovitis.[75] Soon, all these union-supported welfare, education and health activities would be overwhelmed by neoliberalism's rolling back of collective rights and ideals in favour of the "individual", at least in theory.

The Aboriginal issue was the second main area of FILEF's involvement during the late 1980s. The indigenous 'cause' in Australia was closely linked to the rise of new nationalism in white bourgeois Australia where, in the absence of a national language, the nation could seem 'unique' through its '60,000 years of history'. Thus all the absurd mention of tribal land and elders at every Australian public event. The adoption of this ritual did nothing to improve the well-being of the indigenous people or remove them from their last position on every Australian social index.

In 1986, FILEF strongly opposed the proposal to set up a Bicentennial multicultural foundation to celebrate the bicentenary.[76] This stand was taken in support of the Aborigines, who considered the "white invasion" of 1788 as a disaster. At its 4th Congress, on 4-5 December 1987, FILEF declared that "FILEF NSW believes that 1988, the bicentennial anniversary of white occupation of this country, more than a year of uncritical celebration can be an occasion for reflection, dialogue with the Aboriginal community and support for their claims. Our aim is therefore to better inform our community about the history, the rights and the claims by Aborigines such as land rights, the maintenance and development of their language and culture and improvement of living conditions".[77]

In December 1987 FILEF was instrumental in establishing the Migrant Committee for Aboriginal Rights (MCAR), comprising representatives from over 20 migrant groups. The Committee developed close links with Aboriginal groups and worked to explore areas of common concern with the principal aim of promoting greater reciprocal understanding between migrant communities and Aboriginal communities. It did this through cultural events, public

FILEF during the 1980s

forums and conferences. MCAR maintained that "it is not possible to talk about multiculturalism if we continue to live in a society that continues to deny the Aboriginal people of their rights. This inacceptable situation must be redressed…The Aboriginal people should be allowed to manage and control their own affairs. They should be free from the purse-strings of Government and be given every opportunity to form a self-sufficient economic basis…When Australia has given the Aboriginal people back their right to their land and their future so that they can live their life in dignity, can we begin to celebrate Australia as a democratic and multicultural nation".[78] MCAR vehemently opposed the mainstreaming of services to Aborigines and the assimilation of Aborigines into the white community. As was the case for migrants, assimilation held absolutely no positive connotations for people proud of, practising and living their culture. Assimilation was not the recognition of their culture in its own right, but the rejection of a culture to exist and be accepted.[79]

On 10 January 1988, MCAR organised at the Tom Mann Theatre in Sydney a concert in support of the struggle of Aboriginal people for their rights. Among its Committee Members were FILEF and the Circolo Di Vittorio. Key speaker at the event was Aboriginal leader Gary Foley. Activist, academic, writer and actor, Foley was best known for his role in establishing the Aboriginal Tent Embassy in Canberra in 1972 and for setting up an Aboriginal Legal Service in Redfern in the 1970s. A "person of interest" to ASIO for many years, he was kept under surveillance and photographed. The story of ASIO's monitoring of Foley's activities was the subject of a SBS television documentary, *Persons of Interest*, that was screened on 7 January 2014.[80] In his address, Foley quipped that "one of the things I learnt at numerous schools is that you don't have to explain to migrant kids what racism is all about. We know the experience of dispossession. We know the experience of oppression. It is a bond that is common to all of us".[81] Other speakers at the concert pointed out that "over a number of years migrants have called for the right to maintain and develop their languages and cultures as a necessary step to participate fully in this society, that is to achieve a truly multicultural society. It has become obvious to the groups involved in the Committee that it is not possible to talk about multiculturalism if we live in a society where the rights of Aboriginal people are still denied...We as migrants in Australia believe that we cannot attain a truly multicultural society until a full recognition and understanding of Aboriginal people and cultures is achieved. This must be the basis for a new Australian society which respects all cultures and which may then hold its head up in the international community".[82]

*Gary Foley speaking at the Migrant Committee for Aboriginal Rights Solidarity Concert, 10 January 1988. (Photo by Matthew McKee).*

When in 1991 the Hawke Government banned the mining of uranium at the sacred Aboriginal site of Coronation Hill, in Kakadu National Park, Northern Territory, FILEF wrote to the Prime Minister, congratulating the government on its decision: "we appreciate your sensitivity to the rights and beliefs of our indigenous people who for centuries have been the victims of colonial domination both in physical and cultural terms".[83]

Resistance to the "assimilation" of indigenous Australia on the part of the dominant culture brought about also a parallel refusal to comply with the attempt by the CPA to "colonise" its 'ethnic' comrades. During the 1980s, hard-core Italian militants in the ranks of the PCI in Australia, estranged from the internecine ideological struggle between the pro-Moscow SPA and the "Eurocommunist" CPA, and not wanting to be overtly demonised by the Australian public for being Italian communists, even if "with a human face", founded a front organisation, the Associazione Progressista Repubblicana Italo-Australiana (APR). The APR was established on 21 July 1985 at the Circolo Fratelli Cervi in Fairfield. From the outset, it distanced itself from its Australian comrades, explicitly condemning them of backwardness and of neglecting the aspirations, needs and rights of immigrant workers and implicitly charging them of hegemonic tendencies.

"Our organisation", the APR stated in a lengthy letter to the CPA, "consists mainly of Australian communists of Italian origin but also of communists from other cultural backgrounds: Anglo-Saxon, Yugoslav and others. The goal of our organisation is not to compete with other Australian communist parties in order to achieve political hegemony over them. Rather, our goal is to give our contribution to the building of an Australian communist party that is modern, national and hence reflects, among other things, the multicultural nature of the Australian working class. We have the immensely valuable experiences of the migrant workers who have brought with them not only their labour, folk dances, languages and foods to Australia but also their political experiences, so far almost completely untapped by the Australian communist parties. What a wealth of ideas and so often dismissed with that rather banal phrase 'They only care to talk about their home country'. Perhaps it is so because so few care to listen to what they have to say about Australia or because they do not readily identify with the existing communist parties. Was it not the migrant associations who waged the lengthy and successful campaign for the introduction of community languages in state schools?".[84]

Disillusionment was equally meted out to the Australian Labor Party, complicit in ignoring the aspirations of Australians of non-English background, even ten years after the sacking of the Whitlam government. "Ten long years have passed since the fall of the Whitlam government and with it fell many of our hopes for social and economic reform….Today we have once again a Labor government but the lights have not been turned on. This Labor government has not re-kindled in us the hope that Australian society can undergo those deep social and economic changes necessary in order to achieve social and economic justice for the majority of Australians – the working people".[85]

The aims of the APR were the following:

- Peace. To give a contribution to the peace and nuclear disarmament movements.
- Employment. To work towards the development of a national economy that will guarantee employment to every citizen.
- Health. To work towards the creation of a national health scheme based on the right that every citizen should have access to high quality medical services.
- Democracy. To participate at all levels of society to reinforce and develop the democratic and decision making processes in the workplace, in society and the parliament.

Despite the vagueness of its program, APR carried out – without achieving much in the short, let alone the long term - public rallies in support of progressive causes, not dissimilar to those promoted by the Australian Communist Parties, FILEF and the Australian Labor Party, and often sharing the platform with representatives of these organisations. For instance, on 30 August 1985 the Associazione Progressista Repubblicana held a public meeting at Leichhardt Town Hall on Australia's foreign policy and a nuclear free Pacific. Speakers were Claudio Crollini of the APR, Franca Arena MLC, leader of the

Italian Friends of Labor and Bob Howard representing the ALP.[86] Incidentally, even before the funding of Italian Friends of Labor in the mid-1970s, FILEF maintained an ambiguous attitude towards the new formation. The infiltrated ASIO covert agent reported that "FILEF and PCIA have not decided on a line of action. This situation exists because the new group would probably attract many Italians who would not be prepared to join or who have not heard of the PCIA. It has been decided, however, that if the group is formed, it will be PCIA-controlled. By so doing, the PCIA hopes to be able to attract new recruits from Friends of Labor".[87] Again, the wait-and-see approach adopted by FILEF betrayed its Leninist leaning to 'hegemonise' rather than collaborate on an equal standing with like-minded political bodies, in apparent alignment with Berlinguer's appeal, launched on 12 October 1974 in the Party's theoretical journal *Rinascita* for a "constructive dialogue and an agreement between all popular forces, without this meaning confusion or abandonment of the difference and diversity of the policies and ideals that characterise each of these forces"[88], despite the PCI still being anchored to the Leninist ideology of 'democratic centralism'. An important criticism of this methodology was made by politologist and at that time PCI member Salvatore Sechi, with his essay *L'austero fascino del centralismo democratico*, published in Bologna's journal *Il Mulino* (No. 3, May-June 1978, pp. 408-453). APR's stand, encouraging 'diversity' from other communist parties, was favoured at this time by the Eurocommunist PCI, because it enhanced its influence in countries of Italian emigration and heightened its importance in Italian political affairs. The main theoretical foundation of Eurocommunism was Antonio Gramsci's writings about Marxist theory that questioned the sectarianism of the Left and encouraged communist parties to develop social alliances to win *hegemonic* support for social reforms. As late as 1986, Gianni Giadresco, in charge of the Party's Emigration Section, defended the validity of this policy to his Italian comrades in Australia: "Whoever believes that the Italian worker, being a member of an Australian party or organisation, can equally defend his interests and contribute to the political and social growth of the country that is hosting him, expresses a correct opinion, but only in part true. You cannot ignore the fact that the presence of a party like the Communist Party, which enjoys high international prestige, accustomed as it is to collaborate and to act in unity with the progressive forces operating in the world, can encourage a broader participation and commitment of the Italian community to improve its living and employment conditions for the progress and development of Australian society. Based on these considerations we think that both you and we must make an extra effort to strengthen our organisation in Australia. On the other hand, if the characteristics of an organised, mass party, even in countries of emigration would disappear, we would lose many of the reasons for our influence at the international level".[89]

Striving to support and influence as many progressive and left-wing causes as possible was one of FILEF's main strategies. During the 1980s, as before in the 1970s, FILEF and the minority of its members who held a PCI membership card were actively engaged in public rallies, marches, demonstrations, celebrations, conferences, luncheons and gatherings having a distinct political message and finality: to rally in favour of or protest against a number of causes affecting Australia and the world. This was the public face of the Federation, showing its clout, following and success, or lack of it. Countless marches were held, against the dismissal of the Whitlam government, against Pinochet's dictatorship in Chile, against French atomic weapons tests at Mururoa, for the closure of the US base at Pine Gap – in 1986 the Treasurer of the Close Pine Gap Action Committee (Sydney) was Frank Panucci, and in 1987 FILEF was affiliated to the Australian Anti-Bases Campaign Coalition.[90] Marches were also organised against the installation of US missiles at Comiso in Sicily, and in favour of peace, of the Palestinian people, of the right to work, in defence of the environment, for Australia in a nuclear free Asian region, in support of SBS and of Aboriginal rights and advocating no more wars. FILEF's members paraded on May Day, Hiroshima Day and Women's Day (8 March).

The earliest Women's Day observances were held on 3 May

1908 in Chicago, 28 February 1909 in New York, and 27 February 1910, again in New York. In August 1910, an International Women's Conference was organised during the Socialist Second International meeting in Copenhagen, Denmark. Inspired in part by the American socialists, German socialist Luise Zietz proposed the establishment of an annual 'International Woman's Day' and was seconded by fellow socialist and later communist leader Clara Zetkin, although no date was specified at that conference. Delegates, 100 women from 17 countries, agreed to the idea as a strategy to promote equal rights, including suffrage, for women.

*FILEF members and sympathisers march in support of Aboriginal rights, Sydney 1988. (Courtesy FILEF Collection).*

Commemorations of the liberation of Italy from Nazi-Fascism and of the proclamation of the Republic were held annually on 25

April and 2 June respectively. At the end of the 1980s the latter had changed its political character, prompting FILEF's remonstrations. "Unfortunately", wrote Antonia Rubino, "from a couple of years the *Festa* [of the Republic] seems to be losing its previous character as a community event to take a more commercial aspect... Currently it seems that you tend to favour and promote Italian companies at the expense of community groups. We would like to ask the Committee to reverse this trend and give back to the *Festa* its community rather than commercial nature".[91] Rallies were held also for other community causes, as those in support of *Nuovo Paese* and for Italian being taught in State schools.

Several initiatives were held in NSW to combat racism and to engage in "identity politics", with their lights and shadows, for instance in 1984 FILEF endorsed a leaflet printed by the Combined Unions Against Racism opposing changes to the Anti-Discrimination laws proposed by Premier Unsworth[92], and the Circolo G. Di Vittorio organised a luncheon with Anthony Albanese MP on the theme "La cittadinanza e la partecipazione politica come mezzo per combattere il razzismo".[93] Particular attention was given to issues affecting women. On 15 November 1985, FILEF held a 5-week course on "Il movimento delle donne in Italia"[94], on 20 July 1989 a public lecture was given at the Associazione Napoletana, Leichhardt, under FILEF's auspices, by Tina Lagostena Bassi, a renowned Italian barrister expert on Italian law on abortion, domestic violence and drug addiction, who spoke on women's rights,[95] and on 26 August 1989, FILEF organised a public meeting at Annandale Town Hall and hosted Tiziana Arista, member of the PCI's central committee, responsible for the female section.[96] In 1988, FILEF disputed the findings of the Fitzgerald Report on immigration, that it considered "the most offensive and dangerous document on immigration from the repeal of the White Australia Policy".[97] On 5 August 1988 a public meeting was held at Leichhardt Town Hall to muster public support against the report's recommendations.

Throughout the 1980s, as it had been in the 1970s, *Nuovo Paese* remained a problem. Funding, subscriptions, co-ordination between the editorial offices in Sydney, Melbourne and Adelaide, and scarce human resources were ongoing issues. An analysis of the situation, made in 1983 by Frank Panucci, clearly identified the hurdles to be overcome. "The main reason", wrote Panucci, "why we in Sydney arrived at the conclusion that we do not see other alternative than to publish the newspaper *New Country* monthly, is the political question of the future of our organisation and the priorities that must be established to ensure, as far as possible, its future. We believe that the growth and the strengthening of our organisation is more important than to be choked by work in order to keep the publication of the newspaper fortnightly. If you look at the history of our newspaper, we see that it is not an instrument that has grown hand in hand with our organisation, rather an artificial appendage".[98]

The proposal to issue *Nuovo Paese* fortnightly was opposed by FILEF Sydney for sound reasons. As spelled out by Panucci, "there were three errors at the origin of the choice to publish fortnightly: (1) It implies a fortnightly political, financial and human effort that did not reflect (and does not reflect) the strength of the organisation. (2) It commits limited forces that could be used with more profit to bolster the organisation. (3) It assumes that the newspaper is not tied to the organisation, but is published because it is appropriate to print a newspaper (as if it would be possible, from the political point of view as well as the economic one, for the newspaper to progress and continue like other papers). This situation affects not only the organisation but also the quality and the very effectiveness of the newspaper as a tool for information and training. On the positive side, we could free resources that can be used to strengthen and improve our organisation, making it capable to deal with the problems felt by our community and to organise campaigns to solve these problems. If we are able to muster more means to organise and carry out this groundwork, we think that this is politically more important than maintaining a fortnightly newspaper, and does guarantee the future and the continuity of our organisation. More ability to interact and work with our community also implies an improved newspaper, because we acquire a greater knowledge of the situation and a greater capacity to plan".[99]

All FILEF branches accepted the decision taken in 1984 to issue the newspaper monthly, rather than fortnightly, as was the case since 1974. Again, FILEF Sydney explained the reasons for this move in a lengthy memorandum to the Federation: "For an organisation like ours, taking into account our cadres, our numerical strength, our human and financial resources and real possibilities, a fortnightly newspaper was too burdensome a commitment. This hypothesis was confirmed by the fact that FILEF Melbourne, that from the beginning had borne the bulk of the responsibility of the newspaper, periodically encountered enormous difficulty to print it, then...a few times some comrades from Sydney, and in particular comrade Pierina Pirisi , whose enormous effort and contribution have not always been duly recognised by some comrades, had to go to Melbourne to lend a hand in crisis situations. In particular, after the departure of comrade Cira La Gioia (1981), both comrade Pirisi and comrade Edoardo Burani moved to Melbourne to edit the newspaper. Since early in 1982, the alternative to this transfer was to move the paper to Sydney, but a new attempt was made to rebuild a core editorial group in Melbourne – an idea that we had to abandon in front of the evidence. An even more serious fact, structurally speaking, helped to confirm our hypothesis. The newspaper was absorbing, not only from FILEF, but also from the Party, their resources and best cadres. The latter, beleaguered by the unavoidable deadlines to issue the newspaper, were unable to effectively contribute to the activities and growth of both organisations and to play an active and substantial role in FILEF's and/or the party's initiatives taken on behalf of the Italian community and, generally, in Australian politics. This situation made it impossible for Melbourne's FILEF to express itself, participate in things, to act politically in a consistent and continuous way, to develop its own methods and areas of intervention. As a result it did not even create new cadres. This road could lead the organisation to its political death".[100]

In order to validate the decision taken, the memorandum noted that during the previous ten years FILEF had been unable to bring the number of paying subscribers over the 300-400 mark, and that the qualitative and numerical growth of the newspaper could only spring from a qualitative, political and numerical growth of the organisation. Evidently, *Nuovo Paese*'s new editorial look did not please everybody. In February 1984 Ignazio Salemi wrote to the editors of the newspaper two letters, strongly critical of the change. In them, he considered the new monthly to be "evidently, a backward step", atypical (*aberrante*), and lambasted some of its content. For instance, he criticised the editors for having reported the proceedings of FILEF's 1983 Congress only at page four: "*obiettivamente, una notizia ad una colonna in quarta pagina è veramente poco, in un giornale della FILEF*".[101]

*Young readers of Nuovo Paese (Courtesy FILEF Collection).*

Despite criticism, the new look attracted increased interest and readership. At FILEF (Sydney) 4th Congress it was reported that "since two years ago *Nuovo Paese* changed from newspaper to magazine, paying subscriptions have tripled".[102] However, progress on sales was not encouraging. Congress delegates were informed, rather contradictorily, that, "since it became a magazine, we have seen a doubling in paying subscribers and a constant commitment on the part of trade unions (although this will not continue forever). What is most disturbing is the lack of sales, which are about 250 per month nationwide - this means that we have not been able to add to our goal of increasing readers of *Nuovo Paese*".[103]

The same Congress approved the target readership that the publication should aim to attract: "1) the Italo-Australian community that is, first, second and third generation people... It must be an organ in which the community personally can identify itself, meaning it must print articles of human interest, stories of people - activities by associations in the community – dealing with issues of importance or that have a resonance in the community. 2) Government institutions and bodies that are the key stakeholders to resolve the problems raised by us, and we must not forget the issue of trade unions. 3) The third group is that of minority associations and Australian left-wing entities (Anglo-Saxon or solidarity groups)".[104] Despite its editors' efforts and the expectations of FILEF's leadership, *Nuovo Paese* never became a *giornale di massa* (grassroots newspaper), due to scarce financial and human resources, limited membership to the Federation and, most importantly, the innate disinterest, when not apathy, of most Italo-Australians in political, social or cultural matters.

At the end of the 1980s, *glasnost, perestroika* and the enduring structural crisis besetting the socialist system led to the demise of communism in Eastern Europe. On 9 November 1989 the Berlin Wall fell, and on 26 December 1991 the Supreme Soviet, the highest governmental body of the Soviet Union, voted both itself and the Soviet Union out of existence. This event marked the official, final dissolution of the Soviet Union as a functioning state. The disappearance of the *stato guida* (leading State), its satellites and the communist Parties in Western Europe had a profound effect on FILEF's communist members. Carmela Lavezzari remembered that "we were caught spiritually. To us the PCI was everything...we were duped ... at that time there were no shades, either you were with us or you were against us ... then, slowly, we opened our eyes. When Czechoslovakia happened, we could no longer be swindled, by then we were quite shocked, and then Poland happened. At the Fratelli Cervi Pierina [Pirisi] said: 'From now on we do not want the [magazine] *Soviet Union* any more and we have nothing to do with Russia'. A little man, a Calabrian, one of those hard-core comrades, when he heard such a thing, it seemed anathema to him, a thing that was destroying him. He was a person who believed in [the Soviet Union]. He put everything in an ideal that eventually proved wrong ... we were very naive ... all of us were rather upset ... The [Soviet Union] seemed to be a paradise and then, when everything collapsed, we saw that they had committed heinous things".[105] It is a striking fact that, despite more than a decade during which the Soviet system gave countless signs of decay and disintegration, the strength of ideological fervour that for a long time gripped many rank-and-file PCI members blinded them to the obvious, and they "saw the light" only in the twilight years of the communist gods. As Mikhail Gorbachev, the last president of the Soviet Union, would point out many years later, in reflecting on the events of 1989 and 1991, "history punishes those who are late. But it has an ever harsher punishment for those who try to stand in its way".[106]

Also Bruno Di Biase witnessed, during his last months as Secretary, the upheaval caused within FILEF by the decline and fall of international Communism: "It had a pretty disruptive effect, in the sense that until then there was a group of communists who were the ones who basically managed FILEF. There was a hard core of them who were ensuring continuity, who actually contributed financially, who run the association and tried to give it a kind of a strategy, a fairly uniform orientation ... There was discussion but there was no agreement on everything. Even during the days of Gorbachev and *glasnost*, there were those who kept predicting 'moustachioed [Stalin] is going to prevail'... There was a great disillusionment with many of us. Many did not take it well, and somehow left the Federation. There was a lot of disagreement, even within the leadership".[107]

However, as mentioned in chapter 1, dissent within FILEF and the Sydney branches of the PCI in NSW was prevalent from the early 1970s. This dissent was viewed with suspicion by a Party like the PCI, that unquestioningly adhered to the Leninist principles of democratic centralism and the *partito guida*. During the National Conference of the Italian Communist Party in Australia, held on 20-21 April 1973, Giuliano Pajetta had a memorable clash with Salvatore Palazzolo, one of the supporters of the line adopted by the Socialist Party of Australia (SPA), aligned with Moscow. Palazzolo retorted that "he intended to resign as Secretary of the PCI as he had been accused of spying for the SPA and also of embezzling Party funds. He said the PCI had tried to collaborate with the CPA but the CPA had rejected all the proposals put to it". To which, Pajetta responded by saying that "he did not want to hear any criticism of the CPA".[108] It was at this point, as another ASIO informer reported, "that trouble started in the ranks of the Italians. It was clear that some members supported the CPA, others supported the SPA, while others wanted an independent organisation directly linked and supervised by the PCI in Italy".[109] Dissent was created also by some youth who experienced the Italian student revolt in 1968, but their influence was more pronounced in Melbourne than Sydney. Moreover, the few FILEF activists who militated in Italy in the ranks of the extra-parliamentarian groups, *fiancheggiatori* of the ultra-left wing movement, also tended to undermine FILEF's activities. Bruno Di Biase remembered that they were "people with a good deal of antagonism, because they did not recognise themselves in FILEF or in the Party, they were more an element bringing disorder rather than growth... when we moved out of 423 Parramatta Road and bought this house in Marion Street, there was a lot of friction, for instance there were those recently arrived from Italy, who were more to the left than the communists and got really pissed off that the association was in the hands of the communists".[110]

The official disbandment of the Partito Comunista Italiano, on 3 February 1991, although weakening FILEF, did not mark its end. In 1990, FILEF still had 563 members of Italian origin, some of whom at some stage and in their capacity volunteered their labour. FILEF's membership was heterogeneous, comprising blue-collar workers, professionals, secondary school students, unemployed, and pensioners, and amongst all these groups there was a high percentage of women from various areas of NSW. There was a core group of 20-25 persons who regularly volunteered their time and skills to the organisation.[111] During the following decade the Federation adapted to the new reality and continued to carry out activities in support of what was by then an ageing, shrunk Italian community, increasingly out of touch with Italian realities, its umbilical cord with the 'motherland' cut out by the end of Italian mass migration.

## Notes

[1]   Mitchell Library, Sydney, FILEF-NSW Branch Collection (hereafter ML MSS 5288), circular letter, *circa* 1974.

[2]   National Archives of Australia, (hereafter NAA), Series A6122, control symbol 2671, item barcode 13031175, FILEF, vol. 1, confidential reports – 118 -, date censored; - 128 -, dated 29 August 1974; - 133 -, date censored.

[3]   Fondazione Istituto Gramsci, Rome, Fondo Partito Comunista Italiano (hereafter FIG/PCI), 1975/334/144, Pirisi to comrades, 27 May 1975. Also, NAA, Series A6122, control symbol 2673, item barcode 30485695, FILEF vol. 3, confidential report, - 64 -, 28 January 1977.

[4]   Leichhardt Library, FILEF Collection (thereafter LLFC), 1/12, Zaccari to Angelucci & Zol, 19 October 1992.

[5]   LLFC, 1/4, Zaccari to Angelucci & Zol, 18 December 1992 and 22 February 1993.

[6]   ML MSS 5288, Relazione introduttiva al congresso di sezione del PCI del NSW, 9 April 1978.

[7]   Ibid.

[8]   NAA, Series A6119, control symbol 4640, Lavezzari, Carmela Vol. 1, ASIO No.

3349/65, dated 12 July 1965.

9  Ibid., ASIO No, 2876/65, dated 15 June 1965.

10  Ibid., ASIO No. 5198/65, dated 19 October 1965; NAA, Series A6119, control symbol 3820, item barcode 7949852, Pajetta, Guiliano [sic], Vol. 1, ASIO No. 2728/73, dated 23 April 1973.

11  Ibid.

12  NAA, Series A6119, control symbol 3820, item barcode 7949852, Pajetta, Guiliano, Vol 1, ASIO No. 1482/66, dated 23 May 1966.

13  NAA, Series A6119, control symbol 4640, Lavezzari, Carmela Vol. 1, ASIO No. 1135//66, dated 11 April 1966.

14  FIG/PCI, 1973/234/13, copy of *Voce Libera*.

15  *Abbiamo prodotto mille copie di Voce Libera...500 copie per Melbourne, 50 per Adelaide, 15 per il WA, 15 per Wollongong e 15 per Newcastle...le copie del bollettino che ci sono rimaste a Sydney le abbiamo distribuite tutte, solo qualcuno ce le ha pagate...bisogna che la gente cominci prima ad abituarsi a noi e al bollettino* - FIG/PCI, 1973/234/14, Pirisi to PCI, Botteghe Oscure, 1 September 1973.

16  NAA, Series A6122, control symbol 2671, item barcode 13031175, FILEF, vol. 1, Director-General, ASIO to Liaison Officer, Rome, - 143 -, 7 January 1975. In it, the Director-General also mentioned that "at the present time, we have no comprehensive paper on the activities of the PCI in Australia".

17  FIG/PCI, 1973/234/12, Pajetta to Aarons, 19 September 1973.

18  NAA, Series A6119, control symbol 4640, Lavezzari, Carmela Vol. 1, ASIO No. 1135//66, dated 11 April 1966. Also: NAA, Series A6119, control symbol 3820, item barcode 7949852, Pajetta, Guiliano, Vol 1, ASIO No. 3887/73, dated 25 July 1973.

19  NAA, Series A6122, control symbol 2672, item barcode 30485694, FILEF, vol. 2, confidential report, -130 -, date censored.

20  Battiston, Simone, *Immigrants Turned Activists*, Troubadour Italian Studies, Leics, UK 2012, p.45.

21  NAA, Series A6122, control symbol 2671, item barcode 13031175, FILEF, vol. 1, Gentili to compagni, -140 -, 23 December 1974; confidential report, - 148 -, 11 February 1975.

22  LLFC, 2/4, Vescio to members, Circular letter, un-dated.

23  LLFC, 7/5, FILEF Committee meeting minute, 6 June 1991.

24  LLFC, 7/21, CCFC financial statement 1982-83.

25  Di Biase, Bruno, interview with the author, 24 January 2014.

26  *La resistenza e la lotta contro la decisione antidemocratica del governo australiano sono state giuste, ma ci si è lasciati assorbire troppo e se ne è fatto quasi l'esclusivo motivo di mobilitazione dei compagni* – FIG/PCI, 1977/415/33, Informazione di Cianca sulla sua permanenza in Australia (dal 3 al 31 ottobre 1977).

27  LLFC, 5/11.

28  *The Bulletin*, 8 November 1983, p. 41.

29  ML MSS 5288, Pirisi to Editor, 30 June 1977.

30  Di Biase, Bruno, interview with the author, 24 January 2014.

31  Ibid.

32  *quasi mai la sinistra australiana è stata in grado di organizzare la partecipazione degli immigrati alla vita politica australiana: lo dimostra la scarsissima presenza di immigrati nei partiti della sinistra australiana, sia come iscritti che come dirigenti...poca o quasi insignificante è la loro presenza in posizioni dirigenti... il clima di guerra fredda che il presente governo liberale-agrario sta rinfocolando, la schedatura da parte della polizia di militanti o simpatizzanti di sinistra* - ML MSS 5288, Relazione introduttiva al congresso di sezione del PCI del NSW, 9 April 1978.

33  *la mossa per la convocazione della conferenza è partita da alcuni compagni immigrati all'interno del CPA che, con l'appoggio del CPA stesso, hanno deciso di lanciare l'idea della conferenza...col consenso delle unioni, che hanno generalmente dato il loro appoggio, almeno formale, alla conferenza.* - ML MSS 5288, Considerazioni sulle conferenze dei lavoratori immigrati, un-dated.

34  *la seconda conferenza è stata caratterizzata da una presenza molto più massiccia della FILEF e dei lavoratori italiani, e dal tentativo della FILEF di dare un carattere più 'strategico' e di lotta alla conferenza, puntando sul diritto al lavoro come rivendicazione principale sulla quale concentrare l'attenzione, sia per evitare una conferenza che si traducesse in un'altra inutile 'shopping list', priva di indicazioni di lavoro e di lotta e di capacità di orientamento.* – Ibid.

35  ML MSS 5288, Il saluto della FILEF alla 2nd Migrant Workers Conference, 7 November 1975.

36  ML MSS 5288, Zangalis, George, Report to 2nd Migrant Workers' Conference, 7-8 November 1975.

37  ML MSS 5288, Salemi, Considerazioni sulle conferenze dei lavoratori immigrati, un-dated.

38  LLFC, 2/1, ACTU; LLFC5/17, Proposal for discussion at the ACTU Migrant Workers Conference, Melbourne 29-30 June 1981.

39  LLFC, 7/19, Panucci, Frank, Six monthly report of grant-in-aid worker, October 1984.

40  LLFC, 26/9, Peres, Viri, interview with De Re, Caterina, 10 May 1988.

41  LLFC, 26/9, Cooke, Kevin, interview with De Re, Caterina, 23 May 1988.

[42]   Peres, Viri, int. cit.

[43]   LLFC, 26/9, Cook, Bud, interview with De Re, Caterina, un-dated.

[44]   LLFC, 26/9, Mundey, Jack, interview with De Re, Caterina, un-dated.

[45]   Cook, int. cit.

[46]   LLFC, 4/1, Halevi, *FILEF*, paper un-dated.

[47]   *avevamo ragione a non occuparci troppo di cose formali...c'era più orientamento pratico che teorico.*
      - Di Biase, Bruno, interview with the author, 24 January 2014.

[48]   ML MSS 5288, Di Biase, Bruno, circular letter, un-dated.

[49]   *l'interesse dei lavoratori si fa soltanto nell'unità, mai nella frammentazione* - ML MSS 5288,
      Salemi to congress delegates, un-dated.

[50]   ML MSS 5288, Risoluzione programmatica del secondo congresso del PCI del NSW,
      un-dated.

[51]   NAA, Series A6122, control symbol 2673, item barcode 30485695, FILEF vol. 3,
      confidential report, - 19 -, 12 August 1976.

[52]   ML MSS 5288, Terzo Congresso della FILEF del NSW. 1 e 2 ottobre 1983.
      Documento di discussione, un-dated. Also: LLFC, 7/20, Terzo Congresso della
      FILEF del NSW, 1 e 2 ottobre 1983, Orientamenti e line programmatiche.

[53]   LLFC, 5/3.

[54]   *la FILEF deve saper dare una risposta anche organizzativa ad una ripresa delle tematiche dei
      diritti e del multiculturalismo nelle istituzioni di governo, nei partiti, nei sindacati, anche perchè
      siamo convinti che non ci potrà essere uno sviluppo economico senza un parallelo sviluppo sul piano
      culturale e sociale.* – LLFC, 3/16, Documento programmatico, FILEF's 4th Congress.

[55]   *per noi il multiculturalismo vuol dire democrazia, non come fatto puramente formale ma come
      processo di partecipazione, come difesa e promozione dei diritti democratici, in particolare degli
      immigrati e, dato il contesto multiculturale di fatto in cui ci muoviamo, delle minoranze.* – LLFC,
      3/13, Relazione generale.

[56]   *tra campi che hanno avuto ampio sviluppo nell'ambito della FILEF dall'ultimo Congresso
      a questa parte c'è senz'altro il campo delle attività artistiche che sono state avviate e sostenute
      dall'organizzazione allo scopo di coinvolgere particolarmente i giovani e le seconde generazioni. I
      tre spettacoli allestiti negli ultimi tre anni hanno dato un contributo originale allo sviluppo di un
      "teatro dell'emigrazione", e parlo delle mostre multimediali elaborate ed allestite sotto la direzione di
      Dennis del Favero. Tutte queste attività hanno portato prestigio all'organizzazione e l'hanno fatta
      crescere.* – LLFC, 3/13, Relazione generale.

[57]   *i nostri connazionali in Australia si rifanno a dei valori morali. Se si vuole che si avvicinino alla
      nostra organizzazione, non si possono ignorare tali valori. Non ignorare non significa accettare.
      Una delle ragioni per l'allontanamento dalla FILEF è senza dubbio il fatto che l'organizzazione
      ha dato troppo spazio a gruppi di giovani 'trendy' che nulla hanno a che fare (o molto poco) con i*

*valori morali delle vecchie generazioni ed in certi casi non dimostrano nemmeno alcun rispetto in tale riguardo* – LLFC, 3/16, note, un-dated.

58  ML MSS 5288, 4o Congresso della FILEF del NSW, Documento programmatico, un-dated.

59  *In apertura di congresso si è anche parlato di una caratterizzazione politica più marcata dell'organizzazione. Questo va meglio discusso in questo congresso: rapporto con la sinistra e l'ALP, le questioni sociali e politiche più generali, se e quando la FILEF assume posizioni (a livello nazionale/ statale)* – LLFC, 3/16, Documento programmatico, FILEF's 4th Congress.

60  *oggi l'80% della nostra collettività, più propriamente la nostra prima generazione, si trova in Australia ormai da 20 anni o più ed è relativamente stabilita in questo paese. L'invecchiamento della nostra collettività e l'emergere delle nuove generazioni (che ormai superano numericamente coloro che sono nati in Italia) pongono oggi problemi nuovi che anche la FILEF deve contribuire ad affrontare. Tra questi emergono con forza una maggiore domanda di recupero culturale e di assistenza e servizi per gli anziani.* – LLFC, 3/16, Documento programmatico, FILEF's 4th Congress.

61  *è possibile che vi siano stati dei casi di esaurimento delle energie anche a causa di assenze e forse sintomi di stanchezza da parte sia centrale che periferica. Contribuisce a ciò lo stato di disinformazione rispetto agli avvenimenti che si vanno verificando nel mondo socialista, nelle forze di sinistra in Italia ecc. E tutto ciò ha causato un certo disorientamento nell'organizzazione che comunque non riusciva ad avere, a causa della mole di attività in via di completamento, i necessari momenti di discussione, di orientamento politico, di verifica e anche, perchè no, di incoraggiamento e incontro sociale.* – LLFC, 3/16, Documento programmatico, FILEF's 4th Congress.

62  *l'organizzazione del PCI in Australia aveva fino al 1982 assunto una sua funzione come federazione e da quell'anno si è andati sempre meno a svolgere un ruolo e un lavoro formale perchè sono venuti a mancare i mezzi finanziari e i rapporti con la Sezione Emigrazione…Venuti a mancare i rapporti formali con la Sezione Emigrazione ne è derivato un graduale disorientamento politico a vari livelli dell'organizzazione e determinando precarietà ed incertezze nelle attività. Abbiamo poi cercato, in diverse occasioni, un chiarimento con la Sezione Emigrazione al fine di comprendere che tipo di rapporto e impegno volesse mantenere con l'Australia…tuttavia, non siamo riusciti ad avere nessuna risposta in cui si potesse intravvedere una ripresa del reciproco dialogo.* – LLFC, 2/4, Panucci, Greco and Soderini to Giadresco, Sezione Emigrazione del PCI, 7 September 1985.

63  *ci è mancato negli ultimi anni il contatto, proprio quando era più necessario, con le sezioni di altri stati* – LLFC, 2/4, Soderini to Members of Adelaide's PCI Secretariat, 7 June 1985.

64  *le condizioni di comprensibile difficoltà anche in ragione della lontananza dall'Italia rende sempre più difficile il rapporto diretto e frequente tra noi… è necessario intensificare i rapporti tra le organizzazioni del partito in Australia e la nostra sezione di lavoro in tutte le forme che saranno via via possibili, anche in ragione delle grandi ristrettezze finanziarie nelle quali ci dibattiamo e che spesso tagliano le gambe alle migliori intenzioni".* – LLFC, 2/4, Giadresco, Gianni, Sezione Emigrazione del PCI to PCI organisations in Melbourne-Sydney-Adelaide, 20 February 1986.

65   On this, see: LLFC, 19/20, Sgrò to FILEF Sydney, 2 June 1987; Di Biase, Bruno to Presidenza INCA-CGIL Rome, 20 July 1987; INCA Melbourne to INCA Sydney, 18 and 24 April 1990; *dalla vostra lettera traspare chiaramente un orientamento che non tiene in dovuta considerazione l'autonomia dell'INCA come istituzione, bensì emerge la volontà di porre l'INCA in una posizione subalterna* (INCA Sydney to Circolo Di Vittorio, 19 July 1990); Circolo Di Vittorio to INCA Sydney, 10 October 1990. *La presenza nel comitato INCA di Sydney di persone che gestiscono un'agenzia privata che fornisce il servizio pensionistico a pagamento risulta contraria alla politica di tutte e due le organizzazioni [INCA e FILEF] e rappresenta un grave caso di conflitto d'interessi...[INCA's management hanno preso] la decisione di escludere il Circolo Di Vittorio dal Comitato INCA stesso...alla rappresentante FILEF nel comitato INCA è stato negato accesso a corrispondenza che riguardava specificatamente la formazione e il funzionamento del comitato stesso -* LLFC1/13, Segreteria FILEF to INCA Committee Members, 20 August 1990.

66   *La necessità di mettere al corrente la FILEF e il PCI della questione nasce proprio dal progressive deterioramento dei rapporti tra la FILEF e il partito da una parte e l'ufficio INCA di Sydney dall'altra. Un deterioramento che risale ormai a diversi mesi orsono, e che dalla collaborazione tra noi e loro ha portato ora all'aperta ostilità e al rifiuto puro e semplice da parte loro di operare e fare lavoro politico con la FILEF e con il partito...la altrettanto discutibile decisione di ridurre il servizio di consulenza pensionistica nel nostro ufficio di Leichhardt da settimanale a quindicinale. Dopo la nostra protesta per tale decisione...l'INCA ha poi deciso di sopprimere del tutto quel servizio...Un'altra decisione molto discutibile è stata quella di rifiutare la nostra nomina di un compagno di partito per il comitato INCA. Nessuna motivazione è stata data per quel rifiuto, aggiungendo per giunta che l'INCA ritiene 'non necessaria' la presenza di un rappresentante del partito nel loro comitato...Con l'ultima risposta in ordine di tempo, ci hanno comunicato che semplicemente non vogliono avere più niente a che fare con noi. –* LLFC, 13/7, Popoli to Milani, Armellino, 20 September 1990.

67   *Si aggiunga anche a ciò il relativo scombussolamento portato dallo spostamento totale dell'INCA da Leichhardt. Era un passo necessario secondo l'INCA centrale che voleva un ufficio più ampio, moderno, ecc. Ma il fatto di non aver lasciato una presenza a Leichhardt ha finito, a nostro giudizio, per indebolire tutte e due le organizzazioni – l'INCA perchè gli è venuto a mancare lo stimolo politico e quindi rispondeva solo ad esigenze di caratttere amministrativo e non sociale e politico, e la FILEF perchè alla gente che viene ancora qui per pratiche di pensione ora bisogna mandarle a Five Dock e perchè coloro che vanno a Five Dock perdono l'occasione che c'era di mantenersi in contatto anche con la FILEF. –* LLFC, 13/7, Popoli to Milani, Armellino, 20 September 1990.

68   *Una considerazione che ci sentiamo di fare è che abbiamo goduto di una grossa autonomia sulle cose da fare in Australia e, allo stesso tempo, Pajetta aveva una grande capacità di comprendere il nostro punto di vista e di incoraggiare la nostra iniziativa" –* Burani and Pirisi to author, email, 18 July 2014.

69   LLFC, 2/5, FILEF Communiqué, un-dated. Also: NAA, Series A6122, control symbol 2671, item barcode 13031175, FILEF, vol. 1, Public meeting of FILEF, confidential report 946/75 -169 -, 11 March 1975.

70   LLFC, 6/4, FILEF circular letter, 10 December 1985.

[71] LLFC, 6/5, Lidcombe MHC report, un-dated.

[72] LLFC, 6/2, Response to the NSW Government Commission of Inquiry into Occupational Health and Safety, by the EAC of NSW, March 1982.

[73] LLFC, 3/4, Di Biase and Zaccari to Ethnic communities Council, 4 October 1990.

[74] LLFC, 7/19, Di Biase to Oakley, Diane, 10 July 1986.

[75] LLFC, 5/11.

[76] LLFC, 6/8, Di Biase circular letter, 4 July 1986.

[77] *la FILEF del NSW ritiene che il 1988, anno del bicentenario dell'occupazione bianca di questo paese, più che un anno di celebrazione acritica può essere occasione di riflessione, di dialogo con le collettività aborigine e di appoggio alle loro rivendicazioni. Ci proponiamo perciò di informare meglio la nostra comunità sulla storia, sui diritti e rivendicazioni degli aborigeni quali il diritto alla terra, il mantenimento e sviluppo delle loro lingue e cultura, miglioramento delle condizioni di vita* – LLFC, 3/16, Documento programmatico, FILEF's 4th Congress).

[78] LLFC, 7/6, De Re to White, John, 6 March 1990.

[79] LLFC, 7/6, De Re to Zammit, Paul, 26 April 1989.

[80] Rick Feneley, ASIO files: That looks suspicious, doesn't it? Sydney Morning Herald, 4 January 2014, accessed on 28 February 2014. See also Foley's comments on his ASIO file in: Burgmann, Meredith, *Dirty Secrets. Our ASIO Files,* University of New South Wales Press, 2014, pp. 91-111.

[81] LLFC, 1/2, Leaflet, un-dated.

[82] LLFC, 1/2, MCAR Declaration, un-dated.

[83] LLFC, 1/8, Caglieris to Prime Minister Hawke, 24 June 1991.

[84] LLFC, 2/2, Crollini to National Committee, Communist Party of Australia, 22 June 1985.

[85] LLFC, 2/7, Crollini, leaflet, November 1985.

[86] LLFC, 2/6, Poster.

[87] NAA, Series A6122, control symbol 2673, item barcode 30485695, FILEF vol. 3, confidential report, - 141 -, date censored.

[88] *un dialogo costruttivo e di un'intesa tra tutte le forze popolari senza che ciò significhi confusioni o rinuncia alle distinzioni e alle diversità ideali e politiche che contraddistinguono ciascuna di tali forze* –Berlinguer, Enrico, 'Riflessioni sull'Italia dopo i fatti del Cile. Alleanze sociali e schieramenti politici' *Rinascita,* 12 October 1974, accessed on 23 July 2014 in: http://www.ilportoritrovato.net/html/berlinguer2.html.

[89] *Chi ritiene che il lavoratore italiano, militando in un partito o in una organizzazione australiana, può ugualmente difendere i propri interessi e contribuire alla crescita politica e sociale del paese che lo*

*ospita, esprime una visione giusta, tuttavia parziale della realtà. Non si può ignorare il fatto che la presenza di un partito come il PCI, che gode di grande prestigio internazionale, orientato a collegarsi e ad agire concordemente con quanto di più avanzato esiste in ogni realtà del mondo, può favorire la più ampia partecipazione della comunità italiana all'impegno per il miglioramento delle condizioni di vita e di lavoro degli italiani e per il progresso e lo sviluppo della società Australiana. Sulla base di queste valutazioni noi pensiamo che sia noi, sia voi, dobbiamo compiere un ulteriore sforzo per il rafforzamento delle nostre organizzazioni in Australia. D'altra parte, se venissero meno le caratteristiche di partito organizzato e di massa anche nei paesi di emigrazione, si perderebbero molte delle ragioni della nostra influenza a livello internazionale.* – LLFC, 2/4, Gianni Giadresco, Sezione Emigrazione del PCI to PCI organisations in Melbourne-Sydney-Adelaide, 20 February 1986.

90 LLFC, 1/17, Report, 13 August 1986.

91 *Purtroppo, già da un paio di anni la Festa [della Repubblica] sembra stia perdendo il suo carattere comunitario per assumere una veste sempre più commerciale…Attualmente pare che si tenda a favorire e promuovere le imprese italiane, a scapito dei gruppi comunitari. Vorremmo chiedere al Comitato di ribaltare tale tendenza, e di restituire alla Festa il carattere di appuntamento comunitario anzichè commerciale* (LLFC, 1/5, Rubino to Comitato Celebrazione Festa della Repubblica Italiana, 25 August 1990.

92 LLFC, 1/16.

93 LLFC, 1/8, leaflet, un-dated.

94 LLFC, 5/15.

95 LLFC, 5/12.

96 LLFC, 5/14 and LLFC,17/7.

97 *il documento più offensivo e pericoloso sull'immigrazione a partire dall'abrogazione della politica dell'Australia Bianca* – LLFC,17/11.

98 *La ragione principale per cui noi a Sydney siamo arrivati alla posizione che non vediamo altre alternative che portare il giornale "Nuovo Paese" a mensile, è la questione politica del futuro della nostra organizzazione e delle priorità che è necessario stabilire per assicurare, per quanto possibile, questo futuro. Pensiamo che la crescita e il rafforzamento della nostra organizzazione sia più importante che lasciarci soffocare del lavoro per mantenere il giornale quindicinale. Se guardiamo alla storia del nostro giornale, vediamo che non è uno strumento che è cresciuto di pari passo con la nostra organizzazione, ma piuttosto un'appendice un po' artificiale.* – LLFC, 1/1, Panucci to FILEF Adelaide and Melbourne, 7 November 1983).

99 *c'erano tre errori alla base della scelta del quindicinale, cioè (1) un quindicinale implica uno sforzo politico, finanziario e umano che non rifletteva (e non riflette) la realtà dell'organizzazione. (2) impegna forze limitate che potrebbero essere utilizzate con più profitto e a far crescere l'organizzazione. (3) implica una concezione del giornale che non è legato all'organizzazione, ma che si fà perchè è opportuno fare un giornale (come se fosse possibile poi per il giornale andare avanti e reggere come fanno tutti gli altri, sia dal punto di vista politico che quello economico). Di questa situazione soffre*

*non solo l'organizzazione, ma anche la qualità e l'efficacia stessa del giornale in quanto strumento di informazione e di formazione. Il lato positivo è che si liberano energie che possono essere utilizzate per rafforzare e far crescere la nostra organizzazione, che risulta così più in grado di affrontare i problemi sentiti dalla nostra comunità e di organizzare campagne per risolvere questi problemi. Se siamo in grado di avere più forze per organizzare e svolgere il lavoro di "massa" pensiamo che ciò sia più importante politicamente che mantenere il giornale quindicinale e offra più garanzia per il futuro e per la continuità della nostra organizzazione. Più capacità di intervenire e lavorare con la nostra comunità significa anche un miglioramento del giornale, perchè acquistiamo una maggiore conoscenza della realtà e maggiore capacità di proposta.* – LLFC, 1/1, Panucci to FILEF Adelaide and Melbourne, 7 November 1983.

100 *Per un'organizzazione come la nostra, tenendo conto cioè dei nostri quadri, della nostra consistenza numerica, e delle nostre risorse umane e finanziarie e limiti obiettivi, un giornale quindicinale rappresentava un impegno troppo gravoso. Questa ipotesi trovava conferma nel fatto che la FILEF di Melbourne, che aveva a carico il grosso delle responsabilità del giornale dall'inizio, aveva periodicamente enormi difficoltà a mandarlo avanti....più volte alcuni compagni di Sydney, e in particolare la compagna Pierina Pirisi, il cui enorme sforzo e contributo non sono sempre stati dovutamente riconosciuti da alcuni compagni, sono dovuti andare a Melbourne per dare una mano a coprire il buco in situazioni di crisi. In particolare, dopo la partenza della compagna Cira La Gioia (1981), sia la compagna Pirisi che il compagno Edoardo Burani si sono trasferiti del tutto a Melbourne per portare avanti il giornale. L'alternativa a questo spostamento era di trasferire il giornale a Sydney già dall'inizio dell'82, ma si volle fare un nuovo tentativo di ricostruire un nucleo redazionale a Melbourne – idea che dovemmo abbandonare alla prova dei fatti. Contribuiva a confermare la nostra ipotesi un fatto ancora più grave, strutturalmente parlando. E cioè, il giornale finiva per assorbire le forze, i quadri più qualificati, non solo della FILEF, ma anche del Partito, i quali, assillati dale scadenze inevitabili dell'uscita del giornale, non riuscivano ad esprimere un loro contributo nel lavoro più ampio sia per la costruzione e la crescita delle organizzazioni e sia per un intervento attivo e qualificato della FILEF e/o del Partito nella collettività italiana e nella politica australiana più in generale. Questo ha privato l'organizzazione di Melbourne della possibilità di esprimersi, di intervenire nelle cose, di agire politicamente in modo coerente e continuo, di sviluppare propri metodi e campi di intervento. Di conseguenza non si sono generati neanche nuovi quadri. Quella strada poteva significare la morte politica dell'organizzazione.* – LLFC, 1/1, Memorandum "Quali prospettive per Nuovo Paese?", September 1984.

101 ML MSS 5288, Salemi to *Nuovo Paese*'s editors, 23 and 27 February 1984.

102 *da quando nuovo Paese è cambiato da giornale a rivista, cioè da due anni, gli abbonamenti paganti di sono triplicati,* - LLFC, 3/16, Documento programmatico, FILEF's 4th Congress, 4-5 December 1987.

103 *Da quando è diventata rivista abbiamo visto un raddoppiamento negli abbonati paganti e una costanza da parte dell'impegno dei sindacati (anche se questo non continuerà per sempre). La cosa più preoccupante è la mancanza di vendite, che sono circa 250 al mese a livello nazionale – questo significa che non siamo stati in grado di aggiungere al nostro obiettivo di aumentare i lettori di Nuovo Paese.* – LLFC, 3/16, Documento programmatico, FILEF's 4th Congress, 4-5 December 1987.

[104] *La collettività italo-australiana – cioè la prima, seconda e terza generazione…Deve essere una componente in cui la comunità si può identificare in prima persona, cioè significa articoli di carattere di interesse umani, delle storie delle persone – l'attività delle associazioni nella comunità – di trattare questioni di importanza o che hanno una risonanza nella collettività. 2) Autorità governative e le istituzioni che sono gli interlocutori principali per risolvere i problemi che solleviamo, anche qui non dobbiamo dimenticare la questione dei sindacati. 3) Il terzo gruppo è quello minoritario e la sinistra australiana (anglo-sassone o gruppi di solidarietà –* LLFC, 3/16, Documento programmatico, FILEF's 4th Congress, 4-5 December 1987.

[105] *eravamo stati catturati spiritualmente. Il PCI per noi era come se fosse chissà cosa…ci siamo fatti abbindolare…a quel tempo non c'erano sfumature, o eri con noi o eri contro…poi pian piano ti si aprono gli occhi. Quando era successa la Cecoslovacchia, ormai non mi fregavano più, ormai eravamo abbastanza scandalizzati, poi è successa la Polonia. Ai Fratelli Cervi Pierina disse: da ora in poi noi la "Soviet Union" non la vogliamo più e non abbiamo niente a che fare con la Russia. Un omino, un calabrese, di quelli sfegatati, quando ha sentito una cosa del genere, a lui è sembrato un anatema, era una cosa che lo distruggeva. Era una persona che ci credeva. Aveva messo tutto in un ideale che poi non si è rivelato giusto…siamo stati molto ingenui…eravamo un po' tutti sconvolti… Là sembrava che ci fosse il paradiso e poi, quando tutto è caduto, abbiamo visto che avevano fatto dei macelli. –* Carmela Lavezzari, interview with the author, 19 July 2013.

[106] *Russia Beyond the Headlines,* distributed by *The Sydney Morning Herald,* November 2014, p.9.

[107] *È stato un effetto abbastanza dirompente, nel senso che fino allora c'era una base di comunisti che erano quelli che in pratica portavano avanti la FILEF. C'era una specie di zoccolo duro che continuava, e questi erano quelli che effettivamente contribuivano finanziariamente, che tenevano in piedi l'associazione e che cercavano di dargli un certo indirizzo, un orientamento abbastanza unitario…C'era dibattito e non c'era accordo su tutto. Già ai tempi di Gorbaciov, glasnost, c'era chi continuava a dire "ha da venì Baffone"…c'è stata anche una grande disillusione con tanti dei nostri. Non l'hanno presa bene e quindi si sono un po' staccati. C'è stato parecchio dissidio, anche nei gruppi dirigenti.* - Bruno Di Biase, interview with the author, 24 January 2014.

[108] NAA, Series A6119, control symbol 3820, item barcode 7949852, Pajetta, Guiliano (sic), Vol. 1, ASIO No. 2537/73, dated 2 May 1973.

[109] Ibid., ASIO No. 3890/73, dated 25 July 1973.

[110] *qualcuno aveva una buona dose di antagonismo, perché non si riconoscevano nella FILEF o nel partito, erano più elementi di disturbo che di crescita… quando si è usciti da 423 Parramatta Road e si è andati a comprare questa casa a Marion Street, lì c'è stata parecchia maretta, da una parte c'erano quelli venuti recentemente dall'Italia e che erano più a sinistra dei comunisti, che si incazzavano che l'associazione era in mano ai comunisti* - Di Biase, Bruno, interview with the author, 24 January 2014.

[111] LLFC, 3/4, Di Biase and Zaccari to Ethnic Communities Council, 4 October 1990.

# 3

# FILEF and culture, education, language and the arts

Art is necessary in order that man should be able to recognise
and change the world. But art is also necessary
by virtue of the magic inherent in it.
(Ernst Fischer, *The Necessity of Art. A Marxist Approach*, 1984).

Beside political, social, welfare and propaganda activities carried out by FILEF during the 1970s and 1980s, the association was active in organising and promoting artistic, educational and cultural events largely aimed at, but not exclusively, the Italian migrant community. The structure that enabled FILEF to perform this task, the FILEF Cultural Committee (FCC), was set up on 28 February 1977. Its members included Bruno Di Biase (Secretary), Anna Berto (Treasurer), Julie Docker, Aldo Casari (President) Claudio Marcello and Pierina Pirisi.[1] Its Constitution detailed the Committee's aims as follows: "The objects of the Association shall be to encourage Italian migrants (including second generations) to participate more fully in all aspects of Australian society by promoting the organisation of migrants and their families around such issues as: education, the maintenance of community languages, welfare, social security, employment, health, safety, environment, trade union involvement and cultural development, in order to generate a positive sense of identity and greater sense of self esteem and to contribute to the development of a multicultural society in Australia".[2] On 28 June 1977 the FILEF Cultural Committee was registered under the provisions of the Charitable Collections Act, 1934-41[3] and was incorporated on 24 July 1987.[4] It is not surprising that its incorporation took place ten years after its formation. During those initial years FILEF was engaged on several fronts, fighting the battle to avoid Salemi's deportation, circumventing anti-communist criticism for its alleged 'subversive' plans, promoting a membership campaign, distributing the newly published *Nuovo Paese* and looking for an affordable venue in Leichhardt. Knowledge of bureaucratic and administrative practices was scant and, understandably, one of the last priorities. Even the Federation name, FILEF Sydney, was not incorporated. It would be only forty years later, in 2013 (its Australian Business Number being 65 318 748 859).

A plan to commit FILEF to cultural, artistic and educational promotion was part of the overall strategy suggested by Giuliano Pajetta to PCI's branches in Australia. In November 1977, drawing on his international experience as the Party's spokesman on migrant affairs, and following his visit to Sydney the previous year, he wrote: "the areas in which you more successfully can engage yourselves as a 'driving force' of a democratic and popular movement among emigrants, are, in our opinion, a) the general ethnic rights of migrants; b) the special problems facing Italian immigrants in their dealings with consular authorities and Italy; c) educational, school, cultural and welfare issues concerning Italian immigrants; d) participation by Italians to the trade union and social life in Australia".[5] It is interesting to note that, in order of importance, Pajetta seemed to value cultural and educational pursuits higher than industrial and social integration. His elitist definition of culture was in stark contrast with the more popular variety likely to have been treasured among many immigrants. At this time, the PCI pursued a rather double-faced line on 'culture'. Communists believed themselves to hold the moral high ground in Italian cultural life. A kind of Manichaeism took a hold of the mind of the communist militant, a belief in the purity of his/her struggle and in his/her cultural superiority. The cultural aims presumably flowed to Australia from Italy and from the Gramscian myth, whereby a bloody revolution could be avoided by the PCI simply conquering high culture and therefore beguiling the bourgeoisie into dying. It was a pretty doubtful course of action, and even more doubtful in anti-intellectual Australia. Worth noting is also the fact that Pajetta was writing to PCI Branches and not to FILEF. It seems that he was still holding to the Leninist principles of 'democratic centralism' within the party, and that *Botteghe Oscure*, the PCI headquarters in Rome, was bringing to bear its vanguard role over FILEF. In any event, in 1978 this still was the official party line. In one of his speeches, Berlinguer firmly rejected the thesis that 'democratic centralism' was incompatible with a democratic party: "this principle does not aim to ensure preventive unanimity, but is a method to eventually guarantee, after a democratic confrontation of all possible alternatives, the indispensable unity of direction and the concrete work of the party".[6] Of course, this position provided ammunition to FILEF's detractors who alleged with some credit, yet with classical Cold War verbiage, that it was a communist front organisation, ideologically inspired and funded by the USSR. The allegation that Botteghe Oscure was in receipt of the 'gold from Moscow' (*l'oro di Mosca*) was substantiated in an article by *La Repubblica*, dated 12 October 1999, confirming that between 1970 and 1977 twenty three million and three hundred thousand US dollars were handed by staff of the Soviet Embassy to PCI officials in Rome. The United States of America and the Vatican gave rather richer funding to the PCI's enemies. Between 1945 and 1966 the Central Intelligence Agency (CIA) provided more than $65 million in financial assistance to non-communist parties in Italy, mainly the Democrazia Cristiana. The programme of funding was renewed in 1971, to the tune of $11.5 million, and much of it went directly to the Italian secret services. A further $2 million was sanctioned in the mid-1980s.[7]

Even before the formation of FCC, FILEF's Sydney Branch, no doubt inspired by Antonio Gramsci's teachings on the role of 'organic' intellectuals in society, had already earmarked culture as a way of reaching Italo-Australian university students, still presumably a minority of the second generation. The jailed Communist Party leader, whom an American historian rather neatly described as "the Marxist whom you can take home to mother", distinguished between 'traditional' and 'organic' intellectuals. He was interested in the formation of intellectuals who could be organic to the interests of the working class and who therefore would find their place within the revolutionary party: "what matters is [the Party's] leadership and organisational role, which is also educational, therefore intellectual".[8] Already in 1975 Salemi attempted to establish a contact with Sydney's academic world. In a letter to Pajetta, he informed the Head of the Ufficio Emigrazione that it was possible to set up a cultural centre in Sydney, run by FILEF, that would become a pole of attraction for 'traditional' intellectuals.[9] A few months later, the project began with the dispatch to FILEF in Rome of the first order of history books that would constitute the backbone of a library based at FILEF's premises in Sydney. Salemi was very optimistic about this initiative. In a letter to Pajetta, he included "a list of books that are those chosen by Cresciani to kick off his cultural initiative in Sydney. On this question we made some time ago a meeting in Sydney and there is really a chance to link with university circles".[10] In the mid-1970s, the author was researching on the history of Italian anti-fascism in Australia between the two World Wars and was interviewing former communist cadres in Melbourne. It was in Carlton that he met by chance Ignazio Salemi, just arrived from Italy and seeking to contact past members of the communist underground. The two struck a friendship based on their common historical interests. While in Sydney, Salemi sought the author's assistance, although not a PCI nor a FILEF member, to motivate the fledgling association to organise a library at its premises.

During 1976 several book orders were made through Pajetta's secretary, Rita Riccio, charged to ship them to Sydney. In April 1976 Pajetta confirmed to Cresciani that "Rita has received your last orders and is replying to you direct... it seems that your cultural initiative is proceeding well". He closed his letter with a typically gramscian plea to 'organically' lend assistance to the newly established FILEF:

"I am urging you (I've already made it personally several times!) to be very close to our comrades and friends".[11] After a while, having received several orders of history books, Pajetta expressed to Salemi his suspicion that they reflected more Cresciani's interests than those of their eventual readers. Distrust was never far off from the old revolutionary's mindset, although he was not altogether wrong in this instance. Salemi allayed his concerns by detailing the usefulness of the initiative. "I would look with less suspicion", he wrote, "his preference for historical subjects. That is his area of interest and I think it is understandable that those are the things that he better understands. His idea to bring to FILEF, through the library, university students of those subjects, should not be discarded. It is an initiative that already, on a small scale, makes Sydney's comrades feel 'functional'. ... there are many sons and daughters of Italian immigrants who attend the university and if we are the ones to make available to them different and interesting material and not always just propaganda, I think it is a positive step ... Cresciani in his own way is also making the 'Dante' useful by organising for instance a conference on Italy discussing a left-wing alternative. And you know that here these are things that matter".[12] Eventually, an on-going contact, even if not 'organic', was established with some of the teaching staff, among them Alastair Davidson, Maria Shevtsova and Joseph Halevi, and with students at the University of Sydney, through the Frederick May Foundation for Italian Studies and the Centre for European Studies.

In 1978 the May Foundation invited historian and PCI Senator Giuliano Procacci to give a paper at the Foundation's first Australian Conference on Italian Culture and Italy Today, held on 27-31 August. Pajetta endorsed Procacci's mission.[13] It was in the relatively small migrant enclaves of Sydney and Melbourne that during the 1970s and 1980s the PCI 'exported' from Italy the strategy of cultural hegemony and made efforts to compete with the local, predominant Catholic and American, Hollywood-dominated cultures. In Italy, the party relied on the publishing house Editori Riuniti, the journal *Studi Storici* and legions of intellectuals *impegnati* (literally, committed to the cause).

In Australia, the supportive, intellectual humus needed to attempt to achieve 'hegemony' was absent. Of course, as Australian historian Richard Bosworth quipped, the Americans won and the Catholics have never left the field.

Since its foundation in June 1977, FILEF's Cultural Committee informed its activities in response to the perceived needs of the Italian community. As well as setting up a library and an information desk on Australian and Italian services, from 1984 it ran courses on English language and on Australian society; liaised with the trade union movement, promoting a greater awareness by migrants of their union rights and responsibilities; identified Italian migrants' and their families' special needs; promoted the introduction of community languages in schools; provided consultation and information on welfare rights and on issues of social and cultural isolation experienced particularly by the aged and second generation Italians.

FILEF conducted some educational courses since 1982. However, from 1984, with the assistance of the NSW Board of Adult Education, their number increased considerably. They were conducted in Italian, covered a multitude of topics and often served as catalysts for other community-based activities. The courses were held in the evenings, in order to make it possible for workers to participate, and served a dual purpose. They contributed to the maintenance of language, which is important for the maintenance of culture, especially for second-generation migrants. Secondly, they provided education for adults in the Italian community who could not follow similar courses conducted in English. This helped break the situation of cultural stagnation and isolation in which many migrants found themselves.

A majority of Italian migrants came to Australia with a limited education. Many had not been able to finish primary school and often had not even had the opportunity to get to know their own country and its history. Instead, they knew their *paese* and family, perhaps just as good things to know as 'their' country and history. In coming to Australia, they cut off practically all links with Italy, apart from perhaps the exchange of letters – often written by someone else, as many were illiterate – with family members who remained in Italy. The lack of a basic level of literacy made it extremely difficult for them to acquire the skills necessary to play a part within the new society, both from the point of view of language and as far as knowledge of social structures were concerned. Surely, the key issue here was learning English and any knowledge of Italian was merely a distraction, all the more given that Italian is not a global language. FILEF believed that it was necessary, more than ever, to foster the cultural growth and development of migrant workers and their families by promoting a number of cultural activities that directly involved and enabled them to take their place within Australian society whilst at the same time preserving their cultural identity. In doing so, FILEF and, conversely, the PCI sought hegemony and power.

It was for these reasons that in 1984 FILEF launched the idea of a community theatre project in Leichhardt, aimed especially at second-generation Italians, women, workers, aged people and the unemployed. The positive results of that experience highlighted the necessity for continuation of community theatre activities. FILEF wanted to overcome the many social barriers that separated Italians amongst themselves and the rest of the community, and to encourage people to emerge from the ghetto of the family circle and the local Italian club, be it the APIA Club in Leichhardt, patronised mainly be people from the Veneto region, or the Club Marconi in Bossley Park, at the outskirts of Western Sydney, whose membership was predominantly Calabrian. In these venues, they greatly prefer pulling poker machines and watching American plays on TV. For this reason, FILEF involved people of non-Italian origin in its activities, wanting to tear down the barriers that others had built, and work together for a more just society based on respect and recognition of diversity. The ideological framework underpinning the theatre initiative, as other FILEF cultural and educational projects, was spelled out in a lengthy article written by Pierina Pirisi in the February 1984 issue of *Nuovo Paese:* "There is no such a thing as a static and homogeneous society where everybody thinks the same, where there is no struggle of ideas. Moreover, in any society where there are oppressors and oppressed, a struggle is unavoidable, and from this arise different concepts and values within the same culture...In their countries of origin, migrants were part of a complex set of social relations, from family, relatives, friends and neighbours, to local and national social and political organisations...once in a new, alien country, this complex set of social relations generally becomes very simplified: all that remains is, generally speaking, family, relatives, and friends. It is obvious that in this situation old values and concepts tend to remain 'frozen'.... the assimilationist policies pursued by successive Australian governments denied migrants the right to keep in close contact with their language and culture of origin, thereby denying them the right to cultural development...A very fundamental fact was ignored: that knowledge and development of one's own language and culture are essential to establish a fruitful contact with another language and culture, to establish a relationship between the two which is based on equality...If we want to reduce migrant cultures to folkloristic notions and static values, we are doing migrants another injustice, by pushing them further into ghettoes and subcultures, and in fact preventing a fruitful integration...education, and schools specifically, have a big role to play to achieve the aim of integration of migrants on the basis of equality. The teaching of migrant languages and cultures in schools is essential to this end".

With the establishment of the FILEF Theatre Group in 1984 the organisation was able to reach albeit a small section of the Italian community and Italo-Australian children in some primary and secondary schools of Sydney's inner-west. The aims of FILEF's Theatre Group were cogently listed by Maria Shevtsova in her paper *Italo-Australian bilingual community theatre and its audiences:* "Tackle material directly relevant to immigrant communities and which has been neglected by mainstream theatre; show that the issues raised concern the whole Australian society and not merely its ethnic "ghettoes"; validate the history of immigrants...by bringing to light the role they have played in the history of Australia; make theatre accessible to the Italian-born who arrived in the 1950s and 1960s…reach their children, namely the second and third-generation of Italo-Australians who may have been more or less assimilated in the dominant Anglo-Celtic culture…evaluate positively a cultural legacy that had been virtually driven underground by the immigrants in question and derided by their adoptive country".[14] In the end, the shared values of the dominant culture proved overwhelming and Hollywood and TV won by a million to nil over such worthy ventures.

Performances were held at two local schools, Leichhardt High School and Kegworth Primary School, as these venues were in an area with high concentration of children from Italian and other migrant backgrounds. They also were easily accessible to pensioners living in the neighbourhood. Performers were recruited from anyone who was interested in joining, whatever their age or background. Those who were not fluent in Italian delivered lines in English. The Group was composed by a few professional and semi-professional people, who were outnumbered by amateurs. Although presentations were of a good standard, they lacked the polish and finish expected from professional companies. FILEF was something of an umbrella for the Theatre Group without, however, being its political or artistic chief. The relationship between the two entities, though rather loose, was mutually beneficial. The Group, albeit not a cohesive unit motivated by an altogether well defined philosophy or vision, had produced works that sustained some of the cultural principles for which FILEF, at least in part, stood. FILEF, on its part, provided the infrastructural and institutional support necessary for the Group's ventures. FILEF's theatrical practice was a form of social intervention with and for disadvantaged minorities. The use of Italian and English in all productions had political and cultural importance. Each production was trying to find new ways of incorporating both languages in order to make the show comprehensible to all. Of course, communication does not rely only on language; there are many ways to convey feelings, stories and ideas to viewers who do not speak the language, with singing, music, posters, banners and the like. But young Italo-

Australians were interested in exploring Italian history and speaking the language, although modern Italian was often not their parents' language. Anglo-Australians who did not speak Italian and who were part of the dominant culture had the opportunity to experience the discomfort of not knowing exactly what was being said. In the beginning many children refused to speak Italian, but towards the end they spoke it on stage and used it at school.

The first work performed by the FILEF Theatre Group was *Nuovo Paese* (New Country), on a script written by Patrick Cranney and Sonja Sedmak. It was performed on 12-15 December 1984 at the Pioneer Park, Leichhardt and at the Leichhardt High School's Auditorium and courtyard. It was an ambitious project involving about a hundred performers, among them grandparents, parents and schoolchildren from Leichhardt. It began in the park, took to the streets, thereby imitating the processions typical of Italian religious and secular festivals, and finally filled the local school, jam-packed with spectators who had accompanied it along the way or joined it at its destination. The production enacted aspects of Italian immigration to Australia. Drawing on a variety of Italian popular traditions, *Nuovo Paese* was well received by the audience by virtue of its apparent spontaneity, street-theatre dynamic, novelty and, most importantly, because it announced a theatre commensurate with multiculturalism. At last, a minority culture seemed to be an integral component of the national culture. A sample of 315 people interviewed (who attended performances) on their national origin revealed that 66 were Italian, 56 Italo-Australian, 3 Aboriginal Australian, 134 Anglo-Celtic and 56 "other". Two thirds of the respondents were female. The bulk of the respondents (198) were between the age of 21 and 40. Media reception was mixed. Brian Hoad, in *The Bulletin* of 8 January 1985 criticised "the fun loving ideologues of the [Australia] Council, bent over backwards during 1984 to encourage community arts – at the expense of art as such", while James Waites in *The National Times* of January 1985 thought that *Nuovo Paese* was both "celebratory and challenging" (15). On the other hand, The Principal of Leichhardt High School, in a letter to the Australia Council dated 13 March 1985[16], stated that the play had been "highly successful, and has had a strong and lasting impact on the students concerned, the teachers and the school in general…We feel that *Nuovo Paese* was successful artistically and that it fulfilled the requirements of the Board for the development of quality community theatre". On 27 May 1985 the Australia Council congratulated FILEF for staging *Nuovo Paese*: "the Leichhardt project was an extraordinary and highly successful undertaking".[17]

Following its first production, the theatre group set up several bilingual plays, their main character being propagandist, again involving the participation of local community members who generally had no previous experience in theatre. In April 1986 FILEF appointed Roberto Malara to the position of Ethnic Arts Officer, funded by the Community Arts Board of the Australia Council. His brief included the tasks to develop projects for the Italian Pensioners' Group, raise funds, expand the initiatives undertaken in the schools and assist in the co-ordination of FILEF's cultural projects.[18] Also in 1986 FILEF put on stage *Lasciateci in pace* (Leave us in peace), a play that dealt with the question of global and local peace, and in 1987 *L'albero delle Rose* (The Tree of Roses), an account of the experience of Italian women spanning three generations. It was based on the oral histories of Italian immigrant women recorded by FILEF. Sonja Sedmak wrote the script of both plays. Also in 1987 FILEF staged *8 Marzo* (Eight of March), based on the historical events that led to the adoption of 8 March as International Women's Day. Its production was devised in conjunction with FILEF Women's Group. The year 1988 saw the staging of *Storie in cantiere* (Stories in Construction), scripted by Sonja Sedmak and Silvio Ofria and based on stories collected from Italian workers in the building and construction industry and from members of their families. The play explored the nature of racism in the workplace and occupational health and safety and attracted the praise of the trade union movement. The Australian Council of Trade Unions (ACTU) strongly supported the unions' endorsement of FILEF's cultural enterprises. Its President, Simon Crean, stated that "the ACTU believes that the trade union movement has a responsibility to facilitate communication with migrant workers and provide them with a clear understanding of their rights and responsibilities as workers…The ACTU welcomes the initiative by the unions involved in this National Bicentennial Project". The State Secretary of the Building Workers' Industrial Union of Australia (whose telephonic agenda listing also FILEF's number had been surreptitiously copied by ASIO), who was the recipient of Crean's letter, in commenting on FILEF's play, stated that "it is essential that the trade union movement further develop its relationship with programme theatre workers such as yourselves".[19] Alas, in future his good intentions would remain dead letter.

The response from primary school children and young Italo-Australians in general was considered to be so positive that in 1990 FILEF established a young Italians' cultural group.[20] Also, at this time FILEF endeavoured to create partnerships with other theatrical companies. In an application for funding to the Australia Council, the Federal body for the arts, FILEF's President, Claudio Marcello, stressed that "an association with PACT Youth Theatre represents a new and exciting step forward for FILEF. In the past FILEF's Theatre Group has worked with a small group of arts workers and a large number of members of the local community interested in using theatre as a medium through which they could express their experiences and aspirations. The current proposal is unique in a number of aspects. Firstly, it represents a move toward working with established mainstream theatre groups. Secondly, it focuses on young people. Furthermore, the 'end product' – the show – will be quite different in form, style and the way in which two languages (English and Italian) will be integrated".[21] Collaboration with PACT Youth Theatre resulted in 1992 in the performance of *Diavolo zoppo* (The Con Artist), a play written by Carl Caulfield, moving between the fantastic world of Italian folk tales collected by distinguished Italian writer Italo Calvino and the real life experience of today's youth. Two other plays, produced and staged by FILEF, were 'The Story of a Thing" and 'Stories of the Heart'. From then on, FTG's staff began being involved in other theatrical initiatives; one of the most relevant being Sydney's Multicultural Theatre Festival. In 1991 Marcello confirmed "the appointment of Caterina De Re, Rosalba Paris and Sergio Scudery on behalf of FILEF as co-ordinators of the first NSW Multicultural Theatre Festival…the above named individuals will act as co-ordinators throughout the duration of the project and Caterina De Re will act as its principal contact person".[22]

*A moment of the production of Storie in cantiere, 1988 (Courtesy FILEF Collection).*

FILEF's theatrical endeavours were not only the subject of journalistic reviews and peer comments, in the main favourable, but also attracted academic interest. Sydney University's Maria Shevtsova, in her book on bilingual theatre, rather following the party line, presented in June 1990 at the 12th Sociology World Conference in Madrid, analysed the impact of migrant community theatre. "The publication", FILEF's Vera Zaccari commented, "represents the first study of the emerging patterns of the audience of bilingual community theatre in Australia. The study is based on statistical information gathered during the two most recent productions of the FILEF Theatre Group. The publication is the first attempt at providing a qualitative and quantitative understanding of the social composition of the audience and an analysis of their reaction to such productions in terms of the objectives guiding the work of migrant community artists. The study also examines the emerging patterns of the audience and the impact of bilingualism".[23]

However, it must be noted that FTG's productions were not patronised by Sydney's mainstream elitist theatre audience, who rather chose to view the plays staged by the Sydney Theatre Company or Belvoir Street Theatre, that preferably dealt with universal themes and employed professional actors. Performances dealing with 'sectional', 'minority' and 'left wing' issues were shunned, especially if one could not understand part of the dialogue, spoken in a 'foreign' language. Everyone else watched American TV.

Another means adopted by FILEF, attempting to graft into Sydney's mainstream artistic life, was the staging of large exhibitions in the dominant culture's iconic venues, thus engaging in the discourse of the artistic representation of minorities. *Quegli ultimi momenti* (Those Last Moments) by FILEF's member Dionisio Del Favero was exhibited in 1984 at the Australian Centre for Photography. It depicted the struggle of a fictional Italian family during the Second World War in Italy and their subsequent experience as migrants in Australia, in a world threatened by a new and more horrific world war. *Quegli ultimi momenti* was also exhibited at the 1984 Sydney Biennale and at the Art Gallery of NSW, that acquired it for its permanent collection. It travelled to six Australian cities, was seen by an estimated 150,000 people and won the 1985 Award from the Design Institute of Australia. Its total cost was $84,000, funded partly by government grants ($10,400). The exhibition attracted criticism from Michael Cobb, National Party MP and Member of the Waste Watch Committee, who made scurrilous allegations that FILEF had objectionable political aims and criminal connections. Italian Ambassador Eric Da Rin was compelled to rebut them in a public letter to the Australian media, as disingenuous as Cobb's allegations, in which he stated that "FILEF operates with no political prejudice whatsoever, nor is institutionally linked to any Italian political party...the Italian Embassy and the Italian Consulates have always found in FILEF...an indispensable factor in the network of human solidarity...to claim that Mafia style or other questionable political interests are reflected in FILEF is a gratuitous, unfounded and unfair distortion of the real ideals, aims and accomplishments of the organisation".[24]

A second FILEF's high profile event was the exhibition *Mondi diversi* (Different Worlds). It was a community project that started in 1986 and was achieved thanks to the collaboration with workers, students, artists, government institutions and migrant workers' organisations. The installation included photographs, an audio-visual sequence and a documentary in Italian, produced by Radio 2EA. It looked at the working people's struggle to survive in a new land and their efforts to be recognised as a contributing force in the development of post-war Australia. The work was developed through a series of community workshops in which over fifty migrant trade unionists, community members and students worked on various aspects of the exhibition and collected radio material under the co-ordination of artists-in-community. The bilingual exhibition *Mondi Diversi* interpreted in a poetic form the experiences of Italian workers in the construction industry over the previous forty years. It was praised by Bronwyn Watson in the *Sydney Morning Herald* as "a significant and worthwhile exhibition".[25]

*Mondi Diversi* continued the cycle of multi-media, audio visual exhibitions co-produced by FILEF and a group of artists-in-community: *Quegli ultimi momenti* in 1984 on the themes of resistance to Fascism, immigration and peace, and *Linea di fuoco* (Line of Fire) in 1987, dedicated to the defence of democracy and civil liberties from the abuse of power disguised as 'national interest'. The brochure produced for the 1987 exhibition stated that "participating in society means learning about social structures and the way they operate, and forming an idea as to whether they satisfactorily meet the needs of all members of society or not. It means seeking and finding ways of understanding and changing the realities of today's society, learning to collaborate with others, and thus know, understand and better appreciate them and oneself. Participation also means being able to take part in identifying the issues Australia has to face and in the decision making processes of the institutions of the country. Participation has been the key element in this project. It demonstrates how diversity is a valuable resource – it shows how multiculturalism is a reality and not a mere theoretical construct. But to understand the concept of multiculturalism we need to understand the history of racism and discrimination that stem from the first processes against the original inhabitants and later against many other groups that have settled on aboriginal land. Aborigines, like migrants, have been struggling for equality of rights, including rights to maintain their own language and culture. Hence the struggle for equality is one that is common to all non-dominant groups in Australia. The struggle is for a more democratic Australia". Again, the mantra of "identity politics", underscoring this propaganda piece, overshadowed the reality of class struggle and of power relationships imposed by the ruling elite.

More provocative was Carnivale's press release, presciently pointing out that *Linea di fuoco*'s theme was "state terrorism, an issue many artists might consider too hot to handle…the exhibition reveals the way the world now operates as a single organism and no-one, no matter how innocent, is safe from the machinations of certain governments and their security services". The exhibition was held at the Australian Centre for Photography, Paddington and was opened on 14 September 1988 by former Prime Minister Gough Whitlam and Italian Ambassador Eric Da Rin. It received positive reviews; Terry Smith in his review on 6 September 1988 in *The Times on Sunday* wrote: "this is the best of our art…it is superbly well-made and focuses us critically on content crucial to our lives". The Special Broadcasting Service (SBS) made an in-kind contribution of $12,000 to the project and the Italian government provided $10,000, the largest single amount until then made to a community organisation for a community-based arts and media project.

Two years before the impending celebrations for Australia's Bicentenary, FILEF's artistic director Dionisio Del Favero, a former designer with Midnight Oil and photographer for the Sydney Theatre Company, sought financial support from several funding bodies for his projected exhibition entitled *Three Cities/Three Cultures.* The project aimed to involve working people from the Greek, Italian and Turkish communities in Adelaide, Sydney and Melbourne, reiterating their contribution to the development of Australia and reflecting each community's hopes, aspirations and visions for the future. Initially funded by the Federal Government, the project aimed to record and examine the experiences and aspirations of working class migrants in several unions. However, on 7 May 1987 FILEF withdrew from the joint project. In a letter to its national co-ordinator, Vera Zaccari pointed out that "we [are] unable to continue participating to the project, as presently constituted...there needs to be a clarification of the conceptual framework of the project...[that] does not sufficiently reflect the diversity inherent in the three communities...the project, in its present form, creates a superficial unity and would not reflect the reality...the framework we adopt should enable this diversity to be expressed rather than one which conceptually forces homogeneity on three completely different ethnic groups". FILEF's withdrawal was motivated on political grounds, in support of the Aboriginal communities' opposition to the Bicentennial 'celebrations'. However, the severing of the links with the project was made only at the federal level. In a letter to SBS, FILEF advised that "whilst we are not continuing with the project at the national level as this would necessitate accepting money from the ABA, we intend to continue with the project at the state level. We would not like to see the good work carried out over the last two years come to no fruition".[26] It seems that on this occasion expediency had the better over ideological rigour.

FILEF's record of continuous involvement in cultural and artistic activities attracted during the 1980s considerable support from Federal,

State, Local Government authorities and from private concerns and individuals. Not all applications were successful. For instance, In 1987 FILEF applied for a $65,184 grant for a project entitled "Images of Italo-Australian Women: The Changing Profiles from 1976 to 1986". The project aimed to identify changes in the socio-economic, political, cultural and demographic position of Italian women in Australia and to examine the implications that these changes had on policy development. The application was rejected by the Department of Prime Minister and Cabinet.[27] Other applications did not meet with favour from the funding bodies. However, by the late 1980s FILEF's record of successfully applying for grants was impressive and, in retrospect, the state's largesse to culture, somehow defined, seems surprising.

In 1986, the Department of Immigration, Local Government and Ethnic Affairs (DILGEA) granted FILEF $5,415 under the Migrant Subsidy Scheme. With this, FILEF purchased its first Macintosh computer. In 1987, it received $38,700 from the Department of Immigration and Ethnic Affairs (DIEA) for a Grant-in-Aid (GIA) worker and $28,165 from the Department of Employment and Industrial Relations for an oral history publication project. The Australia Council granted $10,000 for the development and production costs of the play *L'Albero delle Rose* and another $10,000 towards the cost of materials of the exhibition *3 Cities/3 Cultures*; $7,500 towards the salary of an Ethnic Arts Officer and $10,320 for an artist-in-residence for *3 Cities/3 Cultures*. The NSW Office of the Minister for the Arts approved a visual arts grant for *Linea di Fuoco*, and Carnivale added another $10,000 to the same project. The NSW Ethnic Affairs Commission granted $6,000 for a Community Development Officer and $500 for the purchase of musical instruments. The NSW Board of Adult Education contributed $2,200 towards the running of courses and the Italian Consulate-General $1,000 for *L'Albero delle Rose*. Also, in September 1987 the Law Foundation of NSW granted FILEF $4,248 to publish the English version of the Italian Labour Law (*Statuto dei Lavoratori*).[28]

In 1988, FILEF received \$38,700 from DILGEA for a GIA worker; also, the Ethnic Commission of NSW allocated funds totalling \$6,500 for a Community Development Officer, \$300 for the printing of a photographic history book and \$1,000 for the printing of an oral history of Italian women. The NSW Board of Adult Education offered a grant of \$2,000 for courses, Carnivale \$5,000 towards the exhibition *Mondi Diversi*, Leichhardt Council \$200 towards the latter, while the Australia Council approved \$33,600 for the play *Damn Those Engineers*.

In 1989 FILEF was given by DILGEA a grant of \$43,280 for a GIA worker; \$1,000 from the Ethnic Affairs Commission of NSW for the printing of a book on community theatre; \$3,500 from the NSW Board of Adult Education for adult education courses in Italian; \$1,000 from Leichhardt Council for venue hire, and \$2,200 from the Centre for European Studies for publication costs.

In 1990, DILGEA renewed its grant of 50,000 for a Pilot Equity and Access Project (PEAPS); the Ethnic Affairs Commission allocated \$1,000 for cultural expenditure and the Australia Council \$2,830 for documentation, marketing and promotion expenses. The Italian Ministry for Foreign Affairs approved \$12,000 for a community education program.

Grants received between 1977 and 1989 totalled the considerable amount of \$ 631,365.96.[29] Despite the perceived worthiness by the funding bodies of the above mentioned initiatives, doubts should be raised about their effectiveness, in view of their complete inability to compete with that popular culture approved and sold by capitalism. FILEF's initiatives may have been humane and good, but they scarcely achieved hegemony.

The third area of FILEF's cultural involvement, beside plays and exhibitions, was education, in particular school activities. Since the late 1970s there had been a School Committee (*Comitato Scuola*) that operated with an annual subsidy of about \$ 30,000 for the creation of educational materials. The Committee, together with the Group for the Promotion of Community Languages, was involved in political and cultural initiatives in the schools. It also monitored the government's budget for the schools and liaised with government officials on ways to advance FILEF's school initiatives, in particular in the field of language teaching. FILEF also organised meetings and conferences, ran training courses for teachers and parents and printed a half-yearly bulletin, *Linguascuola*. It endeavoured to strengthen its ties with teachers and other immigrant groups with similar interests, and in particular it developed contacts and activities with parents.[30]

In order to lend assistance to the programs run by the *Comitato Scuola*, in the early 1980s FILEF set up a publishing company, FILEF Italo-Australian Publications, headed by Vera Zaccari. The company published books for primary and secondary schools, as well as texts of contemporary relevance, like Bruno Di Biase's *Terrorism Today in Italy and Western Europe*, which dealt with Italy's Red Brigades and Germany's Rote Armee Fraktion. By 1989, the company had printed, among others, the following books:

| 1980 | Morag Loh | With courage in their Cases |
| 1985 | Camilla Bettoni | Tra lingua, dialetto e inglese |
| 1985 | Di Biase/Brian Paltridge | Sull'italiano in Australia |
| 1988 | Di Biase/Bruno Dyson | Language rights and the School |
| 1988 | Antonella Reim | The Labyrinths of the Self |
| 1989 | Rubino/Shevtsova | Gramsci: His Thoughts and Influence |

*Educational*

| 1982 | Di Biase/Guaraldi | ItaliaPuzzle |
| 1983 | Rubino/Guaraldi | Garibaldi |
| 1985 | Rubino | Garibaldi. Note storiche |
| 1986 | Bottero | Giornalino |

1986. FILEF's Multicultural Education Co-ordinating Committee published *Che Gelato!*, with text by Ronda Bottero and Nina Rubino, illustrations by Rosemary Nicotina and photographs by Barbara Aroney.

1987. FILEF's Multicultural Education Co-ordinating Committee published, with a School Assistance Grant from the Italian Ministry for Foreign Affairs, *Fusilli e Skateboard*, with text by Ronda Bottero and Nina Rubino and illustrations by Barbara Albury.[31]

By 1990, FILEF Italo-Australian Publications had published 22 titles. During the 1989-1990 financial year, the sale of publications totalled $9,050, and the sale of tapes $1,200, for a grand total of $10,250. Funds held in bank totalled $15,344.[32] In 1985, FILEF began publishing a bilingual *Bollettino Mensile* (Monthly Bulletin)/*Newsletter*, advertising its cultural activities. By May-June it had produced three issues, but the initiative did not last long, being one of the victims of the late 1980s financial *dénuement* of the organisation.

During the 1980s FILEF, beside planning activities and publishing material for the schools, organised educational lectures for adults. The program of courses on Italian language and culture required the active participation from the audience, steering away from the traditional model in which a teacher conducts a course in several classes. Instead, FILEF's program was built around 'nuclei of interest'; the leader not only performed the role of 'teacher' but also of facilitator in the discussion among participants. The attendees were mainly first-generation Italian immigrants and children of Italians. The courses did not take place in schools but at FILEF's premises or in the offices of clubs and community centres in other parts of Sydney.[33]

The following ones were held in 1990:

> 'The Italian regions'. The course was directed to groups of pensioners and first generation unemployed, and the lessons were held in places where different social groups could meet. In total, eight groups averaging 24 people per course (total participants:

191) were involved. Two groups were exclusively formed by first generation Italian women.

'The woman and the environment'. The course was presented by Vittoria Pasquini. It lasted four weeks and was attended by 20 Italian women.

"Women and literature". Course presented by Mirella Scriboni. It was attended by 14 women.

'Theatrical Writing'. Workshop presented by Sonja Sedmak. It was attended by a dozen students.

'Theatre workshops'. Series conducted by Sonja Sedmak. Twenty people took part.

'Introduction to Computer'. Course presented by Vera Zaccari. Close number, limited to eight people.[34]

From 6 September to 11 October 1990 Alistair Davidson, a member of the Politics Department at Monash University and author of a history of the Communist Party of Australia, held a series of five lectures on Gramsci to which 26 people attended.[35]

Also in 1990 FILEF provided a cultural/educational package for Italians in the community. It consisted in 6 lessons examining four Italian regions, Lazio, Sicilia, Calabria and Veneto. The courses[36], run by Roberto Pettini, who during the 2000s would teach Italian Advanced Conversation courses at Sydney's Workers' Educational Association, aimed to:

- Increase the self-esteem of young Italo-Australian women, ageing Italian women, single Italian women and Italian aged.
- Increase access and knowledge of existing community services (both governmental and non-governmental).
- Increase access and knowledge of services and programs available to Italians from the Italian national and regional governments.
- Encourage fuller participation in the community.
- Promote social networking.

In May 1991 a computer course was attended by 10 people, while courses on Italian regions, culture and current Italian development were presented at Bondi, Pennant Hills, Leichhardt, Marsfield, Ryde,

Hunters Hill, Manly, Willoughby, Dee Why and Rockdale. Each course was attended by an average of 12 people[37], and in 1992 FILEF organised an advanced course of Italian, restricted to 12 students, run by Maria Cristina Mauceri, a lecturer in the Italian Department of the University of Sydney.[38] Other courses offered by FILEF were on 'Italian masks', La Commedia dell'Arte, Italian Opera, contemporary Italian cinema, contemporary Italy, 'International crime and drugs', 'Italy, the Euro and Australia', 'Italian Women's Movement in Italy during the 1990's', the use of computers and 'Introduction to the Internet'.[39] On 28 June 1997 FILEF organised a workshop for parents and teachers on the theme of Italian-English bilingualism in the Italo-Australian community. It was aimed to inform participants on the problems and issues associated with bilingualism in general and more specifically to provide practical strategies to promote and maintain bilingualism.[40]

As first generation Italian were ageing and deceasing, in 1991 FILEF's *Comitato Scuola,* also compelled by funding shortages, took the decision to concentrate its efforts on youth and launch a new, more appropriate and challenging initiative, *Vacanzascuola.* The main objective of *Vacanzascuola* was to create a network/link with Italian language teachers in public and catholic primary schools[41], in order to maintain and improve the language skills that Italo-Australians children already possessed, through intensive and planned activities during school holidays. The program was not meant to replace the teaching of Italian at school, but to support and strengthen it through periods of 'immersion' into the Italian language. In this way it was hoped to maintain the language and culture among second and third-generation Italians, in order for them to be able to use this language at home and in the community, to develop contacts with Italy and identify themselves with the language of their country of origin and not just as Australians.[42]

The language immersion program *Vacanzascuola* became one of the main activities of the School Committee. The program involved Italo-Australian children aged 5 to 12 years. The number of attendees grew steadily. During the Easter break in 1992, twenty-five children took part in *Vacazascuola* and in 1994 forty-one children attended its seventh edition. On 5-8 April 1994 *Vacanzascuola* was held at the Kegworth Primary School on the theme 'The Human Body'. Forty-two children took part. The event was co-ordinated by Antonia Rubino and Vera Zaccari.[43] In 1999 the number of courses grew to twelve, with about 15-18 children each. In addition, another eleven courses were held at the elementary school in Concord. All courses had a duration of 5 days each, for seven hours a day. However, the number of pupils reached by FILEF with its courses was negligible, if compared with the overall student population in state and private schools learning Italian at primary level. By this time, the number in the latter institutions was already declining, as did the number of candidates sitting for the final examination at Year 12. In December 1994 Di Biase and Carmela Lavezzari, who were members of COMITES' Gruppo Lingua e Scuola, attended a meeting with John Aquilina, Minister of Education. They were concerned of the "fall in the participation of [Italian language] students in primary schools from 40,000 to less than 700 at the level of leaving certificate".[44]

*Copies of the journal Linguascuola (Courtesy FILEF Collection).*

Despite the ageing of Italo-Australian migrants, during the 1990s FILEF still endeavoured to cater for some of their needs. In October-December 1995 FILEF organised a Cine-Forum during which six Italian films were screened:

- Palombella Rossa (Red Dove)
- La scorta (The Escort)
- Pummaro' (Neapolitan slang for tomato)
- Verso Sud (Towards the south)
- A Soul divided in Two.
- Libera (Free)

Educational courses promoted in 1998 included the following topics:

- Italian language and culture courses, including Italian language and conversation, beginners to advanced.
- Commedia dell'Arte theatre, mask making and performing. Mask making seminars were led by Italian artisan Paolo Consiglio, performing seminars by comedian Elio Gatti.
- Italian women writers
- Contemporary Italian music and songwriters (Calvino, Fo, *cantautori*).
- HSC Option Study Days and teachers' seminars. Preparing students for the Italian HSC exam and providing teachers with professional development.
- Computer courses.

After operating for more than 25 years to promote and spread Italian language and culture, in 1999 FILEF's School Committee was forced to review the strategy to continue its activities at the same level as in the past, as well as of launching new ones. Unexpected circumstances prompted FILEF to take this step, as well as the fact that government grants in the previous five to six years had been kept at the same level. The pioneering character of FILEF's school initiatives in spreading Italian culture and language was recognised by other Italo-Australian organisations, that duplicated activities originally drawn up by FILEF, namely, courses specifically directed to students sitting for secondary schools' leaving certificate examinations in Italian, or courses on Italian regions. With regard to the reasons that made FILEF's work more difficult, some were the following:

- changed working conditions in Australia, with an increase in working hours that made it more difficult to rely on help from volunteers. Therefore, it was necessary to employ a co-ordinator to plan and manage FILEF's programs.

- the competition of other community organisations that were offering a variety of initiatives in the cultural and linguistic fields; it was therefore necessary to carry out a constant and massive promotional work of FILEF's activities.

- as the Italo-Australian community was considered to be satisfactorily integrated in Australian society, there was a dearth of grants for projects aimed at, or managed by, Italo-Australians.

- during the previous years management costs and staff salaries increased considerably, while insurance costs remained unchanged irrespective of the size of the program.[45]

The competition referred to above came mainly from the Catholic, right wing oriented Italian Committee of Assistance (COASIT), that did not miss an opportunity for trying to contain FILEF's influence and impact on community affairs. For instance, FILEF was excluded from participating to the fourth National Conference of Italian Welfare Associations and School Teaching, held in Perth on 6-7 October 1990. In a letter to the Italian Ambassador, FILEF's President Claudio Marcello complained that "it seems to us that the conference was rather a national meeting of COASIT and we regret that FILEF was not able to make its contribution because it had not been invited".[46] On the other hand, FILEF shunned being associated with projects that were promoted by people who, rightly or wrongly, were considered being right wing, like those managing the project for the establishment of an Italian cultural centre in Leichhardt, the Italian Forum. "It must be quite clear" FILEF's committee announced, "that FILEF does not want and must not become a member of the Forum's committee".[47]

One of the principal problems facing the Italian community in Australia was access to information on government programs and services and knowledge of how government structures operate. Lack of English proficiency remained the main barrier to overcoming this problem. In addition to language and communication problems, there existed a generally low level of formal education attained by Italians who emigrated in the post-war period. One of FILEF's principal objectives was to disseminate information on government programs to the Italian community.[48]

In 1986, the policy of multiculturalism, that enjoyed bi-partisan support under the Whitlam and Fraser governments, came under attack by the Hawke government, which was pioneering neoliberal politics in Australia. Funds to 'ethnic' organisations and the Special Broadcasting Service suffered savage cuts. In 1985-1986, Federal funds for English as a Second Language (ESL) to schools across Australia were $62 million. They were cut to $34.3 million in 1986-1987, targeting children of non-English speaking background. FILEF took part in a rally held in Canberra on 14 and 16 September 1986 against the budget cuts to migrant services. In August 1986 the Federal Government withdrew funding ($126,000) from Sydney's Inner City Education Centre. In response, FILEF wrote a letter of complaint to Prime Minister Hawke. It said: "Many community groups, including FILEF, played an important role in the establishment of the Centre as a response to the educational and cultural needs of our local community. For over ten years the Centre has served as a valuable and vital service to students, teachers, parents and community groups... We are extremely disappointed that the Government has made such an ill considered decision and hope that it will be seriously reconsidered. We feel further aggrieved as it is yet another cut affecting migrant density areas".[49] Hawke's government cuts were not only a result of the recession then affecting Australia's economy. It was also a political recalibration to the right of Labor policies on migrants and multiculturalism, as a consequence of the first of the 'history wars' launched by the Liberal Party and its right wing supporters.

It all started with Geoffrey Blainey's Warrnambool lecture on 17 March 1984 and his book *All for Australia*, published in the same year, when he controversially attacked Asian immigration and condemned multiculturalism because it was reducing Australia to 'a nation of tribes'. By 1988, most media jocks, among them Ron Casey and Alan Jones, had come out of the woodworks, brandishing the racial argument to scare public opinion into rejecting multiculturalism, a word that, in the opinion of Greg Sheridan, another vocal right wing 'opinion maker', "must be dropped". By then, multiculturalism as a viable political instrument to achieve reconciliation, equality, 'unity in diversity', had been demonised, reduced to an empty slogan used only to paternalistically praise migrants for their food and folklore. Or, as del Favero feared, it had become "a mere theoretical construct". Respected political commentators claimed that Howard's Liberal Party had opportunistically embraced "the expedient politics of race" (Mike Steketee in *The Sydney Morning Herald*, 5 August 1988) and in so doing, had "abandoned the high moral ground" (Max Walsh in *The Sydney Morning Herald*, 4 August 1988).

In 1991 FILEF strongly criticised the proposals concerning the language policy put forward by Minister Dawkins in his Green Paper 'The Language of Australia'. It debased multiculturalism and wanted to separate language from culture courses. "We object in the strongest terms", FILEF's document stated, "to the total 'obliteration' of the issue of community languages (language development and maintenance for the children of immigrants) that the document is proposing ... you want to create a rift between language and culture, and to reduce the latter to a domestic issue of a specific community, rather than a legitimate part of educational institutions".[50]

During the 1980s and in the following years, FILEF was a staunch supporter of SBS and reacted to governmental attempts to reduce or weaken the multicultural content of its programs. On 20 September 1990 it submitted a recommendation strongly in support of SBS.[51] The following year FILEF issued a media release stating that it "was appalled at SBS's decision to introduce radio programs in English at the expense of community language programs…Any decision to introduce programs in English indicate a move away from the original charter for which many migrants struggled to achieve… At a time of recession it is the most vulnerable members of society who are most deeply affected. It is at times such as these that access to information becomes a question of equality of opportunity and therefore, democracy".[52] The same day FILEF's Italian School Committee condemned "the utterly insensitive and undemocratic decision by SBS to reduce time and make unwelcome changes to the schedule of Italian language programme. At its meeting of 25 July the Committee… judged SBS's decisions as totally inappropriate to meet the needs of the newly arrived immigrants by cutting into the needs of old established communities. SBS is robbing Peter to pay Paul".[53] In 1992 FILEF even encouraged COMITES, its rival in their mutual quest to conquer the allegiance of Italo-Australians, to intervene on the issue of Italian programs of Radio 2EA and SBS, shifted to inappropriate hours.[54] It also wrote to Robert Collins, Minister for Transport and Communications, complaining that "during the restructuring and rescheduling of programs, senior management has demonstrated an incapacity to effectively deal with community concerns and industrial rights of employees. They have also shown an inability to improve program quality and service to make them more responsive to the demands and wishes of the audience. We request that you intervene to ensure that the industrial rights of employees are fully respected.. [and] undertake a review of the management of SBS".[55]

Later, in 1997, FILEF was at the forefront of the protest against government cuts to multicultural educational institutions. In that year, the Federation wrote to Prime Minister Howard complaining against the Commonwealth funding cuts to the Association of Non-English Speaking Background Women of Australia (ANESBWA). "By cutting the little funding that is provided to ANESBWA you are leaving us with no effective advocate. You are well aware of the suffering endured by migrants when they first come to this country and the enormous contribution that they make, not only through their physical labour but also by providing vital economic contacts with their countries of origin...We believe that by saving a few miserable thousand dollars, your government will have to pay a very high price". The assertion that migrants spurred trade with Italy was unfounded. There was not, nor there had ever been, any evidence that migrants provided "vital economic contacts". A study carried out in 2014 by Bruno Mascitelli of Swinburne University of Technology on the effect of Italian immigration on Italo-Australian trade proved that "there is a tenuous relationship between the concentrated presence of Italians and strong trade with Italy".[56]

In FILEF's view, there was no clear dividing line between politics, education, arts and welfare. Every initiative promoted by FILEF influenced each of these spheres. Culture was no different. They played an integral role, in Gramscian terms, in the contest of achieving 'hegemony' in the 'manufacture of consent', a consent that in Australia FILEF did not even remotely achieve. During the period 1984-1986, FILEF received funding for one full-time Grant-in-Aid worker. Its first officer was Franco Panucci (1984-1986), followed by Vera Zaccari (1987-1991). With their employment, FCC was able to maintain and develop existing programs and services and to establish new programs to respond to some of the then evident needs of the Italian community, in particular the lack of industrial rights and appropriate work conditions for migrant outworkers.

Some of the FCC projects that made an impact included the establishment of the Italian Education Committee, which involved parents and teachers in the linguistic development of second and third generation Italians. It enabled FILEF to challenge mainstream services and traditional institutions about the appropriateness and accessibility to a diverse population. So many were FILEF's projects at hand that it was difficult to properly service them, as FILEF had only one person in full time employment and relied for the implementation of its activities on a small number of volunteers. This fact was recognised by the Grant-in-Aid worker, who admitted that "unfortunately, only one person is employed 'full-time' and she cannot follow projects all the way or have the time to be engaged in more visible political activities because most of the time is spent in maintaining the structure and conducting activities that, in the end, do not result in being profitable to the organisation".[57]

In 1988, as already mentioned in chapter 2, through the Grant-in-Aid worker, FILEF had given assistance to 184 clients and a further 2,080 enquiries requiring information or referral were taken. The program's leaders asserted that the 1988 statistics "can be considered to be an average annual figure for our agency".[58]

In 1990, the Department of Immigration, Local Government and Ethnic Affairs approved a special grant of $50,000 to FILEF under the Pilot Equity and Access Projects Scheme (PEAPS). Its aim was to enable FILEF to employ a worker in order "to pursue access and equity objectives, identify alternative sources of funding to ensure FILEF's ongoing viability and to arrange, for longer-term residents, especially women, access to English language classes".[59] The program, to be implemented as from 1 April 1990, was articulated into five action-based objectives:[60]

- Dissemination of information, providing the Italian community with information from government and non-government sources to assist them in fully integrating in their communities.
- Advocacy for implementation of access and equity policies.
- Sensitising non-government organisations to the needs of people of non-English speaking background (NESB).
- Put into effect Italian emigration policies.
- Strengthen FILEF's national network.

FILEF's only salaried position, that of the GIA worker, was not funded beyond 1991. Instead, the organisation was offered the above-mentioned grant of $50,000 for the PEAPS project that ended on 30 April 1991, and afterwards FILEF no longer had a paid worker. For this reason the services of Vera Zaccari, the GIA and PEAPS worker, could not be retained. FILEF was still carrying on with its activities, albeit in a more limited capacity, as it was operating on a purely voluntary basis.[61] In December 1990 FILEF's Secretariat advised its members that "from 1991, FILEF will not receive the federal government grant that is currently funding full-time a person (Vera), and in the light of this, the organisation must be radically restructured".[62]

Again in 1992, FILEF lodged a strong note of protest with the Minister for Community Services, stating that "we wish to express our grave concern regarding the proposals contained in the revised funding arrangements for the Children's Services Program…The period of consultation was not adequate. In the case of non-English speaking background families, there were no consultative mechanisms set in place to enable NESB families to be informed about the report and to make a response to the report. In addition, the report was not made available in other languages, no interpreters were provided at consultations, and there was no publicity through the ethnic media to give NESB families the opportunity to respond".[63]

The following year, in September 1993, a despondent Franco Panucci, then occupying the position of FILEF Administrator, portrayed to the Italian Consul-General FILEF's dismal situation: "The association does not have any salaried staff, but from time to time employs staff on a temporary basis, depending on the specific activities that it is planning to carry out. Approximately twenty volunteers who lend their work part-time carry out the Association's day-to-day administration. Between 400 and 500 people are using the services offered by the Association. Elderly, first generation migrants benefit from advice on Italian and Australian social security and frequent the library; second-generation youth attend courses organised by FILEF (Italian language courses, computer, etc.), second and third generation children attend the language maintenance program *Vacanzascuola*".[64] By 1993, the deepening and negative impact of the rise of governmental neoliberalism on such an always fragile body as FILEF became evident.

During this period, FILEF was involved, nationally and internationally, in activities other than cultural, educational and artistic. It supported other community organisations and trade unions in

Sydney by making available to them its facilities, providing translation and typesetting services and resources such as videos, books, tapes, posters, equipment, taking part in public forums and conferences and bringing its experience and knowledge on migrant issues in Australia. Among the many initiatives, in 1983 FILEF organised with the financial assistance of the NSW Board of Adult Education a ten-week course on the History of the Australian Trade Union Movement, held by Peter Sheldon, a graduate in trade union history, and in 1987 sponsored, with the Centre of European Studies of the University of Sydney, a public discussion on the concept of popular culture and its role in society, to celebrate the 50th anniversary of the death of Antonio Gramsci, who had produced theoretical works on the subject.[65]

FILEF-Sydney took part in the 8th FILEF World Congress, held at Perugia on 1-3 December 1989.[66] Its speaker rejected the commonly held opinion in Italian government circles that the 'problem' of emigration was on the way to be 'solved' or that it was no longer a problem for Italy. The intervention of its delegate dealt with:

- A report on multiculturalism in Australia
- School initiatives held by FILEF in Sydney.
- The request that FILEF Rome develop a multicultural policy and promote an international conference on multiculturalism.
- Solidarity initiatives with migrants from extra communitarian countries.

By 1989 FILEF Rome was on its death throes and the recommendations put forward by its Sydney comrades were not acted upon.

FILEF was a member of the Social Justice for Migrant Workers Coalition, constituted on 14 February 1990 in response of the proposal to change the NSW industrial relations legislation. On 10 April 1990 the Coalition held a conference on the Niland Report on the impact on migrant women and young workers in NSW. "Contrary to what the Government may think" FILEF claimed, "labour market deregulation is a social justice issue and not only one of industrial relations".[67]

On Saturday 14 December 1991 a leaflet distributed by FILEF advertised "a huge JUMBO SALE, when Italo-Australians and Palestinians join efforts for an end of year fundraiser at Leichhardt Public School". "Naturally", the sheet pointed out, "this initiative aims to raise funds in order to make it possible for FILEF to survive".[68] It is indicative that the Federation did not shun, on this as on other occasions, to admit publicly the parlous state of its finances and its detrimental effect on the implementation of its policies.

Also active on the international scene, in December 1990 FILEF made representations against the jailing of Filipino trade unionists by writing to President Corazon Aquino, expressing "our gravest concern at the arrest of Crispin, Beltran and other unionists…we are appalled that in a democratic country trade unionists can be detained for acting in the interest of their members…we call on your government to allow your trade unionists to speak to the people and to the government without the fear of being silenced or locked away".[69]

Industrial relations and the environment remained core issues for FILEF, that did not miss an opportunity to espouse community causes. However, it must be noted that FILEF was making then, as in previous years, rather trendy propaganda and the relationship of such ideas to the 'community' is opaque at best. In 1990, it organised and assisted in the production of radio programs in English and Italian on environmental issues, established a working group on an oral history project focusing on the San Fele community in Sydney and organised and participated in a parliamentary delegation regarding a proposed industrial relations bill.[70] During that year it also praised the NSW Democrats "for having resisted the Government's recent attempt to introduce new industrial relations legislation which would have severely and adversely affected the weakest sections of our workforce: women, non-English speaking migrants and young people. We commend the Australian Democrats' support for industrial relations legislation that is not guided only by economic rationalism but that also addresses the integral issues of social justice".[71] At the same time, FILEF passed a resolution calling on the NSW government to prohibit NSW industries from discharging their waste into the sewer system. "Large companies such as ICI are allowed to continue to pour tonnes of waste, much of which is toxic, into our sewer system...our concern over environmental issues is not a recent development. In fact, it goes back to the very beginnings of our organisation when we argued that economic growth was not sustainable because it led to resource depletion and other unacceptable environmental consequences".[72] FILEF also sought information on the effect of the construction of a third runway on Leichhardt people. "We believe that the detrimental effect of noise on learning is under estimated and would welcome any statistical data that may assist us in our efforts to encourage other ethnic organisations to examine the impact that a third runway at Kingsford Smith Airport may have on the education of their children".[73] FILEF presented a submission to the Environmental Impact Study carried out by Kinhill consulting engineers[74], opposing the third runway for the following reasons:

1. The quality of life of residents would be compromised
2. The quality of education threatened
3. It would be a short-term solution
4. The safety and well being of residents would be put at a greater risk
5. It encouraged greater concentration of population.

It goes without saying that, yet again, capitalism won hands down, the third runway was eventually built and did little to damage inner city lives. The above-mentioned flurry of activities and projects, however worthy, indeed was proof of how 'all over the place' FILEF had become.

In 1990 FILEF set up the Reclaim the Night Committee, being part of a movement against violence on women, that originated in Italy in 1976 and in Australia in 1978. FILEF launched a campaign against sexual violence, *My Daughter Can Walk on the Moon But Not on the Street*. It presented the following log of claims to Gough Whitlam and his wife Margaret, as the Whitlam government had been a pioneer in legislating on discrimination and violence against women:

1. That the State government provide adequate funding to agencies that provide direct service to women and children who have been subjected to sexual violence.
2. Acknowledgement of the extent and gravity of the problem and development of effective strategies for its elimination.
3. That the NSW government provide funding for an education campaign aimed at men, with the aim of countering violence.

On 31 October 1990, FILEF organised a rally in Hyde Park in support of the campaign. It was a great success. Police estimated that over 1,000 women took part in it. The rally started in the Park and moved along William Street "as a compact and cohesive and noisy unit". Some men marched along the footpath in support of the initiative, kept orderly by the presence of over 30 marshals. The event attracted national media coverage, including mainstream radio, commercial television and the press.[75] The pioneering initiative undertaken by FILEF in promoting measures aimed to counter violence against children cannot be emphasised enough, following the unveiling of horrific stories of systematic abuse perpetrated in many religious and secular institutions during the second half of the Twentieth Century.

Activities pursued by FILEF in Sydney during its short history reflected a strong commitment to often very soft 'left-wing causes' by that hard-core of activists who had practically been at its helm since its formation in 1973. FILEF undertook many initiatives to promote cultural development in the Italian community and multicultural development in the general public. It directed much of its work in the cultural field in order to provide working class Italians, most of whom had little formal education, with information and the means with which they could express their opinions, concerns and aspirations on issues affecting them and their families. The cultural activities brought some Italians of all ages together and in contact with other migrant and non-migrant community groups, such as local Aboriginal groups, thus encouraging a reciprocal understanding. The activities also aimed to address problems of cultural and social isolation and to increase self-esteem, break down inter-generational barriers and foster cultural and working-class pride. FILEF's cultural initiatives were recognised by some, although not by the Anglo community at large, as having broken new ground not only in that they were unique examples of community participation in the cultural arena but also because they acted as levers that facilitated the acceptance of community-based culture produced by working class migrants.[76] Again, the often overused term 'community' in FILEF's literature was an endorsement of 'identity politics' and so the surpassing of class. All the chat about 'community' should have troubled Marxists rather more than it did.

*Carmela and Umberto Lavezzari demonstrating in support of SBS (Courtesy FILEF Collection).*

The agents of change were a small group of professionally qualified migrants, undoubtedly representative of that class of 'organic intellectuals' to whom Gramsci entrusted the education and leadership of the working class. By 1990, FILEF's Executive included Claudio Marcello (President), Antonia Rubino (Vice-President), Darco Perusco (Secretary), Cesare Popoli (Vice-Secretary), Chiara Caglieris (Vice-Secretary), Franco Panucci (Administrator) and Carmela Lavezzari (Treasurer). Another 18 members comprised its Committee.[77] They ran FILEF efficiently and were intolerant of incompetence, delays and mismanagement, even on the part of its funding bodies. For instance, Vera Zaccari lambasted the staff of the Ethnic Affairs Commission of NSW for their incompetence, having lost twice FILEF's signed Schedule of Conditions for a grant.[78] By 1990, they felt somehow isolated, orphaned by the death of their 'paternal' interlocutor in Rome, who for almost fifteen years had provided steady guidance and assistance. One of the last significant visits to FILEF by high-ranking PCI members was that of Giovanni Berlinguer, distinguished surgeon and Professor of Social Medicine at the University of Bologna, and brother of Enrico.

In June 1982 Berlinguer represented the Italian Communist Party at the 27th National Congress of the Communist Party of Australia. He was a Member of the Italian Chamber of Deputies representing the PCI and a member of the Central Committee of that Party. He noted the problems facing FILEF in Sydney despite the enthusiasm and perseverance of its members. In a note to Bruno Di Biase, Berlinguer said that he very much appreciated "your commitment in such a difficult situation".[79] Contacts with the *casa madre* (mother house) became progressively infrequent, in view of the chronic problems affecting both the PCI and FILEF, as recognised in 1986 by Gianni Giadresco, then Head of the Emigration Office: "concerning the general problems that we are facing, particularly the peculiar conditions of our organisation in Australia, we are getting a good, reliable picture from information given to us by several comrades who during the last year and a half have visited Australia, by those of you who came to Italy, by your letters and, more recently, by the exchange of views we had with comrade [Vincenzo] Soderini".[80] At that time, telex, telephone and telegraph were widespread communication tools, but apparently they were infrequently used by FILEF on account of lack of funds or because the Federation could not afford to purchase the equipment. In 1994 communication problems were still besetting the Federation, as the Sydney Branch could not contact its Adelaide counterpart. Committee members were advised that "soon as we have money ... we pledge to buy two modems to enable us to immediately begin communicating via telephone between our two Branches".[81]

Among its most active members, the following held important positions in the organisation:

Pierina Pirisi was born in 1950 in Sassari, Sardinia, and emigrated to Australia in 1970 with an older brother and sister, to join a relative who had emigrated sixty years beforehand. In Sydney, she joined the CPA and, during a rally against the war in Vietnam on New Year's Eve in 1972, she met some FILEF members, and later joined that organisation as well as the PCI. Pirisi, as documented in earlier pages, was a stalwart of FILEF – Sydney until her return to Italy in March 1984, together with her partner Edoardo Burani, whom she married in 1985. Her political involvement continued in Modena, where in 1990 she joined Rifondazione Comunista and worked for the Records Office of the local Council.

Edoardo Burani was born in 1948 at Cortile di Carpi, near Modena. A son of tenant farmers, he dropped out of school at the age of sixteen and began working in a shirt manufacturing company in Carpi. In the late 1960s Burani was attracted to left-wing policies and became an activist in the trade union Confederazione Italiana Sindacato Lavoratori (CISL), faithful to the values of democratic Catholicism and secular reformism. While travelling with a friend throughout Asia and Australia in 1974-75, he decided to remain in Sydney, where he joined FILEF. His initial on-and-off involvement with the Federation turned into a full-time commitment in 1976, when he was granted permanent residency. Burani took an active part in the campaign in support of the introduction of community languages in NSW State schools. In 1984 he returned to Modena with Pirisi and began working for a disposal company. They still reside in that city.

Roberto Malara was born at Reggio Calabria in 1948. He graduated in Biology and Medical Technology at the University of Perugia in the 1970s. Malara emigrated to Melbourne in 1978 and in 1979 joined FILEF, briefly holding the position of Secretary. In the 1980s he moved to Sydney and was one of the founders of the FILEF Theatre Group, being one of its active members during the following years. From the late 1980s to the early 2000s Malara was an officer in the Arts and Social Activities Units of the Brisbane, Melbourne and Sydney City Councils. Since 2001 he moved back to Melbourne and worked as Community Grants Officer at the Darebin City Council.

Salvatore Palazzolo, his activities within FILEF-Sydney having been documented in earlier pages, was born on 29 July 1922 in Acireale, Sicily. He died in Sydney on 5 February, 1982.

Frank Panucci was born in Sydney on 6 January 1956 and obtained an Honours Degree in Economics and a Masters Degree in Industrial Relations at Sydney University. From 1979 to 1981 Panucci was engaged as a researcher for the Transnational Corporation. With FILEF-Sydney he performed several tasks, co-ordinating cultural and community projects, being Editor-in-Chief of *Nuovo Paese* and representing FILEF to the Italian and Australian governments. From 1988 to 1993 he was Principal Policy Officer at the Ethnic Affairs Commission of NSW. In 1982 and again in 1993-1994 Panucci worked at FILEF's Head Office in Rome. Panucci was employed by the Australia Council for the Arts in several stints over the last 14 years and has been the Manager of the Council's Multicultural Arts Policy, and the Manager of the Community Cultural Development Board. He returned to temporarily be Manager of the Aboriginal and Torres Strait Islander Arts Board and then was asked to act as the Director of the Policy, Communications and Research Division of Council. Currently he is Executive Director of Arts Funding at the Australia Council for the Arts.

Antonia Rubino was born in Agrigento, Sicily and researched on sociolinguistics, applied linguistics and linguistics, and was appointed to the Chair of the Department of Italian of the University of Sydney. She conducted extensive research in the

Italo-Australian community, focusing on the changes occurring in the Italian language and dialects in the transition from the first to subsequent generations. She published extensively in this area, and presented seminars at a number of universities (Australia, Italy, USA). She co-authored a junior course of Italian in use in Australian secondary schools. A member of the Language and Identity Research Network at the University of Sydney, from 2004 to 2006 Rubino was the Editor of the Australian Review of Applied Linguistics and from 2006 to 2008 one of the Vice-Presidents of the Applied Linguistics Association of Australia. In 2014 she published with Palgrave Macmillan *Trilingual Talk in Sicilian-Australian Migrant Families: Playing out Identities through Language Alternation*. This book is an in-depth study of the linguistic dynamics among Sicilian migrants in Australia, one of the largest regional groups in the context of Italian emigration. The study is placed in the context of the family migrant experience and the shifting attitudes towards immigrant languages in Australia.

Cesare Popoli was born in Naples, Italy. He graduated from the University of Naples in 1985 with a degree in Modern Languages, majoring in Spanish language and literature. Fluent in five languages (Italian, English, Spanish, French and Portuguese) in 1988 Popoli emigrated to Sydney, where he taught Spanish and Italian at both secondary and tertiary level. For many years he was a tutor at the Italian Institute of Culture. He also taught Italian to undergraduates at UTS and UNE and held a full-time position as a senior Spanish teacher at the Open High School.

Francesco Raco was born in Asmara (Eritrea) in 1942 and obtained a Diploma in Surveying. He emigrated to Australia in 1975 and became a member of FILEF in the same year. At that time, he collaborated with Franca Arena, a Labor politician and future Member of the state's Legislative Council, and with Claudio Marcello at the Italian radio program 2EA. Soon after, he returned to Tuscany and became involved in projects of restoration and tourism. He also organised cultural and artistic events in the Region and worked as a carpenter. In 1992 Raco returned to Australia and became active in FILEF, working for 18 months with INCA-CGIL. He also acted and was involved in plays staged by the Compagnia Teatrale Italiana. From 1994 Raco directed radio programs on Italian history and popular culture at Rete Italia,

Sydney. He obtained accreditation as a tourist guide, specialising in Australian colonial architecture and Aboriginal culture.

Vittoria Pasquini was born in Rome in 1946. She had a Degree in Letters and attended a 3-year course in Sociology. In 1983 Pasquini emigrated to Australia, where she obtained a post-graduate Diploma in Modern Language Teaching at the Language Acquisition Research Centre (LARC) of the University of Sydney. Pasquini taught Italian at ANU from 1991 to 1995 and in 1997 was a coordinator of the Italian radio program of Rete Italia, Sydney. She had an interest in FILEFs activities since 1990, when she became a member.

Claudio Marcello was born in Catania, Sicily, in 1941 and grew up in Rome where he graduated in Economics and Commerce and then in Political Science. He emigrated to Sydney in 1967, where he was employed by Electric Power Transmission (EPT), an Australian subsidiary of Società Anonima Elettrificazione (SAE) of Milan, a large company manufacturing and installing steel towers for high voltage transmission lines and TV transmitters. Since 1975, Marcello was engaged as a journalist for the Italian language newspaper *La Fiamma*, then with the Ethnic Affairs Commission of New South Wales and with the Italian program of Radio 2EA (later SBS Radio). From 1981 Marcello worked as correspondent for Australia, New Zealand and the Pacific for ANSA, the Italian National Press Agency, initially part time and then full time. He is also an accredited Italian interpreter and translator. Claudio Marcello joined FILEF Sydney in 1975, and became its president since 1977.

Vera Zaccari was born at Circello, in the province of Benevento, Campania. During the 1960s Vera and her parents emigrated to Switzerland for two years, and in 1967 settled in Adelaide, where she graduated in psychology and sociology, aiming to work in welfare and counselling. Early in the 1980s, Vera moved to Sydney, where she found employment with COASIT. In 1984 she came in contact with FILEF and began helping in the editorial committee of *Nuovo Paese*. In 1986, Vera returned to Italy, where she attended a three-months course in Italian at the University for Foreigners in Perugia and a six-months course at Albinea, in the province of Reggio Emilia, run by the PCI for its cadres. Back in Australia in 1987, Vera became full time grants-in-aid worker at FILEF until 1991. She remained active in FILEF until the early 2000s, when she and her partner moved on a property bordering the Macdonald River and the Greater Blue Mountains World Heritage Area, just outside St Albans. In 2012 she received from the Federal government a $175,000 grant for weed removal and restoration work on her property.

Bruno Di Biase was born at Crotone (Calabria) on 31 January 1946. Already before turning thirty, he had emigrated to Venezuela, where he stayed for nine years, and to Great Britain, for a period of two years. In 1970, Di Biase came to Australia, benefiting from an assisted passage. During the 1970s he attended Macquarie University, where he obtained a BA, and later the Australian National University, which awarded him with a PhD. In 1974 Di Biase joined FILEF and became its Secretary until 1989. From the mid-1980s until the early 1990s he was also Editor of *Nuovo Paese*. From the 1990s Di Biase was employed by the University of Western Sydney in the School of Humanities. Currently, he is Associate Professor in the Dean's Unit – School of Humanities and Comm. Arts. He is the author of several books and articles on community languages and obtained NAATI III National Accreditation Authority for Translators and Interpreters.

Throughout FILEF's history, the above mentioned people and other members made special contributions to the Federation's activities in view of their particular expertise and knowledge in specific fields; namely in political strategy and community affairs (Edoardo Burani, Pierina Pirisi and Frank Panucci), school activities (Rhonda Bottero, and Cinzia Guaraldi), Bella Ciao (Bruno Di Biase), photography (Denis Del Favero), film (Fabio Cavadini) theatre (Sonia Sedmack and Rosalba Paris), *Vacanzascuola* (Nina Rubino and Gloria De Vincenti), relations with institutions, including the union movement ( Frank Panucci and Vera Zaccari).

As already mentioned in chapters 1 and 2, this group of young and energetic people worked out FILEF's strategies and policies, in consultation with FILEF's headquarters in Rome, at the organisation's congresses, convened every two or three years. During the 1980s, FILEF's fourth congress, held on 4-5 December 1987 in the premises of Associazione Puglia in Leichhardt, and the fifth one, that took place on 3-4 November 1989 at the Annandale Neighbourhood Centre, concentrated on the successes achieved in the cultural, artistic and educational fields. The delegates shunned the many critical issues confronting the organisation: the progressive severing of the links with Rome, the ageing and hastening death of the Italian community, the consequences following the end of Italian mass immigration, the alienation of second and third-generation Italo-Australians eschewing FILEF's functions, the frustrating decline in membership, the economic crisis that affected Australia in the second half of the 1980s, multiculturalism being under attack from Howard's Liberal opposition and the ever-present stigma, in the eyes of an easily swayed public opinion, of FILEF allegedly being a dangerous 'communist front organisation', just to mention a few. Instead, the fourth and the fifth congress also delved on cultural success stories. The minutes of the fifth congress read, in an apparent self-congratulatory mood, that "we received considerable help from the Builders Workers Industrial Union for the theatre group staging in the production of *Storie in cantiere* and the distribution of *Nuovo Paese* to that union has improved. During the past two years we have carried out several cultural initiatives, among them the photographic exhibition *Mondi diversi*, the theatrical production *Storie in cantiere*, in collaboration with the building union, and the publication of a book on language rights and the school".[82]

Its inability to see the dark clouds looming large on its political horizon, threatening, in the long term, the organisation's existence, did not deter FILEF from undertaking a short term appraisal of its options and strategy, following INCA's moving elsewhere and in view of the marked change in the political scenario. The organisation's program for 1989-1990 warned that "in recent years the premises have been seen more as an office and less as a meeting place, for an exchange of ideas and so on. In part, this was due to the requirements of the job we were doing and to the fact that we were also preparing the newspaper. This fact, however, had a negative impact, because it turned away several comrades, but also co-nationals who happened to call in the premises. In addition, INCA moved to Fivedock and now there are few people who come to this place unless there is some particular activity. Now, working conditions have changed, for example, the journal is now produced in Adelaide, therefore we must ask the question of how to create a group of people, as well as of comrades, who could use the venue and its resources. This should enable us, through well-defined and useful activities, to make the organisation grow, and to let us better understand the people's real problems, and what are the needs and aspirations of the community, and for us to act accordingly. This is precisely the characteristic that distinguishes FILEF from other associations: the will to understand the problems, to put them in a social context, and to organise ourselves and try to solve them. The premises could function as a reference point for information and advice on many issues:

- Australian Social Security and assistance on pensions, subsidies, benefits, home care, workcare school (Austudy, teaching Italian). We could also offer to assist in filling out forms.
- Italian Pensions (referring them to INCA).
- Specific services and facilities to women.
- Information on unions (registration, health issues and safety at work)
- Immigration, citizenship and questions on family reunions.
- Information on programs by Italian regions for those who wish to repatriate". [83]

One would have expected that, after 18 years of activities, FILEF would have a firm grasp on people's problems and aspirations, rather than aimlessly asking itself the same questions, originally raised in 1973. If need be, this was yet another proof of the rudderless political journey undertaken by the Federation on the eve of the new millennium.

The obvious, widely agreed solution to the above problems and for FILEF to re-invent itself was to move away from 423 Parramatta Road, Leichhardt to a larger, more accessible building, as if a new building could really resolve all the political and social dilemmas. In 1992 FILEF advised its members that "for some years FILEF began to raise money to purchase its own premises ... buying a venue would mean a step forward in the life of our organisation and enable us to carry out more political and social activities...in the last three years we have managed to put together $ 40,000 for this purpose ... [we have found] a house in Leichhardt ... the price is $165,000 ... we hope to raise another $ 40,000, thus seeking a loan of about $ 85,000.[84] The contract for the purchase of a house, situated at 157 Marion Street, Leichhardt, was signed on 30 November 1992 with a loan of $120.000 from Monte dei Paschi at 2% interest.[85] A few months earlier, on 10 August 1992, the name and identity of FILEF's new offshoot, the Italo-Australian Community Centre Inc. (IACC), had been formulated. Legal advice on how to incorporate a new entity was provided by the Redfern Legal Centre.[86] Funding members of its Management Committee were Stefano Albore, Bruno Di Biase, Armida Croccolo (Treasurer), Dante Diomedi, Claudio Marcello, Carmela Lavezzari, Frank Panucci (President), Franco Raco and Vera Zaccari (Secretary and Public Officer). The Committee met annually. Most of its members had joined FILEF since its formation, evidencing continuity in management as well as a weakness in being unable to renew itself by co-opting to the Committee new, young blood. In April 1993, FILEF, FILEF Italo-Australian Publications and *Nuovo Paese* moved in their re-christened new premises.[87] On 19 January 1994 Leichhardt Council gave FILEF consent to its B.A. application to refurbish the venue.[88]

The Circolo G. Di Vittorio contributed $8,000 to the purchase of the asset, and was granted residency. In November 1996 it signed a Memorandum of Agreement with FILEF, whereby the Circolo held a 40% share of the property and FILEF 60%. Also, the Circolo contributed monthly $200 towards loan repayments as well as 40% of the Centre's running costs. However, IACC's overall financial situation continued to worsen by reason of the chronic difficulty in honouring the loan repayments. A special meeting was convened on 5 February 2000, when it was decided to "place the premises on the rental market, with the view of leasing the said premises for up to six years, with the option to extend, at current market rates to a suitable tenant, including a commercial enterprise". Instead, on 4 May 2001, 157 Marion Street was sold to Richardson & Wrench Lending Service for $370,000.00. After paying creditors, legal fees and the sale commission, the net amount credited to FILEF was $272,354.05.[89] As FILEF had been bankrolling the Centre's costs over the previous years to the tune of tens of thousands of dollars, it was decided at a meeting on 30 January 2002 between IACC and FILEF to reimburse FILEF from the proceeds of the sale. A first tranche of $20,000 was to be paid during 2002, while yearly interest on the investment of the capital was earmarked to finance FILEF's future projects. At the same meeting, one of FILEF's members, betraying the disarray, disunity and stagnation gripping the association, expressed his trust in the "common will that disagreements within FILEF be reconciled as far as possible, so that the organisation soon return to be operational".[90] Obviously, many members felt that the sale of the property marked the end of an era.

It had been hoped that the purchase of a new Centre would re-ignite the Italo-Australian community's interest in FILEF's activities and would signal a new beginning for the embattled association, destabilised by the recent, momentous events in the communist world and, to an equal extent, by an Australia that was increasingly becoming more affluent, socially insensitive and politically conservative, where radicalism was widely regarded to be anathema. A new ideological approach was needed to rejuvenate the organisation in order to combat the impending neo-liberal onslaught that would envelop Howard's Australia (1996-2006) and Berlusconi's Italy (from 1994 to 1995, 2001 to 2006 and 2008 to 2011), although Berlusconi was too anxious to stay out of gaol to be a real neoliberal, while the current Prime Minister, Matteo Renzi, is trying to be one. A neoliberalism that, as previously mentioned, in Australia had been pioneered by Hawke and Keating, and would takeover the Australian Labor Party. In Italy, promoted by Craxi and D'Alema, it would emasculate the various leftist groupings. Class struggle and multiculturalism would soon be concepts relegated to the dustbin of intellectual and political discourse, and become what economists call 'stranded assets' (i.e. lost value and obsolete). In the process, FILEF saw the momentum of its educational, cultural and artistic initiatives wane. The ideological battle for the minds and hearts of Australia's population had now changed its epicentre, from social amelioration to economic fundamentalism, from internationalism to chauvinism, of which Prime Minister Abbot's slogan 'Team Australia' is the latest manifestation, to core values of neo-liberal philosophy. Migrant rights and cultural retention by minorities had been, at best, relegated to the periphery of the national concerns or, at worst, rejected outright. However, in Australia, organisations like FILEF, despite shortcomings in their activity, did help the survival of aspects of the humane over the brutal. The new millennium was not bidding well for FILEF, increasingly marginalised and weakened in a changed Australia that was hosting a progressively less influential – if it ever existed – Italo-Australian community.

# NOTES

[1] LLFC, 4/6, FILEF Cultural Committee minute book.

[2] LLFC,17/12.

[3] LLFC, 4/14 and LLFC, 17/12.

[4] LLFC, 4/10 and 11.

[5] *i settori in cui potete impegnarvi con maggior successo come 'forza motrice' di un movimento democratico e popolare tra gli emigrati sono, a parer nostro, a) diritti etnici generali degli emigrati; b) problemi particolari degli emigrati italiani verso autorità consolari e in legame con l'Italia; c) problemi educativi, scolastici, culturali e assistenziali degli emigrati italiani; d) partecipazione degli italiani alla vita sindacale e sociale australiana* – FIG/PCI, 1977/449/208, Pajetta to Comitato Direttivo delle Organizzazioni del PCI in Australia, 10 November 1977.

[6] *questo principio non vuole assicurare unanimismo preventivo ma è il metodo per garantire alla fine, dopo un confronto democratico di tutte le possibili alternative, l'indispensabile*

*unità nell'orientamento e nel lavoro concreto del partito* – www.cronologia.leonardo. it/mondo25c.htm accessed 4 July 2014.

[7] http://www.repubblica.it/online/fatti/kgb/caporale/caporale.html accessed 4 July 1014. On US funding, see: Bull, Martin J. and Newell, James L., *Italian Politics*, Polity Press, Cambridge, UK 2005, p. 100.

[8] *importa la funzione che è direttiva e organizzativa, cioè educativa, cioè intellettuale* - Gramsci, Antonio, *Gli intellettuali e l'organizzazione della cultura*, Einaudi, Torino 1949, p.13.

[9] *il progetto in linea generale va bene...bisogna utilizzare bene tutte le esperienze di una specie di 'centro di informazioni italiane' che abbiamo qui a Melbourne...per avere una voce in più da inserire sulla piazza e un organismo in più che aderisce alla FILEF* – FIG/PCI, 1975/334/144, Salemi to Pajetta, 31 October 1975.

[10] *un elenco di libri che sono quelli che Cresciani ha scelto per dare il via alla sua iniziativa culturale a Sydney. Su questa questione abbiamo fatto tempo fa una riunione a Sydney e c'è veramente la possibilità di legarci gli ambienti universitari* – FIG/PCI, 1975/334/144, Salemi to Pajetta, 16 February 1976.

[11] *la Rita ha avuto le tue ultime ordinazioni e ti risponde lei stessa...vuol dire che le vostre iniziative culturali vanno avanti... ti raccomando ancora (l'ho già fatto di viva voce tante volte!) di stare molto vicino ai nostri compagni e amici* –FIG/PCI. 1976/383/216, Pajetta to Cresciani, 8 April 1976.

[12] *Io guarderei con meno sospetto le sue preferenze per quelle materie storiche. Questo è il suo settore di interesse e mi pare comprensibile che quelle sono le cose che capisce di più. La sua intenzione di convogliare presso la FILEF, attraverso la biblioteca, gli studenti universitari di quelle materie, non è da scartare. È la cosa che già, nell'attuale piccolo, fa sentire 'funzionanti' i compagni di Sydney. ...ci sono molti figli di emigrati italiani che frequentano l'università ed essere noi a mettere a disposizione materiale vario, interessante, e non sempre propagandistico soltanto, mi pare positivo...Cresciani a suo modo fa rendere utile anche la 'Dante' organizzando per esempio una conferenza sull'Italia di fronte alla proposta della sinistra. E tu sai che quì sono cose che contano.* – FIG/PCI, 1976/383/216, Salemi to Pajetta, letter un-dated.

[13] FIG/PCI, 1978/464/88, Cresciani to Pajetta, 21 April 1978; Pajetta to Sezione Esteri, 8 May 1978. Also, FIG/PCI, 978/482/60, Pajetta to Sezione PCI di Sydney, 7 July 1978.

[14] LLFC, 3/10.

[15] LLFC, 26/2, Hoad, Brian, 'Jollity in the suburbs masks decline', in: *The Bulletin*, 8 January 1985; LLFC, 31/5 and LLFC, 29/3, Waites quoted in:

Neeskens, Sonja's reply to Hoad, un-dated.

[16] LLFC, 28/8, Taylor, Trevor to the Australia Council, 13 March 1985.

[17] LLFC, 28/8, Ward, Anna to Panucci, 27 May 1985.

[18] LLFC, 29/7, Panucci to Mills, 29 April 1986.

[19] LLFC, 32/Crean, Simon, ACTU President to McDonald, Don, State Secretary, Building Workers' Industrial Union of Australia, 11 August 1986. Also: LLFC, 27/4, McDonald, Don, to FILEF Theatre Group, 12 August 1988.

[20] LLFC, 1/9, Marcello to Bates, 3 July 1991.

[21] LLFC1/9, Marcello to Australia Council, 29 November 1991.

[22] LLFC, 1/8, Multicultural Theatre Alliance to Marcello, 8 August 1991.

[23] LLFC, 1/9, Zaccari to Australia Council, 26 July 1990.

[24] LLFC, 13/1, Da Rin to Australian media.

[25] LLFC, 31/5, Watson, 'Portrait of a Community', in: *Sydney Morning Herald*, 16 September 1988.

[26] LLFC, 13/3, Zaccari to Eugenia Hill, 7 May 1987. Also: LLFC, 20/9, Zaccari to SBS, 20 November 1987; LLFC, 20/9, Zaccari to Building Workers Industrial Union, 20 November 1987.

[27] LLFC, 5/5, Brooks, Sue, to Zaccari, 29 June 1987.

[28] LLFC, 5/4, Purcell, Terence to Di Biase, 14 September 1987.

[29] LLFC, 3/3, FILEF Cultural Committee: Funding Details.

[30] LLFC, 1/1, Memorandum "Quali prospettive per *Nuovo Paese*?, September 1984.

[31] LLFC,16/3.

[32] LLFC, 7/8, Financial Statement 1989-1990.

[33] LLFC, 1/9, Zaccari to Mirisciotti, 8 November 1990.

[34] LLFC, 1/12, Marcello, Relazione sulle attività svolte nel 1990.

[35] LLFC, 1/9, Glasson to Davidson, 22 November 1990.

[36] LLFC, 1/9, Zaccari to Canterbury-Bankstown Migrant Resource Centre, 16 July 1990.

[37] LLFC, 4/3.

[38] FC1/14, Press Release.

[39] LLFC, 7/7.

[40] LLFC, 16/4.

[41] LLFC, 3/2, Zaccari to De Vincenti, 24 February 1998.

[42] LLFC, 10/15, Consuntivo 1996.

[43] LLFC, 1/9, Zaccari to Di Girolamo, 29 April 1994.

[44] *crollo nella partecipazione degli studenti da 40,000 nelle elementari a meno di 700 a livello di maturità* – LLFC, 1/3, Rapporto sulle attività del COMITES del NSW. Anno 1995.

[45] LLFC, 7/7.

[46] *ci sembra che il convegno sia stato piuttosto una riunione nazionale dei COASIT e ci rammarichiamo che ad esso la FILEF non abbia potuto portare il suo contributo in quanto non invitata* - LLFC, 1/9, Marcello to Ambassador Cardi, 26 October 1990.

[47] *Rimane chiaro che la FILEF non vuole e non deve partecipare al comitato del Forum* – LLFC, 7/5, FILEF Committee meeting minute, 25 April1991.

[48] LLFC, 3/3, Marcello to Department of Immigration, Local Government and Ethnic Affairs, 12 July 1990.

[49] LLFC, 7/1, Di Biase to Hawke, 25 August 1986.

[50] *Non possiamo che obiettare nel modo più netto alla "cancellazione" totale della questione delle lingue comunitarie (mantenimento e sviluppo linguistico dei figli degli immigrati) che il documento opera...si vuole creare una frattura tra lingua e cultura, e ridurre quest'ultima a questione interna ad una specifica collettività, piuttosto che parte legittima delle istituzioni scolastiche* - LLFC, 1/9, Risposta della FILEF (Sydney) al Green Paper "The Language of Australia", 4 March 1991.

[51] LLFC, 1/12, Submission, 20 September 1990.

[52] LLFC,1/9, FILEF Media release, 26 July 1991.

[53] LLFC, 1/9, Press release, 26 July 1991.

[54] LLFC, 1/3, Panucci to COMITES, 27 February 1992.

[55] LLFC, 1/6, Panucci to Collins, 17 September 1992.

[56] LLFC, 1/8, Zaccari to Howard, John, 17 June 1997. On the issue of trade, see: Mascitelli, Bruno, 'Australia-Italy: A Not So "Special" Trade Relationship', in: Cresciani, Gianfranco and Mascitelli, Bruno (Eds), *Italy and Australia. An Asymmetrical Relationship*, Connor Court Publishing, Ballarat 2014, pp.177-209.

[57] *purtroppo una sola persona impiegata nonostante che è a tempo pieno non può seguire progetti fino in fondo o avere il tempo per fare attività più politica e visibile perchè la maggior parte del tempo viene trascorso nel mantenimento della struttura e lo svolgimento di attività e quindi, alla fine dei conti, non da dei risultati che portano un profitto politico dell'organizzazione* - LLFC, 3/11, Report of the GIA worker, 2 February 1990.

[58] LLFC, 3/4, Di Biase and Zaccari to Ethnic Communities Council, 4 October 1990.

[59] LLFC, 3/4, Ray, Robert to Marcello, letter un-dated.

[60] LLFC, 3/4, Zaccari to Tam, Ivy, 4 December 1990. Also: LLFC1/8, Zaccari to Department of Immigration, Local Government and Ethnic Affairs, 4 December 1990.

[61] LLFC, 1/8, Marcello to Harbaum, Carl, Chairperson, Federation Ethnic Communities Council of Australia, 26 July 1991.

[62] *dal 1991 la FILEF non riceverà più il sussidio del governo federale che attualmente finanzia una persona (Vera) a tempo pieno in sede, e alla luce di ciò l'organizzazione dovrà essere radicalmente ristrutturata* -LLFC, 1/12, Secretariat to members, 3 December 1990.

[63] LLFC, 1/8, Zaccari to Hannaford, J., MLA, Minister for Health and Community Services, 11 May 1992.

[64] *L'associazione non dispone di nessun personale salariato, ma assume di volta in volta del personale su base temporanea a seconda delle attività specifiche che intende svolgere. L'attività regolare dell'Associazione è svolta grazie ad una ventina circa di volontari che prestano la loro opera a tempo parziale. Fra le 400 e le 500 persone si servono dei servizi offerti dall'Associazione. Ciò comprende anziani di prima generazione che usufruiscono di consulenza sui servizi previdenziali italiani ed australiani, e della biblioteca; giovani di seconda generazione che frequentano i corsi popolari organizzati dalla FILEF (corsi di lingua italiana, di computer, ecc.); bambini di seconda e terza generazione che frequentano il programma di mantenimento linguistico Vacanzascuola* - LLFC,4/7, Panucci to Consul-General, 10 September 1993.

[65] LLFC,1/12, Marcello to Horin, 11 February 1992. Also: LLFC, 15/10,

Di Biase circular letter, 28 April 1983; LLFC, 26/7, Di Biase to Australia Council, 8 September 1987.

[66] LLFC, 3/11, Report, un-dated. Also: LLFC, 6/9, Rapporto sull'ottavo Congresso FILEF mondiale, Perugia 1-3 December 1989.

[67] LLFC, 1/7, Zaccari to Nori, Sandra MP, 2 May 1990.

[68] *questa iniziativa ha naturalmente lo scopo di raccogliere fondi per la sopravvivenza materiale della FILEF* – LLFC, 1/12, Scudery to members, 28 November 1991.

[69] LLFC, 1/8, Marcello to President Aquino, Corazon, 13 November 1990; to Defence Secretary Ramos, Fidel, 13 November 1990.

[70] LLFC, 1/12, FILEF Activities 1990. Workers Report.

[71] LLFC, 1/8, Marcello to Senator Bourke, Vicky, 30 October 1990.

[72] LLFC, 1/8, Perusco to Premier Greiner, Nick, 27 September 1990.

[73] LLFC, 1/8, Zaccari to University of Sydney, 8 October 1990. Also: LLFC, 1/8, Perusco to Ethnic Affairs Commission of NSW, 4 October 1990.

[74] LLFC, 1/8, Perusco to Kinhill Engineers, 17 May 1990.

[75] LLFC, 1/8, Zaccari to Whitlam, Gough and Margaret, October 1990. Also: LLFC, 20/2, Reclaim the Night March Committee, meeting of the 31 October 1990. On the Whitlam government legislation on women, see: Whitlam, Gough, *The Whitlam Government. 1972-1975*, Penguin Books, Ringwood, Vic. 1985, pp.509-521.

[76] LLFC, 1/9, Marcello to Bates, 3 July 1991.

[77] LLFC, 3/3.

[78] LLFC, 1/8, Zaccari to Kerkyasharian, 9 August 1990.

[79] *Ho apprezzato molto il vostro impegno in condizioni così difficili* – LLFC, 32/ Correspondence, Berlinguer to Di Biase, 26 June 1982.

[80] *circa i problemi generali che abbiamo di fronte, particolarmente per le peculiari condizioni della nostra organizzazione in Australia, il riferimento più valido lo ricaviamo dalle informazioni dateci dai vari compagni che nell'ultimo anno e mezzo hanno visitato l'Australia, da quelli tra voi che sono venuti in Italia, dalle vostre lettere e, recentemente, dallo scambio di vedute avuto con il compagno Soderini* – LLFC, 2/4, Giadresco, Sezione Emigrazione del PCI to PCI organisations in Melbourne-Sydney-Adelaide, 20 February 1986.

[81] *non appena avremo...soldi, ci impegniamo a comprare due modem per poter così subito*

*cominciare la comunicazione via telefono tra le due sedi.* – LLFC, 32/Contributo della redazione di NP di Sydney alla riunione di Melbourne del 6 agosto, 5 August 1994.

[82] *Abbiamo avuto notevoli aiuti dalla Builders Workers Industrial Union per il gruppo teatrale nella produzione di Storie in cantiere ed è migliorata la distribuzione di Nuovo Paese in quel sindacato. Negli ultimi due anni si sono portate a capo diverse iniziative culturali tra cui spiccano la mostra fotografica Mondi diversi, la produzione teatrale Storie in cantiere in collaborazione con gli edili, la pubblicazione del libro sui diritti linguistici e la scuola.* – LLFC, 9/13.

[83] *La sede è stata vista negli ultimi anni sempre più come ufficio e sempre meno come luogo di ritrovo, di scambio di idee ecc. In parte ciò veniva imposto dalle esigenze del lavoro che si faceva e dal fatto che vi si faceva anche il giornale. Questo fatto ha però avuto conseguenze negative in quanto ha allontanato parecchi compagni e compagne, ma anche connazionali che 'capitavano' dal frequentarla. Inoltre, anche l'INCA si è trasferita a Fivedock, e quindi sono poche le persone che ora 'capitano' in sede a meno che non ci sia qualche attività specifica. Ora le condizioni di lavoro sono abbastanza cambiate, per esempio il giornale ora si produce ad Adelaide, quindi ci si deve porre la questione di come creare un giro di persone oltre che di compagne e compagni che utilizzino la sede e le risorse che esistono. Questo ci deve consentire, tramite attività ben definite ed utili, di far crescere l'organizzazione, di farci conoscere più da vicino i problemi concreti che la gente si pone, di capire meglio quali sono le esigenze e le aspirazioni della collettività e di muoverci di conseguenza. Questo è proprio l'elemento che distingue la FILEF da altre associazioni: la volontà di capire i problemi, di socializzarli e di organizzarsi per cercare di risolverli. La sede è in condizioni di funzionare come punto di riferimento per informazioni e consulenze di vario genere:*

- *Sicurezza sociale australiana e assistenza pensioni, sussidi, benefici, home care, workcare, scuola (Austudy, insegnamento dell'italiano). Si può anche offrire di assistere nella compilazione di moduli.*

- *Pensioni italiane (facendo riferimento all'INCA).*

- *Servizi e strutture specifiche per le donne.*

- *Informazioni sindacali (iscrizione, problemi di salute e sicurezza sul lavoro)*

- *Immigrazione, cittadinanza e domande per ricongiungimenti familiari.*

*Informazione sulle provvidenze delle Regioni italiane per coloro che intendono rimpatriare* - LLFC, 4/15, Programma FILEF Sydney 1989-1990.

[84] *da alcuni anni la FILEF ha cominciato a raccogliere dei fondi per acquistare una sua sede...l'acquisto di un sede significherebbe un grande passo avanti nella vita della nostra*

*organizzazione e ci permetterebbe di svolgere più attività sia di carattere politico, sia sociale. ..negli ultimi tre anni siamo riusciti a mettere assieme $40,000 per il fondo sede... [abbiamo trovato] una casa in Leichhardt...il prezzo è $165,000...speriamo di mettere insieme altri $40,000 richiedendo così un mutuo di circa $85,000.* – LLFC,1/12, Zaccari to members, 29 September 1992.

[85] LLFC, 17/3. Also: LLFC, 9/i.

[86] LLFC, 9/j. Also: LLFC, 17/5, Zaccari to Perkins, Mary, letter un-dated.

[87] LLFC, 17/2.

[88] LLFC, 17/1.

[89] LLFC, 9/i. Also: LLFC, 32/Correspondence, Zaccari to members, Notice of Special Meeting, 13 January 2000; Income Statement for 2001; Newsletter of the Italo-Australian Progressive Association G. Di Vittorio, February-March 1997; Ordinary Meeting of IACC at Marketplace, report, 28 June 2001.

[90] LLFC, 32/Correspondence, Zaccari to members, 21 January 2002; *confidando nella volontà comune di appianare per quanto possibile le divergenze in seno alla FILEF affinchè l'organizzazione ritorni quanto prima ad essere operativa* - LLFC, 32/Correspondence, Sidari to Zaccari, 23 January 2002.

# 4

# Towards the new Millennium
# and Beyond

*"The political and social context changed.*
*The ideological centre of gravity of FILEF*
*moved towards the great themes of the environment.*
*Our attention then shifted to the big problem*
*of human rights and the great global emergencies".*
(Sonja Sedmak, appraisal of FILEF's role by
the end of the 1980s, email, May 2014).

The end of communist history, to paraphrase American political scientist Francis Fukuyama, represented the watershed for FILEF's engagement in class-oriented political activities. In his book entitled *The End of History and The Last Man*, Fukuyama argued that "as it conquered rival ideologies like hereditary monarchy, fascism and most recently communism, liberal democracy may constitute the 'end point of mankind's ideological evolution' and the 'final form of human government, and as such constituted the 'end of history' ".[1] Although Fukuyama's eschatological predictions would not pass the test of history, *vide* the rise of fundamentalist Islamist thought at the beginning of the 21st century, he was correct in attesting to the end of communism, the collapse of the Soviet Union, its satellite states and the communist parties around the world, the Italian one included.

In the 1970s and 1980s, relationships between the PCI and the Soviet Union gradually felt apart as the party moved away from Soviet obedience and Marxist-Leninist orthodoxy, and toward Eurocommunism and the Socialist International. Instead, the

PCI sought to form an alliance with the Socialist and Christian Democratic (DC) parties (the Historic Compromise). However, DC party leader Aldo Moro's kidnapping and murder by the Red Brigades in May 1978 put an end to any hopes of such a compromise, that was largely abandoned as a PCI policy in 1981. The Soviet invasion of Afghanistan led to a complete break with Moscow in 1979. In 1980, the PCI refused to participate in the international conference of communist parties in Paris.

In January 1991 the Italian Communist Party split into the Democratic Party of the Left (PDS), led by Achille Occhetto, and the Communist Refoundation Party (PRC), headed by Armando Cossutta. Occhetto, leader of the PCI since 1988, stunned the party faithfully assembled in a working-class section of Bologna with a speech heralding the end of communism. The collapse of the communist governments in the Soviet Union and Eastern Europe had convinced Occhetto that the era of Eurocommunism was over, and he transformed the PCI into a progressive left-wing party, the PDS. Cossutta and a third of the PCI membership refused to join the PDS, and instead founded the Communist Refoundation Party. What was happening to the PCI in the transition from the 1st to the 2nd Republic strongly influenced FILEF's members and its leadership. Many militants, whose lives had been dedicated to the party, felt betrayed and disoriented. They resented being asked to renounce their history.

After 1989, for FILEF, culture and the environment were pre-eminent over political mobilisation. From then on, as one of its activists years later recollected, the Federation carried out "activities that lay outside the classical scheme ... It is true that these were the years of disengagement, especially for the younger (but also for elderly people). But it is also true that it was society and the new rules related to the labor market that forced us to turn away from those activities defined as 'communitarian', organised to benefit society, the community".[2] Obviously, the onslaught of neoliberal economics and politics overwhelmed FILEF's previous ideological convictions and practices.

*The Common Seals of the Italo-Australian Community Centre Inc. and of FILEF-Sydney.*

One tangible effect on FILEF of this momentous shift was the decision taken to maintain a low profile, with the creation in August 1992 of the Italo-Australian Community Centre. FILEF eschewed its former image of a militant, left-wing working class body to adopt the one of a Federation in search of less politically confronting issues. Class struggle and the pursuit of hegemony, if that ever was its goal, had by then gone out of the window. This crisis of identity is evident in perusing the minutes of FILEF's annual General Meeting held on 18 December 1988. A review of past activities brought to light a spate of critical comments: Panucci highlighted the need to "carry out local initiatives but in a wider political sense" (*è necessario fare attività locale ma in senso politico più ampio),* and pointed out that "another area where we should have been involved was the radio; instead we have done nothing" (*altro campo dove avremmo dovuto lavorare, la radio – e invece non abbiamo fatto niente*), also that it was necessary to "maintain closer links with other community associations" (*vedere anche in che modo tenere di più i contatti con le altre associazioni della comunità*). Panucci concluded his intervention by advocating "a re-thinking of [FILEF's] structure, because until now it has been inefficient" (*ripensare le strutture dell'organizzazione perchè finora non hanno funzionato bene*). Chiara Caglieris made the point that "FILEF stalled the political debate within as well as outside the organisation, for this reason many people left it" (*FILEF ha fatto cadere il dibattito politico all'interno e all'esterno, per questo molta gente va via*). Claudio

Marcello recommended "an increase in cultural activities" (*più sforzi nel settore culturale*), while Antonia Rubino lamented the breakdown in communications with the *casa madre*: "I do not trust FILEF and INCA in Rome. This means that we cannot expect anything from Rome and must try to work out our own strategies...we must try to salvage what is possible" (*non ho fiducia nella FILEF e INCA di Roma. Questo significa che non possiamo aspettarci niente da Roma e dobbiamo cercare di elaborare tutte le direttive qui...dobbiamo cercare di recuperare il recuperabile*). Vera Zaccari proposed to "scale down our activities and give priority to the elderly, *Nuovo Paese*, schools, Co.Em.It [the Italian Committee of Emigration] and culture" (*ridurre attività e dare priorità anziani, Nuovo Paese, scuola, Co.Em.It e cultura*) (3). The divergent opinions expressed by FILEF's leadership at this time reflected the confusion and disorientation gripping its ranks and the obviously difficult task of devising a new policy that would attest that FILEF still was a viable alternative.

FILEF realised, however sound was this assumption, that it had to radically change its target audience. A memo drafted by Vera Zaccari on 15 December 1990 and tabled at FILEF's General Assembly, held on the same date, emphasised that "FILEF's future is more and more dependent on second-generation immigrants and the recent newcomers. By saying this it does not mean at all to forget the first generation, but we must acknowledge that there are few among FILEF's 'activists' or cadres who belong to the first generation, and it does not seem very likely to find new ones".[4] The organisation's Secretary, Bruno Di Biase, added to Zaccari's concern by rhetorically asking for the reasons of FILEF's decline in popularity: "for one reason or another, of all Italians with whom we came in contact ... very few are now in FILEF. Why is that? I do not propose, in making this observation, that FILEF should only be doing proselytism, because it would be stupid and unproductive. However, one cannot forget that women and men, that is, its members, are the lifeblood of the association. Without them, the association does not exist".[5]

FILEF's Committee *autocritica* (self-criticism) continued in 1991-1992. On 23 August 1991 Sergio Scudery pointed out that "we have worked badly because we are not known...we should join several committees (Republic, Forum, etc.) and not snub the clubs...Rome has abandoned us, we can count only on ourselves".[6] Panucci lamented FILEF's "shortcomings in the political field", and Carmela Lavezzari that "nobody knows what FILEF is doing", while Franco Raco pointed out that "FILEF must be re-invented". Marcello remarked that "had we had a more elastic structure, some people would not have left us", while both Rubino and Lavezzari proposed "to review our profile...we are known as communists and we should get rid of this tag".[7]

Despite years of painful navel gazing, the situation did not improve and FILEF, instead of re-inventing itself, was dragged to stagnation by international and local events. Traumatised by the ideological earthquake and by the flight of its cadres, FILEF did not become a mass organisation, as Pajetta naively dreamt in much more politically auspicious times. What remained was a search for a reason to exist, and culture, the environment and 'boat-people' causes proved comfortable niches in which to take refuge.

In fact, a new area of engagement at the beginning of 1991 was FILEF's initiative Città Verde Movement. Its political manifesto asserted that "in the current global context environmental issues are becoming increasingly unifying themes for all movements alternative to the Western system and to the philosophy of economic rationalism, and for this reason [Città Verde Movement] wants to promote an ongoing campaign of counter-information and political activism".[8] The initiative attracted media coverage by the Italian language radio, SBS and Sydney 2000 programs and by *La Fiamma* newspaper that published a weekly column on 'green' issues. The Movement promoted information campaigns on genetically modified food in collaboration with GeneEthics, a non-profit educational network of citizens and kindred groups, as well as on sustainable use of water with Water is Life, an organisation that provided advice on clean water, sanitation and hygiene. FILEF also supported, in collaboration with the Italian Welfare Committee (COASIT), programs on renewable energy and on saving electricity with an initiative called Energia alle Stelle – How to be Energy Wise. Environmental policies became the catch cry of the day. Zaccari declared that in FILEF, "we believe it is important to participate in the World Environment Day rally, which will be held on 3 June 1990, as Italo-Australians, to demonstrate that Australians, irrespective of their background, are concerned about the environment which we share".[9] Some of the Movement's programs were quaint, for instance research carried out "on the possible causes (linked to pollution) of the illness affecting the lack of growth of lemons in Sydney".[10] FILEF also spread information on Città Verde through the 'ethnic' media. To this purpose, in 1992 it held courses on broadcasting at 2SER and 2EA, facilitated by Claudia Taranto, who at that time was employed by ABC Radio National. Ten first and second-generation Italians working for Città Verde attended the seminars, learning technical aspects of production and putting them to practice in their weekly broadcasts on environmental issues at 2EA.[11]

On 16 November 1991 FILEF celebrated the first year of operations of the Green City Movement by organising a *Festa* in Petersham, and on 7 December a flea market (*mercatino dell'usato*) in Leichhardt, that also aimed to rekindle subscriptions to *Nuovo Paese* and to "contribute to the economic survival of our association".[12] The previous year, only 119 people took part in a *festa* in support of *Nuovo Paese*, contributing a meagre $192.[13] In effect, FILEF's financial situation progressively worsened throughout the early 1990s. In July-August 1991 expenditure amounting to $4,100 dwarfed the revenue of $2,009.[14] Its financial report for the period January to December 1994 recorded a deficit of $2,634, expenditure totaling $ 33,229 over an income of $30,595. The largest receipt was a grant of $11,274 by the Italian Ministry for Foreign Affairs.[15] Compounding the financial difficulties, in February 1992 FILEF's office was broken into and a facsimile machine, a transcriber and $200 were stolen.[16] Also, by 1992, not only grants from State organisations were drying up and FILEF had to consider to finance its activities from its resources, but trade unions' subscriptions to *Nuovo Paese* were dwindling.[17] Federation members' generous donations contributed in part to stem the financial crisis. In 1992, Committee member Sergio Scudery in his will left his estate to FILEF, and his motorcycle to Rosalba Paris.[18]

As in the past, during the 1990s FILEF's policies and strategies were reviewed at the Federation's biennial congresses. During this period four were held, the sixth in 1992, the 7th on 20 February 1994, the 8th on 25 August 1996 and the 9th in 1998. The sixth Congress was held on Saturday-Sunday 4-5 April 1992, for the last time in FILEF's premises at 423 Parramatta Road, Leichhardt. In his introduction, Bruno Di Biase pointed out that the Congress marked the twentieth anniversary of FILEF being established in Australia, at a time when politics "were sliding even more to the centre, if not to the right" (*la politica slitta sempre più al centro se non a destra*). He also made reference to the changed political scenario that caused difficulties to Sydney's INCA and the Circolo del PCI Di Vittorio in re-defining their role on how to operate within the Italian community. Concerning FILEF, Di Biase, glossing over the Federation's identity crisis, vaguely reiterated its main function: "to assist to the spread of democracy in society and…to contribute to change society so that Italo-Australians can take part in its political, social and cultural life". More specifically, he highlighted that "FILEF began to widen its cultural activities, and specifically [by becoming involved in] women issues and in more general society concerns such as health and the environment".[19] As repeatedly done in the past, FILEF reiterated its attack on COASIT's attempt to monopolise the teaching of Italian: "In FILEF's opinion any attempt to remove from the Australian educational system the direct management and responsibility of teaching Italian tends to ghettoize its teaching in the school and/or outside of it".[20]

FILEF's Seventh Congress was held on 20 February 1994 at the INCA premises, since the Federation had already vacated its venue at 423 Parramatta Road, Leichhardt. Claudio Balzamonti from FILEF Rome was in attendance, Its 8th Congress, on the theme: *Verso il duemila, vivendo il presente* (Towards 2000, living the present), was held on Sunday 25 August 1996 at its new premises, the Italo-Australian Community Centre, 157 Marion Street, Leichhardt. The long, pre-congressional background paper best summarised, although with unduly optimistic overtones, the situation that developed since 1992: "With the purchase of a new home in central Marion Street, Leichhardt, the organisation has been able to make a quantum leap by offering on-site services and cultural and recreational activities. The current situation reflects FILEF's physical and political change. Physically, there was a long period of transition, during the refurbishment of the house. This transition has also meant a stall, waiting for the venue to be fit for use".

The pre-congressional paper went on, emphasizing that "politically, the character of the organisation and its goals, translated into practical action, have also changed. From the defence of rights, FILEF moved forward by intervening in the social and cultural areas. The composition of members and sympathisers has been changing. Quantitatively, FILEF had grown in enrolment and participation, with a turnover in recent years that has seen several new people becoming members (and, of course, some 'old' people leaving). This allowed members and supporters not only to continue with the already established activities of education and language maintenance (Italian evenings, *Vacanzascuola* and, in future, a weekly after-school program for children who speak or study Italian) but also with cultural initiatives as the film club, the review of Italian songwriters and social initiatives such as regular parties or dinners that are held in FILEF's premises. Cultural activities and social initiatives have been made possible thanks to funding from the Italian Government and the voluntary effort of members who took part, especially on the occasion of initiatives to raise funds for the payment and maintenance of the home".

The pre-congressional document concluded, in flight of predictable, vacuous rhetoric, by pointing out that "the current Australian situation naturally requires a political response to the massive onslaught by the federal Liberal government on any right conquered at a price. Just 5 months before the elections, nothing is more certain: the savage cuts to higher education and the State TV, the attacks on the aboriginal right to the land enshrined in MABO, the rights of immigrants and those who want to immigrate, to the various subsidies and benefits for those most in need. These are all things that are likely to disappear or empty of all meaning all recent democratic achievements in Australia. It is obvious that FILEF must organise themselves and move along with other groups to deal with this rampant right-wing attack that threatens to bring us back by 30 or maybe 50 years".[21] Another congress was held in 1998 and yet another Congress, the tenth, *La FILEF del Terzo Millennio* (FILEF of the Third Millennium), was held on 20 May 2001 at COMITES' offices in Norton Street, Leichhardt. It apparently was the last one called by the Federation. Its agenda, vaguely announced, included "political, organisational and economic-financial aspects".[22] All these regular "Congresses", a rather pompous and silly appellation, since at best they numbered a few dozen people, were at the base of Stalinist bureaucratic centralism, still conditioning FILEF's way of doing politics.

*Participants at FILEF's 1998 Congress (Courtesy FILEF Collection).*

Despite protestations to the contrary by some of its members, FILEF's appeal to Sydney's Italo-Australian community witnessed a steady but inexorable decline. A discussion paper tabled at the Eight Congress admitted that "we are few and with few resources".[23] In 1991 FILEF had at least 446 paid members. By contrast, on 13 May 1997, in an application for funding to the Italian Consulate-General, FILEF declared that it had 200 members (Italian) and 20 members (Australian). This figure seems to be widely inflated, since in 1997 the Federation accounted for only 26 members. On 6 April 1998 Vera Zaccari sent a letter to 221 people, "members and friends", urging them to renew their membership for 1998, which obviously they had not yet done nor, it seems, would in future do. At FILEF's Committee meeting of 10 February 1998 it was reported that only 15 people had paid for the 1998 membership.[24] After 2002, the year in which there were only 19 members, FILEF discontinued the distribution of membership cards. These were indeed disastrous numbers and made the pomposity of Congresses all the more silly.

In 1997 its aims (*finalità statutarie*) still were the "Defence and development of Italian culture and civil rights of citizens. Social Activities: various courses of language / Popular theatre / school radio / participation in public events / musical groups".[25] Notable was the absence of the "defence of political rights", so vociferously claimed during the previous twenty years. At the end of the twentieth century, the Italian government was the main provider of funds to the Federation. In 1990 it granted $10,000 annually towards popular courses for Italian children. In particular, disbursements made to FILEF by the Italian Consulate-General, Sydney were the following[26]:

| 22 February 1993 | $12,222.22 | (Lire 11.6 million) |
| 24 June 1996 | $10,833.34 | (Lire 13 million) |
| 5 September 1996 | $4,166.66 | (Lire 5 million) |

This was of course ironical. Still in 2014, Italy was not properly "reformed" as neoliberals would wish and, however corruptly, still indulged in welfare, especially cultural welfare.

Other funds were sought and approved, mainly for cultural activities. A report tabled at its 8th Congress details FILEF's success and failure in its grant applications for the period 1992-1993[27]:

Australia Council, 1992. Sought $12,000 – Granted $ 3,000 for the *Con Artist* Theatre Project, for the employment of 3 artsworkers.

Australia Council, 1992. Sought $ 10,000 – Granted $ 7,500 for the *Con Artist* Video Project, to produce a video documentary.

Australia Council,1992. Sought $ 6,900 – Granted $ 5,990 to write a book on the FILEF Theatre Group.

Italian Ministry for Foreign Affairs, 1993. Sought $ 18,871 – Granted $ 10,298.

NSW Ethnic Affairs Commission, 1993. Sought a capital grant to purchase the new premises. Not approved.

Carnivale, 1993. Sought $ 1,900 for the presentation of the video on the *Con Artist*. Not approved.

NSW Ministry for the Arts, 1993. Sought a grant to employ artists to begin a program on school theatre. Not approved.

Beside artistic, educational, cultural and language initiatives already illustrated in chapter 3, during the 1990s FILEF embarked in other campaigns. Already in 1991 it signaled its support for Franca Arena, MLC and Foundation Secretary of the Australian Republican Movement and of the Italian Friends of Labor (IFL).[28] ASIO was skeptical about FILEF's endorsement of Arena's association. One of its agents reported that: "it would seem that there is a considerable amount of jealously between these two groups. FILEF and PCIA [the Italian Communist Party in Australia] claim that they do all the work, but IFL are claiming the credit. IFL also works in a 'middle class' area, instead of the working area, 'grass-roots' level. It was finally decided that the IFL was of no benefit to FILEF or the PCIA, and therefore they would have no affiliations with this group. They added, however, that they will "use" IFL whenever the opportunity presents itself. My impressions of IFL are that they are not really a force with which to contend".[29]

From 1997 FILEF intensified its involvement in public forums by taking part in the debate on the republic, on constitutional reform and on the election of delegates to the Constitutional Convention. On 21 June 1997 it organised a public meeting at the Annandale Community Centre on the theme "Australia – What type of republic?" Speakers were Franca Arena, Judy Mundey, a feminist and left-wing activist who in 1979-1982 became the first female president of the Communist Party of Australia, and Frank Panucci. (30). Following the rally, it distributed a leaflet reporting that "Australians of Italian background met in Annandale, NSW today to discuss the type of Republic they want for Australia. Five Italian organisations in addition to FILEF were represented at the public meeting. These included: The National Italo-Australian Women's Association, Associazione Lucana, Associazione Liguri nel Mondo, Associazione Giuliani nel Mondo, Circolo G. Di Vittorio. The following resolutions were passed unanimously following an animated discussion:

1. All participants and organisations represented strongly support the move for Australia to become a Republic by the year 2000.

2. All participants and organisations represented urge to Government to conduct the election of delegates to the Constitutional Convention as it would for any other election, i.e. compulsory and at the polls.

3. All organisations represented agreed to promote a broader debate within the Italian community in Australia".

According to FILEF, the meeting felt strongly that the government has failed to involve Australians in shaping the future of the nation by trying to derail the debate on constitutional reform. The Federation also ludicrously claimed, as there was no public outcry by the community, that the meeting demonstrated that Australians of Italian background were keen to be involved in the debate and voiced concern that, like many other Australians, they had not been given an opportunity to contribute to the development of a national identity.[31]

During the following months FILEF raised the profile of its

attacks on the Liberal Government's plan to derail the move in favour of the Republic by printing several leaflets. Indicative is the one that charged the Prime Minister as follows: "The Howard Government wants to retain the monarchy and the current Constitution and that can be ascertained by the fact that it has not bothered to disseminate information about the Constitutional Convention, and for the election of delegates to happen through a postal vote that is not mandatory. We must also remember that the Australian population is being asked to elect 76 delegates while the Howard Government will nominate another 76 – and this would be democracy!"[32] The Australian Republic Referendum was held on 6 November 1999 and was comfortably defeated due to sustained opposition from monarchist groups and to division among republicans on the method proposed for selecting the president.

Throughout the 1990s FILEF continued in its traditional activities in favour of what it thought to be the "Italian community", if such a body ever existed. On 15 February 1996 it organised a public meeting on "Elections 1996. A step forward or a return to the past?" The gathering was addressed by Federal Member Anthony Albanese.[33] In 1998 Italian film nights were held every eight weeks, on Sunday nights, ending with a delicious pasta meal and a discussion on the movie. FILEF's *feste* to celebrate important dates such as International Women's Day, May Day and Italian Liberation Day were a yearly occurrence. As well, discussion evenings and public meetings were held on current issues such as multiculturalism, women's issues, Aboriginal rights and reconciliation, the Republic debate, the environment and contemporary Italy. A special event was the celebration of FILEFs 25th anniversary, held on 6 December 1997 at the Dobroyd Acquatic Club, Five Dock. On that occasion also in attendance were Pierina Pirisi and Edoardo Burani who in March 1984 had 'emigrated' back to Modena and were in Sydney in December 1997-January 1998 for a brief visit. At a public meeting, held on 16 January 1998, Pirisi and Burani spoke on the political situation in Italy.[34]

However, a perusal of FILEF's committee meetings from December 1992 to April 2001[35] reveals the Federation's steady decline during this period. Liaison and activities with the trade union movement practically ceased, mainly due to the fact that governments of both political persuasions in pursuit of neo-liberal policies had emasculated unions, and unions had amalgamated to stem their steady decline in influence and power. Moreover, the number of Italian-born union members declined through retirement and death, cutting the umbilical cord that in previous years linked FILEF with unions. Campaigns to support *Nuovo Paese* became infrequent, most probably because the monthly journal was by then available on the internet, and in view of the fact that successive subscription drives had proved eminently unsuccessful. Records of NSW subscriptions attest to their steady decline[36]:

| | |
|------|-----|
| 1988 | 195 |
| 1989 | 146 |
| 1990 | 130 |
| 1993 | 61  |

In September 1993 FILEF-Sydney hoped to reach by the end of the year the number of subscribers who acquired the paper in 1988.[37] In December 1996 the organisation in Sydney determined that "for the moment it was not in the position to financially support" the paper. It also suggested that "in view of changed times for the media, [it was necessary] to make the paper more modern, more useful, interesting".[38] At the same time, membership to FILEF declined to a record low. By May 1993 it stood at 22, comprising 17 renewals and 5 new members, and by the end of the year it grew to only 59.[39] It was a far cry from the three digit figures that were the norm until 1991, undoubtedly a consequence of the collapse of communism and the void created by the bankruptcy of its ideology, that caused many disoriented FILEF members to desert it in droves. Following a meeting with Melbourne's FILEF, Francesco Raco testified to the existence of "problems common to all branches (of cultural and political identity), coupled with a general feeling of discouragement".[40]

Emblematic of the personal crisis that at the time deeply affected many stalwart supporters of communism is the testimonial given by Carmela Lavezzari in her autobiography: "For a few years already, the Italian Communist Party had not subscribed to Soviet policy, many intellectuals had left the party after the events in Hungary, others did so after Czechoslovakia, but simple people, the populace so to speak, continued to believe in socialism and in the Soviet Union. After years of faith in redemption by socialism, that I wouldn't hesitate to describe as blind, they found themselves wrong-footed, so to speak, without anything to believe in. It was as if a Christian had been told that Christ had never existed. The people were not able to evaluate, to understand that the socialist experiment had failed and the ideals in which they believed did not correspond to reality".

When the uprising erupted in Poland, where the Solidarity trade union emerged on 31 August 1980 in Gdańsk at the Lenin Shipyards and the Communist government attempted to destroy it with the martial law of 1981 and several years of repression, the Italian Communist Party criticised the Soviet Union. Carmela Lavezzari remembered that "it was during a FILEF meeting in Fairfield, that a representative from Sydney informed us that the Party was disassociating itself from the Soviet position. From then on, Italian communists would maintain an autonomous position. It was like a bolt from the blue. There was a Calabrian comrade, who was beside himself, crying that it was high treason to socialist ideals, and he was furious when he learned that the *Unione Sovietica* magazine would no longer be delivered. For me it was a traumatic meeting, to say the least, even though I had disagreed for some time about what was going on in Russia, with the censorship forbidding the publication of certain Russian and foreign authors. (In this regard I remembered reading that when Sartre was received by the Russian Government he learned, from a meeting with students, that his books had been banned). During the uprising in Hungary I had believed what the Italian Left was saying. In those years the political clash was head on, to criticise Russia was like defecting to the other side, but then I could not accept what was happening in Czechoslovakia. The events in Poland were the confirmation of a system that was not working, it was the last straw. History demonstrated that the Italian communists had waited even too long to disassociate themselves. From then on my mind had lost any point of reference, it was clear by then that "real socialism" had failed. However, as Pope John Paul II had stated, it did not mean that capitalism was fair and just. When the Italian Communist Party also disappeared, each of us, in his or her own way, had to deal with his or her conscience, but maybe even more with his or her intelligence. At first I felt betrayed, having believed for all my life in an ideal that had never existed. I had believed in lots of lies and started calling myself stupid, naïve for having believed in an utopia of a better world dictated by someone like Stalin or Brezhnev. I fully realised how absurd was the equation that socialism equalled social justice, a better world etc. I swore that I would never allow myself to be involved again".[41]

Paradoxically, the loss of political compass led the Federation to shun even its traditional supporters, among them left-wing Labor Members of Parliament. When in February 1996 FILEF invited Leichhardt's Federal Member of Parliament Anthony Albanese to address the above mentioned public meeting, some Committee members objected to it, on grounds that "it would have been appropriate to have had a public meeting with all the candidates as this would better reflect FILEF's political position which is not aligned to any party".[42] Again, in December 1997 FILEF kept its distance from the establishment of a new left-wing body: "it supported the formation of the *Forum della Sinistra*. However, the *Forum* and its activities will not be a focus for the organisation".[43]

It seems that at this time FILEF found it difficult to seriously engage with other organisations, apart from paying lip service to their public causes. Probably, this withdrawal from active mobilisation, this inward looking, was also due to lack of human resources. Its few members, forced to rotate themselves in the Committee positions due to lack of 'new blood', were busy administering the organisation. During the first half of the 1990s an inordinate amount of time was spent in search of a new venue, eventually identified at 157 Marion Street, Leichhhardt, then to negotiate for its purchase and later to carry out major refurbishment works. At that time FILEF was also managing ongoing projects like film nights, celebrations, *feste*, HSC courses for year 12 students and *Vacanzascuola*. This last activity remained popular throughout the 1990s. In 1993 it attracted 45 children, and "many were turned back as there were no more places".[44] In May 1999 it still enrolled 44 pupils and 54 in July.[45] A typical list of activities carried out during the 1990s is the one tabled at FILEF's 8th Congress, detailing events for the period 1992-1993 and the amount of funds raised[46]:

Jumbo Sale in association with Palestine Cultural Centre ($603).
Games Party at Wigram Road ($339).
*Festa* for the 25th April 1992 ($366).
Two excursions to Canberra in 1992 ($593).
*Festa* for FILEF's 20th Anniversary on 28 November 1992 ($547).
*Festa* for the 48th Anniversary of Italy's Liberation on 25 April 1993.
Italian Trivia Night on 29 June 1993 ($559).
*Festa* of the Italian Republic, 2 June 1992 ($84).
Two excursions "around Sydney".
End of Year Barbecue, 19 December 1993 ($350).
FILEF Lottery.

From the above it is clear that FILEF found it increasingly difficult, even more than in the past, to engage the Italian "community" to take part *'en masse'* in its activities and to significantly contribute financially to the same.

During the 1990s, Sydney's Italo-Australian organisations, facing FILEF's reluctance to engage in joint projects, took the initiative and sought its collaboration, probably because they also were going through a recruitment crisis. Perhaps this was a turning point for FILEF, that for many years was in need of "a blood transfusion", as colorfully advocated by one of its members, Paolo Potente.[47] In May 1999 Dante Alighieri Society's Director, Elio Gatto, asked for two of FILEF's members to "sacrifice themselves", by joining Dante's Committee and collaborate on cultural initiatives.[48] In July 2000 Frank Panucci and Francesco Raco accepted the position of Committee members to the previously ostracised Italian Forum.[49] FILEF even agreed to combine forces with its traditional adversary, COASIT, to campaign in support of Aboriginal claims. The public rally "Italiani per la Riconciliazione" was held in August 2000.[50] At times old ghosts reappeared: in October 2000 FILEF was invited to attend the 80th birthday celebrations of the Australian Communist Party at the Search Foundation in Surry Hills, a body advocating "21st Century Democratic Ecological Socialism". One of the speakers was Meredith Burgmann.[51] However, by now FILEF's heart beat ecological, at least for the next few years. In 2001 all resources were committed to "follow the activities of the global green", to ensure the success of the Global Green Conference and to encourage participation to the anti-globalisation rally to be held on 1 May 2001.[52]

A major initiative undertaken by FILEF to occupy a space on the electronic media was its involvement in the commercial website *Bravaitalia*, created by FILEF's headquarters in Rome with a budget of 100 million lire (approximately 75,000 euro at 2014 rate).[53] On 31 October 2000 some 500 people attended the launch of *Bravaitalia* at the Le Montage Convention Centre in Leichhardt. The launch was organised by FILEF-Sydney, that had an on-line section dedicated to its activities. "This is an exciting combination of community and business" said FILEF's President. "The concept of community is a central one to *Bravaitalia*, and through this virtual community Italians can gain access to information, participate in discussions and forums that provide them with opportunities for new cultural, social and business projects". *Bravaitalia* claimed, rather spuriously, that being Italian did not simply mean having Italian origins. It meant sharing the values and tastes that "made Italy what it is". It was alleged that *Bravaitalia* was intended for those who, though they felt being foreigners, maintained ties with Italy and had "Italian sensitivity". The webpage www.bravaitalia.com was the first of four language portals that offered a mix of contents, services and products to Italians all over the world.[54]

*Bunting advertising the forum on refugees at Leichhardt Town Hall, 2002 (Courtesy FILEF Collection).*

The other big issue affecting Australia and the world, and to which FILEF signalled its commitment to intervene, was the crisis of biblical proportions of refugees, asylum seekers and the so-called boat people. Some escaped war, danger and famine (situations almost always caused by the very nations, as was the case for Australia, that invaded these countries) and, once on Australian soil, they were locked up for years in concentration camps or transported to off-shore *gulags*, euphemistically called 'reception centres'. Others were transferred from their sinking boats to reasonably 'seaworthy' plastic orange boats and towed towards Indonesia. Among the several initiatives and public meetings was the public forum held on 24 July 2002 at the Leichhardt Town Hall, in association with the Scalabrinian Fathers, with the aim to provide information to the Italo-Australian community on asylum seekers and refugees. The theme was: *Who are the Refugees? From the Migrant Ships to the Tampa. What has changed? What to do?* On that occasion FILEF printed a booklet entitled *On Refugees*, debunking some myths about these "wretched of the earth", to quote Frantz Fanon, one of these falsehoods being that they were seeking refuge 'illegally'.

The feather in FILEF's cap in the cultural field was The Weird Mob Film Festival, a wonderfully ironical title given the assimilationist politics of that film and the original novel. The Festival held three editions, in 2005, 2007 and 2009, devoted to Italo-Australian directors, dealing with the life of Italian migrants around the world and with immigration to Italy. Another film festival was organised in 2010, the year of the Soccer World Cup. FILEF's entry, Soccer Unites, dealt with social and human aspects of soccer and on its impact on society.

On a smaller scale, cultural activity continued in the new millennium, with several music and theatre evenings in collaboration with the Neapolitan Association, at the latter's premises in Leichhardt. Events included soirées dedicated to singer-writer Fabrizio De André and actors Edoardo De Filippo, Totò and Massimo Troisi. FILEF also held a forum on gypsies in Italy and in Australia, in collaboration with the cultural group Cani Sciolti, followed by a lively concert by the gypsy music band Lolo Lovina. It also cooperated with the theatre group I Carbonari della Commedia in the production of the play *This War has Nothing to Fear*.

In 2009 FILEF re-activated its environmental initiatives that had remained dormant for some years. Linked to the Sustainable

Living project of the Ethnic Communities Council, it launched an information-awareness campaign on energy conservation. The purpose was to explore the Italian "community's" knowledge and attitudes to energy conservation and current practices. *La Fiamma* newspaper and the Italian program of SBS Radio advertised the initiative for several weeks. Information included advice on energy efficiency and sustainable living in general. A similar campaign on water conservation at home and in the garden had been carried out in 2007. Following the same model, FILEF operated in conjunction with COASIT, that provided speakers and distributed material through their mailing list and website.[55] Two years later, the Federation was involved in a campaign aimed to fight global warming by reducing $CO2$ emissions. It advertised statements by Leichhardt's Labor Councilor Darcy Byrne, NSW MLC for the Green Party John Kaye, and Professor Mark Diesendorf of the Institute for Environmental Studies at the University of New South Wales, explaining why climate change is real and harmful, and why a carbon tax on industrial pollution was necessary.[56]

The year 2012 was an important year for what was left of FILEF. Not only Leichhardt Council Library agreed to receive FILEF's archival documents ranging from the 1980s to 2012, but Council approved a grant for the Federation to stage an exhibition of its history at Associazione Napoletana. At the opening of the exhibition, on 27 May 2012, a round table was held on the theme "A celebration of the past, a vision for the future". In November 2012 Council approved a $5,000 grant to catalogue the collection, and on 28 December 2012 another $5,000 grant to write a history of FILEF. In 2013 Council approved yet another grant by the same amount to digitise the most historically important documents of the FILEF Collection.

In 2013 FILEF celebrated the 40th anniversary of its establishment in Sydney. On that occasion, Leichhardt Council Library hosted a series of activities between 18 April and 31 May 2013. Under the banner "Four Decades of Social Activism", it presented an exhibition, curated by Francesco Raco, on "the long standing efforts and milestones achieved by the FILEF group". The exhibition showcased posters, photographs, newspaper articles, theatrical presentations, films and displays of significant events. On 30 April the library hosted the launch of Simone Battiston's book *Immigrants turned Activists. Italians in 1970s Melbourne,* being an account of FILEF's activities in that city. This event was followed by three presentations. On 9 May the history of FILEF Multicultural Theatre was illustrated by two of its protagonists, Sonja Sedmak and Rosalba Paris. On 16 May, the theme was "Migrants for Aboriginal Rights – Solidarity with Refugees". The presentation was followed by the screening of Fabio Cavadini's film *Protected* (1975), concerning Palm Island Aborigines. The last event, on 23 May, moderated by Bruno Di Biase and Antonia Rubino, dealt with the *Vacanzascuola* program conducted by FILEF for 25 years, a week of 'full immersion' in the Italian language during school holidays.

The main activity in 2014 was another film initiative. Early in that year, in partnership with the Sydney Film School, FILEF called for entries to the Il Viaggio-The Journey Short Film Competition, a feature event of the Double Belonging Italian/Australian Cultural Festival, which was held in November 2014. The competition attracted 17 entries and was won by Eelan Elanko's documentary *Misinterpretation,* dealing with the perilous sea voyage and the hardships experienced on Australian soil by a Tamil woman.[57]

In assessing FILEF's decline after 1989, several of its historical leaders concurred on many crucial points. Francesco Raco, barely concealing the Leninist roots of his lament, decried the loss of 'democratic centralism' that, in his opinion, brought about a "crisis of identity, of administrative capacity, of keeping records". He regretted "the demise of the [Italian migrant} working class, either alienated from us or deceased". By this time, Raco commented, "the main reason for FILEF's existence, that is its support to the working class, had been exhausted...emigration was no longer a problem. Italian migrants had learnt English, were active in the trade unions, had lost their initial shyness". In the following years, FILEF embarked on more intellectual, creative pursuits, *il tesseramento non era così più importante* (to solicit membership was no longer important). As political advocacy progressively diminished, cultural and artistic initiatives increased. In reality, Raco remembered, FILEF had always been engaged in the latter pursuits since its beginning, when he wrote for FILEF a theatrical piece, *Il drago e il cinesino* (The Drake and the Little Chinese Boy) that he performed with Claudio Marcello's son Agostino in celebration of May Day 1975. Even the acquisition of a new venue in 1992 at 157 Marion Street proved a mixed blessing. If it was true that it represented a pole of attraction for the Federation's supporters who came to take part in *feste*, raffles, meetings, concerts and other social activities, it kept FILEF's cadres busy in organising events and cook food in order to raise funds to pay for the mortgage. Raco characterised these years as *il periodo delle frittelle* (the period of the pancakes). Once the premises were sold in 2001, FILEF's members were again free to pursue political, environmental and cultural initiatives. Meetings and *feste* were seldom held, and FILEF had lost its premises as well as a large part of its constituency.[58]

Claudio Marcelllo, long-time President of FILEF, also characterised the years following 2001 as a *periodo di crisi, di rallentamento, di transizione, di stanca* (period of crisis, of slowing down, of transition, of stagnation). His view was that FILEF was now seen as a body operating at the margins of the Italian "community", no longer being its political pivot. In reality, it never had been the pivot of a "community' whose existence is historically questionable. Having taken distance from party politics, the Federation endeavoured to ally itself with other organisations, with *forze nuove* (new agents of change), "ethnic" and majoritarian, among them even COASIT, that maintained widespread contacts with the "community" at large and would benefit from FILEF's logistic and organisational skills. The traditional instrument of public rallies was no longer working. FILEF, in Marcello's opinion, attempted to renew itself, in particular by seeking to attract the young, but it had been rather difficult and "it did not work". However, in reviewing the past, Marcello acknowledged that, despite many shortcomings, FILEF had left its mark in five important areas, namely the contacts with the trade union movement in order to help the migrant newcomers, the introduction of community languages in the State primary schools system, the support for Aboriginal rights, the film festivals The Weird Mob and the bilingual theatrical productions of the FILEF Theatre Group. FILEF's future, concluded Marcello, rest in its capacity to organise itself and this can only be achieved "if we will be able to attract new people". At present, the Federation's President dryly remarked, *siamo un club di vecchietti* (we are an association of nice old people).[59]

Vera Zaccari remembered the enthusiasm, commitment and sacrifice of FILEF's members during the 1980s, of "people who scraped a living because of what they believed in". In her view, the Federation succeeded in reconnecting many old-time migrants with their cultural background, at a time when they were urged to forget it. Also, FILEF held up an image of Italians that broke the predominant stereotypes, portraying them as people who were concerned about their life, their future and the politics that conditioned it. Italians were creative, worked easily together with others, were a living proof that there is no homogeneity in any group. The third of FILEF's achievements, in Vera Zaccari's opinion, was that the Federation established a bridge between other community organisations, women's groups, ethnic bodies, environmental and migrant associations and a section of the Italian community. FILEF's future, Zaccari believed, rested in establishing closer links with mainstream concerns dealing with issues affecting the environment and refugees.[60]

Despite occasional bursts of activism, by 2014 FILEF was dying. The hard core, the *zoccolo duro* of its members, the young, ideologically motivated activists of the late 1970s, by the new millennium had reached pension age or had comfortably settled in their middle class lifestyle or professional jobs. Moreover, for most and for all of their children, English had become their first language and the Italy of Silvio Berlusconi seemed an alien place or a tourist destination, little different from Phuket or Barcelona. Although in many of them the political fire in the belly had not been extinguished, the will, strength and drive was no longer there. By 2012 *Nuovo Paese* was still seeking financial assistance from its former 'comrades' in Sydney, and FILEF's website was "still in need to be publicised, too few people are looking at it".[61] However, they still cherished the years spent fighting to secure migrants' rights and to address wrongs. One of these stalwarts, Francesco Raco, in 2012 reminded *La Fiamma*'s readers of "an old slogan-song of the Italian Left that said: 'We come from afar and we are going further ahead'. FILEF in Australia is coming from afar concerning both the spatial distance and that of its principles: those of universal and eternal brotherhood, justice and solidarity. And we want to go further ahead ... to continue to operate with the guarantee of our history, adapting ourselves to changing social, political and technological achievements intervened in the meantime".[62]

It is this spirit that set FILEF apart from other Italian associations. In 2013 Carmela Lavezzari, a 'person of interest' not only because for many years spied upon by ASIO, but for her indomitable character, well captured FILEF's peculiar identity when she said: "With FILEF there is more. We have a political conscience, we are people who think, who are not afraid of the reality around us. With FILEF we have won a place in Italian-Australian history".[63] In the final analysis, despite Raco's optimism and Lavezzari's historicism, it could be argued that the season of Italian communist and left wing militancy in Sydney, that began with zest and enthusiasm in the late 1960s, ended forty-five years later in the melancholia of celebrations that resembled more a wake. Almost to underscore the dwindling of FILEF's endeavours, at the same time, in Italy, *L'Unità*, mouthpiece of the PCI, ceased publishing. It was founded by Antonio Gramsci on 12 February 1924, as the "newspaper of workers and peasants", and was the official organ of Italian Communist Party. The newspaper closed on 31 July 2014, beset by economic difficulties. Perhaps, after all, these events are two of the many markers that signal the end of history, of that history which inspired many to fight for a better world, also in an Australia where, from a long time, capitalism is deeply rooted. Already in the 1840s, in the colony of Victoria, tradesmen could easily become employers, petty capitalists, and in 1855 Karl Marx, commenting on the Eureka Stockade rebellion, noted that the colonial government had skillfully quashed the revolutionary zeal of its participants.[64]

# Notes

[1]  Fukuyama, Francis, *The End of History and The Last Man*, Penguin Books, London 1992, p. XI.

[2]  *attività relative che uscivano dallo schema classico... È vero che questi sono stati gli anni del disimpegno soprattutto per i più giovani (ma anche per i senior). Ma è anche vero che è stata la società stessa e le nuove regole legate al mercato del lavoro che ci hanno imposto di allontanarci da quelle attività definite "comunitarie", organizzate nell'interesse della società, della collettività.* - Civili, Max, email to Marcello, Claudio, 4 December 2013.

[3]  LLFC, 6/9, FILEF Annual General Meeting, 18 December 1988.

[4]  *il futuro della FILEF si trova sempre di più fra la seconda generazione di immigrati e i più nuovi arrivati. Dicendo ciò non significa per nulla dimenticare la prima generazione ma bisogna chiarire che fra gli 'attivisti' o quadri della FILEF della prima generazione rimangono pochi, e trovare dei nuovi non mi sembra molto probabile.* – LLFC, 6/9, Zaccari, memo, 15 December 1990.

[5]  *per una ragione o l'altra, di tutti gli italiani con cui siamo venuti a contatto...ben pochi sono oggi nella FILEF. Perchè? Non propongo facendo questa osservazione che la FILEF debba fare solo proselitismo, perchè ciò sarebbe stupido e improduttivo. Tuttavia non ci si può scordarsi che donne e uomini, ossia gli iscritti, sono la linfa dell'associazione. Senza di loro l'associazione non esiste.* - LLFC, 6/9, Assemblea Generale FILEF. Relazione del Segretario, 15 December 1990.

[6]  *abbiamo lavorato molto male anche perchè non siamo tutti molto conosciuti personalmente... dovremmo entrare nei comitati (Repubblica, Forum, ecc.) e non snobbare i clubs...Roma ci ha abbandonato, [dobbiamo] contare solo su di noi* – LLFC, 7/5, Verbali Comitato e Segreteria, 23 August 1991.

7   *sulle mancanze dell'organizzazione in campo politico...non si sa quello che fa la FILEF...c'è da re-inventare la FILEF...se avessimo avuto una struttura più elastica certe persone non se ne sarebbero andate...naturalmente c'è il discorso dell'etichetta che deve essere risolto...noi siamo identificati come comunisti e dovremmo scrollarci l'etichetta* - LLFC, 7/5, Verbali Comitato e Segreteria, 24 February, 4 and 5 April 1992.

8   *riconosce che nell'attuale contesto mondiale i temi ambientali stanno diventando sempre più temi unificanti di tutti i movimenti alternativi al sistema occidentale e alla filosofia del razionalismo economico, ed è per questo che vuole promuovere una campagna permanente di contro informazione e di attivismo politico.* – LLFC, 16/6, Movimento Città Verde, brochure, un-dated.

9   LLFC, 1/12, Zaccari to Zambetti, Frank, 2 May 1990.

10  *una ricerca sulle possibili cause (legate all'inquinamento) della malattia/cattiva crescita dei limoni a Sydney* - LLFC, 7/5, Verbali Comitato e Segreteria, 23 August 1991.

11  LLFC, 19/10, Attività FILEF 1990, 1991-1992.

12  LLFC, 18/5, circular letter, 3 November 1991.

13  LLFC, 6/9, Assemblea Generale FILEF. Relazione del Segretario, 15 December 1990.

14  LLFC, 7/5, Verbali Comitato e Segreteria, Rapporto sommario delle attività dal 6 giugno 1991.

15  LLFC, 17/15, FILEF Financial Report, January to December 1994.

16  LLFC, 7/5, Verbali Comitato e Segreteria, 10 February 1992.

17  LLFC, 7/5, Verbali Comitato e Segreteria, 31 July and 11 September 1992.

18  LLFC, 16/9, Copy of Will.

19  *la FILEF ha cominciato a dare più spazio ad attività culturali, a questioni più generali come la salute e l'ambiente* – LLFC, 32/VI Congresso della FILEF NSW, 4-5 Aprile 1992, Relazione Introduttiva.

20  *A giudizio della FILEF qualsiasi tentativo di sottrarre alle strutture scolastiche australiane la responsabilità e la gestione diretta dell'insegnamento dell'italiano tende a ghettizzare l'insegnamento dell'italiano nella scuola e/o fuori di essa* - FC1/6, Pre-conference discussion paper, un-dated.

21  *Con l'acquisto di una nuova sede nella centralissima Marion Street a Leichhardt l'organizzazione ha potuto fare un salto di qualità nell'offerta dei servizi e di attività culturali e ricreative svolte in sede. La situazione com'è adesso discende da un cambio fisico e politico della FILEF. Fisicamente, c'è stato un lungo periodo di transizione, durante i lavori per mettere a posto la casa. Questa transizione ha anche significato uno stallo, in attesa che la sede fosse agibile. Politicamente, la fisionomia dell'organizzazione e dei suoi scopi tradotti in iniziative pratiche è così cambiata. Dalla difesa dei diritti, la FILEF ha allargato il campo verso una diversificazione degli interventi nel sociale e culturale. Anche la composizione dei soci e simpatizzanti è andata*

*cambiando: quantitativamente, la FILEF è cresciuta nelle iscrizioni e nella partecipazione, con un ricambio negli ultimi anni che ha visto avvicinarsi diverse persone nuove (e naturalmente, allontanarsi qualche persona 'vecchia'). Ciò ha permesso ai soci e simpatizzanti non solo di continuare con le già consolidate attività di istruzione e mantenimento della lingua (serate di italiano, Vacanzascuola e, in progetto, doposcuola settimanale per bambini che parlino o studino l'italiano) ma anche con iniziative culturali come il cineforum, la rassegna della canzone d'autore italiana e iniziative sociali come le periodiche feste o cene che vengono organizzate in sede. Le attività culturali e iniziative sociali si sono rese possibili grazie soprattutto ai fondi del governo italiano e allo sforzo volontario dei soci che vi hanno partecipato, in particolare in occasione di iniziative per raccogliere fondi da destinare al pagamento e mantenimento della sede. La situazione australiana attuale esige naturalmente una risposta politica al massiccio attacco del governo federale liberale a qualsiasi diritto acquisito. Ad appena 5 mesi dalle elezioni, niente è più sicuro: i tagli selvaggi agli studi universitari e alle TV di Stato, gli attacchi al diritto aborigeno alla terra sancito dal MABO, ai diritti degli immigrati e di quelli che vogliono immigrare, ai vari sussidi e benefici per le persone più bisognose, sono tutte cose che rischiano di far sparire o svuotare di ogni significato tutte le conquiste democratiche recenti dell'Australia. È ovvio che la FILEF deve organizzarsi e muoversi assieme ad altri gruppi per fare fronte a questa destra rampante che rischia di riportarci indietro di 30 o forse 50 anni.* - FC1/6, Eight Congresso FILEF, Sunday 25 August 1996, Background degli ultimi anni di vita dell'organizzazione, un-dated.

[22] LLFC, 32/Circular letter, 12 April 2001.

[23] *siamo pochi e con poche forze* - LLFC, 19/10, Verso il duemila, vivendo il presente, un-dated.

[24] LLFC, 17/4, Zaccari, circular letter, 6 April 1998. Also: LLFC, 32/Minutes of the FILEF Meeting, 10 February 1998.

[25] *Difesa e sviluppo cultura italiana e diritti civili dei cittadini. Attività sociali: corsi vari di lingua/Teatro popolare/scuola radio/partecipazione manifestazioni popolari/gruppi musicali.* - FC1/5, Consulate-General Form of Aggiornamento 1997.

[26] FC1/5, Ricevute per fondi elargiti alla FILEF dal Consolato Generale.

[27] LLFC, 32/8th FILEF Congress - Attività svolta nel 1992 e 1993.

[28] LLFC, 7/5, Verbali Comitato e Segreteria, Rapporto sommario delle attività dal 6 giugno 1991, Riunione Comitato FILEF, 23 August 1991.

[29] NAA, Series A6122, Control symbol 2677, FILEF, Vol. 4, ASIO report – 116 – date censored.

[30] FC1/7, leaflet, un-dated.

[31] FILEF Media Release, 21 June 1997.

[32] *Il governo Howard vuole mantenere la monarchia e la Costituzione attuale e questo lo si può costatare dal fatto che non si sia curato di diffondere informazioni a proposito della Constitutional Convention e che l'elezione dei delegati avvenga attraverso un voto postale che non è obbligatorio.*

*Bisogna anche ricordare che si chiede alla popolazione australiana di eleggere 76 delegati mentre il governo Howard ne nominerà altri 76 – e questa sarebbe democrazia!* - FC6/9, FILEF leaflet, un-dated.

33 LLFC, 1/8, Leaflet.

34 LLFC, 20/10, Minutes of FILEF's Committee Meetings 1993-1998, Committee meeting minute, 13 January 1998.

35 LLFC, 20/10, Minutes of FILEF's Committee Meetings 1993-1998; LLFC, 20/7, Minutes of FILEF's Committee Meetings, 1999-2001.

36 LLFC, 20/10, Riunione FILEF Nazionale, 31 July 1993.

37 Ibid., Committee meeting minute, 1 September 1993.

38 Ibid., Committee meeting minute, 10 December 1996.

39 Ibid., Financial Report, 13 May 1993.

40 *problemi comuni a tutte le sedi – di identità culturale e politica – con un generale senso di scoraggiamento*). (Ibid., Committee meeting minute, 9 August 1994.

41 Cresciani, Gianfranco and Silversmith, Jane (Eds), *Carmela Lavezzari. Memoirs of a "person of interest"*, Padana Press, Sydney 2014, pp. 71-72.

42 Ibid., Committee meeting minute, February 1996.

43 Ibid., Committee meeting minute, 9 December 1997.

44 *molti sono stati respinti per mancanza di posto*) (Ibid., Committee meeting minute, 6 October 1993.

45 LLFC, 20/7, Committee meeting minutes, 5 May and 14 July 1999.

46 LLFC, 32/8th FILEF Congress - Attività svolta nel 1992 e 1993.

47 LLFC, 20/7, Committee meeting minute, 5 May 1999.

48 LLFC, 20/7, Committee meeting minute, 5 May 1999.

49 LLFC, 20/7, Committee meeting minutes, 12 July 2000.

50 LLFC, 20/7, Committee meeting minutes, 12 April, 10 May and 14 June 2000.

51 LLFC, 20/7, Committee meeting minute, 26 September 2000.

52 LLFC, 20/7, Committee meeting minute, 11 April 2001.

53 LLFC, 20/7, Committee meeting minutes, 12 July 2000.

54 LLFC, 19/2.

55 LLFC, 32/FILEF Project for the Italian community. Energy conservation education campaign, September 2009.

[56]  LLFC, 32/Riunione pubblica sul tema "Carbon Tax, questa sconosciuta", 30 October 2011.

[57]  *La Fiamma*, 11 August 2014.

[58]  Raco, Francesco, interview with the author, 8 May 2013.

[59]  Marcello, Claudio, interview with the author, 13 August 2013.

[60]  Zaccari, Vera, interview with the author, 1 November 2014.

[61]  *ancora da pubblicizzare, troppo poche le persone che lo guardano* - LLFC, 17/12, Riunione FILEF 25 Febbraio 2012, Verbale.

[62]  *un vecchio slogan-canzone della sinistra italiana diceva: "Veniamo da lontano e andiamo lontano". La FILEF in Australia viene da lontano sia sotto la dimensione spaziale sia sotto quella dei principi: quelli universali ed eterni della fratellanza, della giustizia e della solidarietà. E vogliamo andare lontano...per continuare a operare con la garanzia della nostra storia, adeguandoci ai cambiamenti sociali, politici e tecnologici nel frattempo intervenuti.* – *La Fiamma*, Speciale 40 anni FILEF, 17 May 2012.

[63]  *Con la FILEF c'è di più. Noi dimostriamo che abbiamo una coscienza politica, che siamo gente che pensa e che non abbiamo paura della realtà che di circonda. Con la FILEF abbiamo conquistato un posto nella storia italo-australiana.* - Lavezzari, Carmela, interview with the author, 19 July 2013.

[64]  Marx, Karl, 'Buying Jobs – from Australia', in: *Neue Oder-Zeitung* (Breslau), 7 March 1855, quoted in : Mayer, Henry (Ed), *Marx, Engels and Australia*, Melbourne 1964, pp. 112-114.

# Conclusion

"Emigration, in reality, is servitude, a colonial condition,
a ritual sacrifice, mutilation and racism,
the latter being an instrument of power and a means of
conservation.
When our consciousness is awaken, it becomes
the point of departure for the total renewal of society,
the instrument of a new culture,
the driving force of a functioning organisation,
the lever to move old structures,
the new element of working class struggle,
the yeast that moves stagnant countries".
Carlo Levi

The history of FILEF spans through a period in Australian affairs that witnessed four major and conflicting stages. In the first place, the country witnessed an unparalleled period of economic development, starting in the 1950s, when "it got off the sheep's back" and changed from a predominantly agrarian to an industrial economy. This take-off stage transitioned through a situation of entrenched unionism and class struggle to unbridled pro-market economic reform that resulted in the demise of unionism and the predominance of neoliberalism.

Economic growth had as its precondition an increase in the labour force, made possible by a steady flow of immigrants. It was between the 1950s and the 1970s that Italian emigration to Australia, the largest non-English speaking group, peaked, to abruptly contract soon after in result, among other factors, of the Italian "economic miracle". In the new country Italians, as well as other immigrants, found themselves *deraciné,* rooted up from their familiar cultural, social, religious and linguistic environment, and for many years were politically marginalised, even when they took their Certificate of Naturalisation.

Immigrants who in their homeland had joined or sympathised with left-wing parties found themselves under surveillance from the Australian Security Intelligence Organisation (ASIO) because considered by the latter to euphemistically be "persons of interest". Anti-communist paranoia reigned supreme, and abated only after 1989, with the collapse of the communist world order.

During these forty years, the country transmogrified from a period of blatantly adhering to the ideology of assimilation to a phase when multiculturalism was preached, provided it limited itself to extoll the virtues of pasta and pizza and did not advocate a change in power relationships. Maybe "identity politics" were themselves part of the rise and rise of neoliberalism. Recently, even the fig leaf of multiculturalism was cast away in favour of an aggressive ideology of national chauvinism, where the old anti-communist bogey was replaced by the new one of "Team Australia", which demonised people "of middle eastern appearance", allegedly not sharing "our values".

All of the above situations represented a serious obstacle for FILEF to make inroads and be accepted by Italian migrants and the Australian community. In the first place, the "stigma" of being a communist front organisation disqualified it to the eyes of the bulk of Italians who had come from the Southern regions of Italy, where from the late 19th century trade unionism and political militancy had been effectively stifled by the Catholic Church, the mafia and the predominant climate of fear, *omertà, clientelismo* and conformism. For the same reason, FILEF was not considered by the dominant conservative culture as a honest broker of political, social and economic change. Australian media, political parties and other organisations took comfort in the staunch opposition against FILEF manifested by the Catholic Church, Comites, Coasit, Catholic trade unions and, with few exceptions, Italian consular and diplomatic authorities, as well as by Italian newspapers in Australia, always subservient to their political masters. A letter by ASIO's Director-General to the Secretary of the Department of Immigration and Ethnic Affairs in 1981 accurately stated that "FILEF is well-known in the Italian community as a PCIA 'front' organisation, therefore it is probable that the Federation attracts mostly those relatively few Italians who are already in sympathy with the PCIA's political line. Thus FILEF is considered largely unsuccessful in attracting new members to the PCIA from local Italian communities".[1]

An added reason explaining the limited success in signing up new cadres to the PCIA and to FILEF was the lure of individualism, of consumerism, of a steady job, of *benessere* (affluence). Edoardo Burani, in his speech at the PCIA's Sydney Branch Conference on 9 April 1978, condemned "the negative attitude of some comrades, when judging the Australian reality 'difficult' or even 'impossible'. This fatalistic attitude [explains] the difficulty of seeing the reasons of being communists in a country like Australia where it was possible for us to obtain a job, a house, a car and a TV, maybe in colour".[2] Even a seasoned revolutionary like Giuliano Pajetta had to admit that "Australia has several unique problems – isolation, most ethnic people are now second generation and the general apathy of youth and women. Australian living standards is (sic.) also not conducive to the communist cause".[3]

Affected by the predominant climate of underlying McCarthyism, fear of losing their job and apathy were also factors contributing to Italians' detachment from FILEF and the PCIA. In 1978, Valentino Laudi, speaking about the problems besetting the party's Fairfield branch, said that "the Branch is not very active, which is mainly due to the apathy in that area. Sales of *Nuovo Paese* were also very low".[4] In 1979, an unsuspecting Bruno Di Biase, speaking to an ASIO informant, "claimed to have gained two PCIA and four FILEF new members. He said that he saw many more people but they were hesitant in taking out membership because they were afraid of the authorities".[5] Again, in 1980 an ASIO agent commented that "FILEF are having trouble finding persons with the right attitude and the individual capacity to be a union activist. It appears that some workers will probably not volunteer due to possible repercussions with their employers".[6]

As detailed in previous chapters, FILEF's relations with Australian political parties and trade unions were at best patchy. For different reasons, the ALP, PCA and SPA maintained an ambiguous relationship with FILEF and the PCIA, irked by the latter's ideological 'heresy' of declaring to be 'communists with a human face', and occasionally scathing of its 'Mediterranean' exuberance and unreliability. Their prejudices were confirmed by Salemi's coming to Australia to fund PCIA branches, set up FILEF and publish *Nuovo Paese*. This proved that, also in the opinion of the PCI in Rome, there was no Italian migrant in Australia who could take a leadership role. In 1980, an ever-present ASIO agent to FILEF's meetings reported that "FILEF has always been considered an outsider" by the union movement, and that "a major problem for FILEF is that it does not know many Italian trade unionists in Australia. It has approached trade unions and asked for lists of Italian union members but the unions have refused to assist".[7] Another ASIO mole confirmed that "the Amalgamated Metal Workers & Shipwrights Union (AMWSU) is not prepared to give FILEF any names or addresses of union members of Italian origin".[8]

As discussed earlier, the main obstacle for FILEF in interacting with Australian institutions was the widespread claim that it was a communist organisation. An ASIO report in 1978 noted that "it was local policy, to a large extent, [for the PCIA] to hide behind the apron of FILEF. Most members are aware that membership of FILEF and PCIA is virtually synonymous. The PCIA executive, however, considers it prudent to work out of FILEF, which is basically a welfare organisation. Pajetta suggested that the PCIA declare itself a communist party but to use FILEF for the more delicate issues".[9]

Indeed, it was the unremitting surveillance carried out by ASIO on FILEF, the PCIA and its members that contributed to keep these organisations, to a large extent, isolated from the mainstream. Even the most insignificant minutiae were recorded in the agents' and case officers' reports, and most, if not all, PCIA's and FILEF's meetings were attended by ASIO's informants. Federation's members taking part in these meetings had one or more files opened on them, among them Pierina Pirisi (P/23/79; P/45/3), Nicola Vescio (HQ V/13/53; V/6/59), Mario Abbiezzi (A/5/20; A/4/52), Edoardo Burani (72/8/4), Bruno di Biase (HQT 78/939; D/45/21), Salvatore Palazzolo (P/11/41; P/24/13), Claudio Marcello and his wife Silvia (UI SE 80/2/87, UI SE 80/2/88), Margaret Gloster (UI SE 80/2/83), Claudio Crollini (HQT 77/1101), Fulvio Chicco (HQ C/58/108), Nicola Di Franco (D/16/99; D/39/100), Antonio Agresta (A/14/75), Dimitri Oliva (O/5/84; O/12/27). Non-communist participants, like Franca Arena MLC, also had a file opened on them, in her case no. T/72/665 (10). Even overseas visitors, members of the PCI, like Ignazio Salemi (T/73/524), and members of the Italian Parliament, like Giuliano Pajetta (P/21/3; P/40/56), had been index carded. It is safe to assume that, when ASIO's records on FILEF after 1986 will be released, it will be revealed that more FILEF cadres had a file opened on them.

As pointed out by Justice Elizabeth Evatt, "Although ASIO cannot be compared with the Stasi in East Germany, central to its outlook was the credo of guilt by association". ASIO believed that if a person was a member of a front organisation, like FILEF was deemed to be, he or she was a potential subversive agent and needed to be watched. The Organisation's Director-General of Security, Charles Spry, calculated that 60,000 Australians "could come within this category", and already in 1951 directed that "those with an adverse pro-communist security record should be listed automatically either for internment or restriction, depending on the degree of their subversive activities". As historian David Horner points out, "Spry and his officers were taking a very broad view of the subversive potential of many people who had naively voted for the Communist Party, but would probably never have countenanced the violent overthrow of the Government, or were idealistic members of front organisations who also would not have supported the CPA's more extreme policies. There was little subtlety in ASIO's approach".[11] It is not clear, in perusing ASIO's documents, of what crime the above mentioned people were guilty, apart from being PCIA members or sympathisers. In the absence of unearthing conspiratorial plots, sabotage, espionage activities or plans to undermine state security, ASIO's plants resigned themselves to report gossip, innuendo, boring ideological diatribes and information that had nothing to do with treason or subversion. Typical of it is an agent's entry on Joseph Halevi, one of PCIA's most prominent members: "Halevi is about 5'10" tall, heavy built going to fat, 13½ stone, born approx. 1945, with dark brown thinning hair. He is a lecturer in economics at Sydney University and associates with a woman named Maria who is a tutor or lecturer. He is getting divorced from his wife, Rita, and lives at 12 Catherine Street, Leichhardt. He is currently overseas".[12] Another ASIO field officer was attracted more by the physical appearance of a suspected 'subversive', Carmela Lavezzari, than by her possibly dabbling with "subversion". In his report, he emphasised that the "target" was "young, attractive, waist length hair, has a 12 months old daughter, Linda Brigitte, was formerly an active communist in women's organisations in Europe, will be joining the Union of Australian Women but does not speak good English, is attending classes". In her file there is no report by the Swiss Strategic Intelligence Service (SND) endorsing ASIO's agent's allegations.[13]

Obviously, information recorded by ASIO cannot be taken at face value. Some reports contain glaring examples of misunderstanding or manipulation of issues. Typical is the one that relayed that "Pirisi suggested that *Nuovo Paese* does not reflect the policies and views of the PCIA and the Federation of Italian Migrant Workers & Their Families".[14] Yet, on the whole, they were fairly accurate on major policy issues. An obsessive concern for the danger of communist subversion transpires from ASIO's documents of the time. Paradoxically, FILEF was not a priority target, as clearly spelled out in 1977 in a letter by ASIO's Director-General: "ASIO's interest in FILEF arises from the Organisation's Priority Two requirement to study the international links of the Communist Party of Australia (CPA) with such parties as the Italian Communist Party (PCI). A continuing close relationship between the CPA and the PCI, and consequently between the CPA and members of FILEF, has been noted in other states...With regard to FILEF, therefore, the requirement is to monitor PCI members and their activities, and contact between FILEF and the CPA. That the PCI established FILEF and uses it as a political platform does not deny the work of FILEF as a welfare organisation for the Italian community, nor does it make it a target in itself".[15] Three years later, in 1980, ASIO reiterated its disinterest in FILEF unless involved in communist activities. A telex message from its Melbourne headquarters to the Sydney office relayed the instruction that "FILEF is of interest only insofar as it is used by the PCIA and/or CPA in the pursuit of their aims. Would you please ensure that future reporting of FILEF reflects the nature of our interest".[16] It was nevertheless impossible to report separately on FILEF's and CPIA's activities given the "hegemonic' role played by communist cadres in the leadership of the Federation.

ASIO's concerns about an international communist conspiracy involving Italian migrants, and FILEF and PCIA in particular, were much exaggerated, as it transpires from a study of records held by ASIO, FILEF-Sydney and the PCI archives held at the Fondazione Istituto Gramsci in Rome. Surprisingly lacking in ASIO's files is an overall analysis of the potential threat represented by FILEF and the PCIA. Not that the organisation lacked human resources and confidants, as it must have employed dozens of agents to gather such a vast amount of facts, figures and figments of the spies' imagination. Not surprisingly, little attention was paid to FILEF's policy that pursued migrants' rights, not revolution. No evidence was unearthed on the PCI funding FILEF or the PCIA, apart from petty cash and few airline tickets to attend meetings and courses in Italy. It also seems that ASIO fell for the revolutionary rhetoric uttered by Giuliano Pajetta during his frequent visits to Australia, in particular his prodding to attract new members to the PCIA, because "increasing membership is also important. This achieves two main objectives; one is that it allows for greater PCIA activity and the other being a victory against anti-communist propaganda".[17] Eventually, neither of these goals was achieved. Membership drives did not produce "mass" results and the strength of anti-communist propaganda on the part of the Australian Establishment and its Italian 'fellow travellers' thwarted FILEF's and PCIA's attempts to become national political players.

In reality, even Pajetta fell victim of his own propaganda, of his pipedream to create a "mass party" among Italians in Australia, on the model of the Italian experience. In Italy, the PCI had been less than successful in mobilising Southern Italians, immovable in their atavist mistrust for authority and change. In 1978, FILEF-Sydney set out five main strategies to achieve "hegemony' in New south Wales.[18]

They were:

> "Addressing the issue of the young.
> Addressing the issue of women and their participation, now very poor.
> Increase our presence in the Australian labour movement.
> Improve contacts with the unions.
> The need for a more honest and democratic information addressed to the Italian community".

Thirty-six years later, the results achieved in all five areas were dismal. FILEF did not succeed in exercising a significant appeal on second-generation Italo-Australians, and glaring evidence of this failure is that its leadership remained during these long years overwhelmingly in the hands of the "historic" founders of the Federation, of men like Marcello, Panucci, Raco and Di Biase. There was no generational *ricambio* (turnover). Female participation was modest, migrant women being anchored to the traditions, rituals and influence of the Catholic Church and its ancillary organisations. In the preceding chapters ample evidence was given of the difficulties encountered in persuading the labour movement and the trade unions to include on an equal footing the newly arrived comrades. It seems that Karl Mark and his slogan "Proletarians of the World, Unite!" had been relegated to the dustbin of history and that factionalism and jingoism, with few, remarkable exceptions, prevailed on the Australian Left. As far as the issue of alternative information to the Italian community was concerned, *Nuovo Paese* never became a serious competitor to the conservative press, namely *La Fiamma* and *Il Globo*. As already mentioned, FILEF's news sheet was grudgingly accepted by Italian workers, even when freely distributed, and its circulation remained chronically small.

In short, many and unsurmountable were the obstacles barring the road for FILEF to "agitate" and "activate" Italian migrants to vocally pursue their rights and to transplant on Australian soil a Communist Party that would mirror the heady success of its Italian counterpart, which steadily ran down after 1976 and ended with a D'Alema whimper about Italy as a "normal country". Everything in Australia was different from Italy, climate, language, history, culture, traditions, educational standards, size of the population.

However, although the PCIA was ineffective as a political party, among many reasons for its "original sin" of being considered "Red", FILEF proved to be effective as a pressure group, especially in its cultural, educational and welfare endeavours. One would argue that its main historical legacy was of having attempted to awaken Italian migrants from their generational apathy, indifference and numbness, a product of the shock of the new more than of FILEF's inability to galvanise them into action. In having committed itself with determination to this mammoth task, it could be argued that FILEF succeeded, if only in part. By itself, this was by all means a remarkable result.

## NOTES

1  NAA, Series A6122, control symbol 2679, FILEF Vol. 6, – 51 –, Director-General of Security to Secretary, DIEA, 26 July 1981.

2  *l'atteggiamento negativo di alcuni compagni, quando giudicano la realtà australiana 'difficile' o addirittura 'impossibile'. Questo atteggiamento fatalistico [spiega] la difficoltà di vedere le ragioni di essere comunisti in un paese come l'Australia dove ci è stato possibile avere un lavoro, una casa, un'automobile, una TV, magari a colori -* NAA, Series A6122, control symbol 2677, FILEF Vol. 4, - 174 – Burani's address to PCIA's Sydney Branch, 9 April 1978.

3  NAA, Series A6122, control symbol 2678, FILEF Vol. 5, - 116 –, Report no. 2511/79, 5 September 1979.

4  NAA, Series A6122, control symbol 2677, FILEF Vol. 4, - 186 -, Crollini to PCIA's Second NSW State Congress, 28 April 1978.

5  NAA, Series A6122, control symbol 2678, FILEF Vol. 5, - 104 – Report dated 30 May 1979.

6  NAA, Series A6122, control symbol 2679, FILEF Vol. 6, - 13 -, date censored.

7  NAA, Series A6122, control symbol 2679, FILEF Vol. 6, - 4 -, Report No. 200/80, dated 25 January 1980.

8  NAA, Series A6122, control symbol 2679, FILEF Vol. 6, - 7 -, Report number and date censored.

9  NAA, Series A6122, control symbol 2678, FILEF Vol. 5, - 78 -, Report No. 37/79, dated 19 December 1978.

10  NAA, Series A6122, control symbol 2678, FILEF Vol. 5, - 118 -, Report No. 2511/79, dated 5 September 1979; NAA, Series A6122, control symbol 2679, FILEF Vol. 6, - 9 -, Report No. 536/80, dated 20 February 1980.

11  Evatt, Elizabeth, in: Burgmann, Meredith (Ed.), *Dirty Secrets. Our ASIO Files,* New South Publishing, Sydney 2014, p. 328. Also: Horner, David *The Spy Catchers. The Official History of ASIO,* Allen & Unwin, Crows Nest 2014, pp.186-187; 397-398.

12  NAA, Series A6122, control symbol 2679, FILEF Vol. 6, - 7 -, Report number and date censored.

13  NAA, Series A6119, control symbol 4640, Lavezzari, Carmela, Vol. 1, ASIO's Field Officer report, 8 June 1961.

14  NAA, Series A6122, control symbol 2677, FILEF Vol. 4, - 191 -, Report number and date censored.

15  NAA, Series A6122, control symbol 2677, FILEF Vol. 4, - 80 -, Director-General to Regional Director, WA, 11 November 1977.

16  NAA, Series A6122, control symbol 2679, FILEF Vol. 6, - 17 -, ASIO Headquarters to Sydney Office, telex no. 4976, dated 21 April 1980.

17  NAA, Series A6122, control symbol 2678, FILEF Vol. 5, - 113 -, Report No. 2300/79, dated 22 August 1979.

18  *Affrontare il problema dei giovani. Affrontare il problema delle donne e della loro partecipazione, ora molto scarsa. Accrescere la nostra presenza nel movimento operaio australiano. Migliorare i contatti con i sindacati. Esigenza di una informazione più onesta e democratica nella comunità italiana.* - NAA, Series A6122, control symbol 2677, FILEF Vol. 4, - 163 -, Burani, Edoardo, Relazione introduttiva al Congresso di Sezione del PCI del NSW, 9 April 1978.

# Selected Bibliography

## Archives

**Archivio Centrale dello Stato, Rome**, Casellario Politico Centrale

Busta 2936, Abbiezzi Mario di Francesco.

**Fondazione Istituto Gramsci**, Rome, Fondo Partito Comunista Italiano

| SERIES | YEAR | BUSTA | FASCICOLO |
|---|---|---|---|
| 500 Organizzazioni di massa | 1972 | 170 | 191 |
| 800 Esteri | 1972 | 177 | 254 |
| 800 Esteri | 1972 | 183 | 331 |
| 800 Esteri | 1973 | 217 | 244 |
| 6 Ufficio Emigrazione | 1973 | 234 | 12 |
| 6 Ufficio Emigrazione | 1973 | 234 | 13 |
| 6 Ufficio Emigrazione | 1973 | 234 | 14 |
| 3 Sezione Esteri | 1974 | 262 | 14 |
| 3 Sezione Esteri | 1974 | 263 | 26 |
| 9 Ufficio Emigrazione | 1974 | 275 | 110 |
| 9 Ufficio Emigrazione | 1974 | 276 | 111 |
| 4 Sezione Esteri | 1975 | 321 | 35 |
| 11 Ufficio Emigrazione | 1975 | 334 | 144 |
| 4 Sezione Esteri | 1976 | 360 | 25 |
| 800 Sezione Esteri | 1976 | 354 | 101 |
| 14 Ufficio Emigrazione | 1976 | 383 | 216 |
| 3 Sezione di Amministrazione | 1977 | 409 | 9 |
| 5 Sezione Esteri | 1977 | 415 | 33 |
| 14 Ufficio Emigrazione | 1977 | 448 | 205 |
| 14 Ufficio Emigrazione | 1977 | 449 | 208 |
| 800 Esteri | 1978 | 464 | 88 |
| 6 Ufficio Emigrazione | 1978 | 482 | 60 |
| 6 Sezione Emigrazione | 1980 | 585 | 73 |

**Leichhardt Library**, FILEF Collection

Boxes 1 to 37, containing 371 files.

**Mitchell Library, State Library of NSW**, Sydney, Manuscript Collection, Italians in NSW , ML MSS 5288.

### National Archives of Australia, Canberra

A6119 Australian Security Intelligence Organisation, Central Office

A4556 Australian Legation, Italy [Rome]

A437 Department of Immigration, Central Office

A9696 Department of Defence [III], Central Office

A6122 Australian Security Intelligence Organisation, Central Office

A432 Attorney-General's Department, Central Office

A2559 Department of Immigration, Central Office

A10756 Cabinet Office

A12389 Royal Commission on Intelligence and Security

M1336 The Rt Hon John Malcolm FRASER AC, CH

A9111 Australian Legation, Italy [Rome] - Migration Office

A6980 Secret correspondence files, single number series with block allocations and 'S' [Secret] prefix

A10074 High Court of Australia, Principal Registry, Melbourne [Victoria]

### National Archives of Australia, Sydney

C320 Security Service, New South Wales

C321 Department of Immigration, New South Wales Branch

SP908/1 Department of Immigration, New South Wales Branch

M4174 Hon Michael John Randal MACKELLAR

C115 Australia Council

C123 Security Service, New South Wales

### National Archives of Australia, Brisbane

BP242/1 Investigation Branch, Queensland

## Interviews

Di Biase, Bruno, 24 January 2014.

Lavezzari, Carmela, 19 July 2013.

Marcello, Claudio, 13 August 2013

Paris, Rosalba, 24 November 2014.

Raco, Francesco, 8 May 2013.

Zaccari, Vera, 1 November 2014.


## Videos

*Persons of Interest. ASIO's Dirty War on Dissent,* DVD, Produced by Gai Steele, Directed by Haydn Keenan, Distributed by Smart St Films Pty Ltd, 2014.


Fabio Cavadini, *The Other Side of the Coin (Il rovescio della medaglia),* Frontyard Films, Sydney 2012.


## Un-published works

Simone Battiston, *History and Collective Memory of the Italian Migrant Workers' Organisation FILEF in 1970s Melbourne,* PhD Thesis, La Trobe University, Bundoora, Victoria 2004.


## Publications

Aarons, Eric, *What's Left? Memoirs of an Australian Communist,* Penguin Books, Ringwood, Victoria 1993.

Aarons, Mark, *The Family File,* Black Inc., Melbourne 2010

Agosti, Aldo, *Storia del PCI,* Laterza,Bari 1999.

Australian Bureau of Statistics, *Overseas Born Australians 1988. A Statistical Profile,* Canberra 1989.

Battiston, Simone, *Immigrants Turned Activists. Italians in 1970s Melbourne, Troubador Publishing, Kibworth Beauchamp, UK 2012.*

Berlinguer, Enrico, Opening Report to the XIV National Congress of the PCI, in: *The Italian Communists, Foreign Bulletin of the PCI,* N. 2-3, March-May 1975.

Berlinguer, Enrico, 'Riflessioni sull'Italia dopo i fatti del Cile. Alleanze sociali e schieramenti politici', in: *Rinascita,* 12 October 1974.

Bosworth, Richard, 'Conspiracy of the Consuls? Official Italy and the Bonegilla Riot of 1952', in: *Historical Studies*, No. 22, 1987.

Bull, Martin J. and Newell, James L., *Italian Politics*, Polity Press, Cambridge, UK 2005.

Burgmann, Meredith, *Dirty Secrets. Our ASIO Files*, University of New South Wales Press, 2014.

Cain, Frank, *The Origins of Political Surveillance in Australia*, Angus & Robertson Publishers, Sydney 1983.

Cain, Frank, 'ASIO and the Australian Labour Movement – An Historical Perspective', in: *Labour History*, No. 58, May 1990.

Canali, Mauro, *Le spie del Regime*, Il Mulino, Bologna 2004.

Cresciani, Gianfranco and Mascitelli, Bruno (Eds), *Italy and Australia. An Asymmetrical Relationship*, Connor Court Publishing, Ballarat 2014.

Cresciani, Gianfranco and Silversmith, Jane (Eds.), *Carmela Lavezzari. Memoirs of a "person of interest"*, Padana Press, Sydney 2014.

Davidson, Alastair, *The Communist Party of Australia*, Hoover Institution Press, Stanford University, 1969.

Faulkner, Arthur and Storer, Des, *The 1982 Campaign against Illegal Immigrants: a Critical Response*, Clearing House on Migration Issues, Richmond, Vic. 1982.

Ginsborg, Paul, *Italy and its Discontents. 1980-2001*, Penguin Books, London 2001.

Gramsci, Antonio, *Gli intellettuali e l'organizzazione della cultura*, Einaudi, Torino 1949.

Hardy, Frank, *But the Dead are Many*, Triad/Panther Books, Frogmore, St Albans, UK 1976.

Horner, David, *The Spy Catchers. The Official History of ASIO*, Vol. 1, Allen & Unwin, Sydney 2014.

Kertzer, David I., *Politics & Symbols. The Italian Communist Party and the Fall of Communism*, Yale University Press, New Haven 1996.

Loh, Morag, *With Courage in their Cases*, FILEF Publications, Melbourne 1980.

Macintyre, Stuart, *The Reds*, Allen & Unwin, Sydney 1998.

McKnight, David, *Australia's Spies and their Secrets*, Allen & Unwin, Crows Nest 1994.

Moorhouse, Frank, *Australia under Surveillance*, Random House, 2014.

Morissey, Michael and Jakubowicz, Andrew, *Migrants and Occupational Health: A Report*, Social Welfare Research Centre, University of New South Wales, November 1980.

Pajetta, Giuliano, *Russia 1932-1934*, Editori Riuniti, Roma 1985.

Pajetta, Giuliano, *Ricordi di Spagna*, Editori Riuniti, Roma 1977.

Pavone, Claudio, *Una guerra civile. Saggio storico sulla moralità nella Resistenza*, Bollati Boringhieri, Torino 1998.

Ricci, Rodolfo, *1997-2007. Dieci anni di migrAzioni*, Editrice Filef srl, 2007.

Sechi, Salvatore, 'L'austero fascino del centralismo democratico', in: *Il Mulino*, Bologna, No.3, May-June 1978, pp. 408-453.

Sgrò, Giovanni, *Mediterranean Son. Memoirs of a Calabrian Migrant*, Scoprire il Sud, Coburg, VIC. 2000.

Solling, Max and Reynolds, Peter, *Leichhardt: On the Margins of the City*, Allen & Unwin, Sydney 1997.

Storer, Des, *Italians in Australia : a social overview / written by Des Storer on behalf of F.I.L.E.F.* Centre for Urban Research and Action, Fitzroy, Vic. 1975?

Storer, Des, (Ed.), *Ethnic Rights, Power and Participation Toward a Multi-Cultural Australia*, Clearing House on Migration Issues, Richmond, Vic. 1975.

Storer, Des, *"But I wouldn't want my wife to work here…". A Study of Migrant Women in Melbourne Industry*, Centre for Urban Research and Action, Fitzroy, VIC. 1975?

Storer, Des, *Migrant Families in Australia: a Review of some Social and Demographic Trends of non Anglo-Saxon Migrants, 1947 to 1981*, Institute of Family Studies, Melbourne 1981.

Zaccari, Vera, *FILEF, Italian Migrant Women and Australian Trade Unions*, Clearing House on Migration Issues, Richmond, Vic. 1986.

# About the Author

*Gianfranco Cresciani at the Fondazione Istituto Gramsci, in front of Gramsci's death mask, Rome, April 2014.*

Gianfranco Cresciani was born in Trieste, Italy and emigrated to Australia in 1962. He worked for Electric Power Transmission Pty Ltd, the Ethnic Affairs Commission and the Ministry for the Arts of the NSW Government. In 1989 and 1994 he was a member of the Australian Delegation re-negotiating with the Italian Government the Italo-Australian Cultural Agreement. Master of Arts, First Class Honours, from the University of Sydney in 1978. Doctor of Letters, honoris causa, from the University of New South Wales in 2005. In 2004 the Italian Government awarded him the honour of Cavaliere Ufficiale dell'Ordine al Merito. Member of the Scientific Committee of the journal Altreitalie, published by the Centro Altreitalie, Turin, Italy. In 2014 he was awarded the C.H. Currey Memorial Fellowship by the State Library of New South Wales, to research on Italian communists in Sydney 1970-1990 and was appointed Library Fellow. He has researched the history of Italian migration to Australia since 1971, and is the author of many books, articles, exhibitions, radio and television programs and web sites in Australia and Italy on the history of Italian migration to Australia.